For Better, For Worse

Biblical Relationships & Modern Marriage

For Better, For Worse

Biblical Relationships & Modern Marriage

Mark Vincent

The Christadelphian

404 Shaftmoor Lane, Hall Green, Birmingham B28 8SZ, UK

2015

First published 2015

© 2015 The Christadelphian Magazine and Publishing Association

ISBN 978 0 85189 294 8 (print edition)
ISBN 978 0 85189 295 5 (electronic edition)

Printed and bound in Malta by
Gutenberg Press Limited

Contents

Personal introduction

MY guess is that anyone who writes on marriage does so with some trepidation. My own marriage, in its eighteenth year as I write, has its strengths for which I am very grateful, but also its weaknesses; it is a work in progress. While my wife and I pray for the best and by and large focus our efforts in that direction (with occasional lapses on both sides to be sure), neither of us knows with certainty how our marriage will continue to develop.

I'm also conscious that many have longer life experience and some have professional expertise, perhaps as trained counsellors or psychologists. There are many stages of marriage through which we have not yet passed; I am merely a fascinated layman who has spent a lot of time reading on the subject and reflecting on the relevant Biblical passages.

There could therefore be an argument for saying nothing. However, I for one am grateful that other writers, equally aware of their own inadequacies, have not taken that approach. After all, it is a subject of tremendous importance: for those of us who marry (and it is most of us) it is the most important earthly relationship we have, one with the potential for so much joy but which also carries the risk of so much pain. These thoughts are therefore offered in the spirit of a person who is trying better to understand the subject himself in the hope of becoming a more spiritual person in his own marriage.

This book is primarily a series of studies of married couples we meet in the Bible. These Biblical studies are then expanded into some practical thoughts on how the principles might apply to marriage in the modern day. I have not come across another book which approaches the topic of marriage quite like this, so I hope this will be a genuinely useful contribution and not simply a rehash of what can be found elsewhere. I have been surprised at how many highly relevant and practical principles have come out from seemingly brief and in some cases obscure passages.

Some of the material was first published as a series of twelve character studies in *The Christadelphian* in 2013. I then wrote another twenty or so studies of other Biblical marriages and relationships which have not been published before, organised them into eight broad themes, and then appended an introductory chapter and sometimes a postscript to each of these eight sections.

The book can be read in several ways – either by topical section or in totality, or by reading the chapters on specific Biblical characters you might be interested in. Each chapter outlines what marriage topics are covered within it at the start in the hope that this will make it easier to find the relevant material. It's perhaps worth mentioning that the first section ("Foundations") deals with Adam and Eve at some length (three chapters for one couple rather than the usual one chapter throughout the rest of the book) as well as the central pattern of Christ and his bride around which the whole subject revolves. These portions of the Bible are so rich with meaning that it has taken quite a bit of space to do them justice and some readers may find these chapters a bit heavier going than the rest of the book (it's also in these chapters that I've tackled some gender issues which may well be a side topic for some readers but may be critical to the discussion for others). I beg readers' indulgence here – these chapters of early Genesis are so amazing and incredibly relevant that I felt unable to pass them by quickly – the rest of the book then endeavours to pick up the pace! As far as possible I've tried to write so that the individual chapters of the book stand on their own, and readers should be able to dip in and out as desired.

In terms of acknowledgements I have been particularly influenced by talks on marriage by Harry Tennant that I heard in my younger years and the framework they provided. I've also appreciated Christadelphian material by John Martin, Olive Dawes and Andrew Collinge. I'm also grateful to Ryan Mutter for sharing material he has developed on dating, some of which I have passed on in Part 2. Amongst many non-Christadelphian resources with a religious slant I've found Nicky and Sila Lee, Tim Keller, Voddie Baucham and Selwyn Hughes to be especially worthwhile. My biggest influence, however, has been my wife Anita with whom I've been blessed to experience something of the wonderful potential of marriage. The journey – still incomplete – has been at turns exciting, comforting, strengthening, challenging, and energising. It has always been an adventure and it has always been a great source of learning and personal development for both of us. I am grateful to Anita for allowing me to say the things I have said in this book and in doing so to share publicly something of our own relationship. But most of all I am grateful for her love and her care and for the fact that she agreed to be my wife. She is my one among a thousand, and I dedicate this book to her.

Mark Vincent
Stirling
September 2015

Part 1
Foundations:
God's recipe for marriage

1 |

Introduction: losing the recipe

Topics: Marriage in crisis – the lost recipe; Unrealistic expectations; The consumer model; The covenant model; Marriage as a spiritual opportunity.

MARRIAGE hasn't fared well in the Western world over the last hundred years: about half of all marriages end in divorce, and some of those that do survive do so in the face of meaningful unhappiness. In some marriages there may be a coldness, for instance, in which two people come to live increasingly separate emotional lives to mask the pain of their aching hearts; what was meant to be a fairy tale, Cinderella's 'happily ever after', has ended up as a confining emotional cage. 'How can it have come to this?' a couple might ask themselves while simultaneously feeling completely powerless to do anything about it.

Of course not all marriages are like this – there are any number of wonderful examples, including many of those conducted with no awareness of God. Nevertheless, given the sheer number of failed and troubled marriages it is not exactly surprising that society has begun to question the very institution of marriage. "Till death do us part" might seem a nice sentiment in theory but in the modern world many are increasingly taking the view that it is just not realistic. The problem is not marriage however; it is people's expectations and approach to it that is the issue. It's probably not unreasonable to say that marriage as an institution in modern society is in a state of crisis.

How has this state of affairs come about? The answer to that would probably take its own book, one involving a good deal of cultural and social history. One might point to the increasing atomisation of society in which 'everyone does that which is right in their own eyes'. There can be a tendency to think first of one's own interests before those of others, adopting an essentially selfish approach towards relationships which takes a drastic toll on their sustainability. Another factor might be the decline of belief in God and with it a sense that there is a standard to strive for and an accountability which transcends one's personal interests. Or again, one might point to the lack of role models – the all-encompassing celebrity culture providing far more examples of dysfunction and short-termism than consistency, faithfulness and lasting love.

In short, we might say that society has lost the recipe for marriage. It no longer knows either *what* marriage is supposed to be, or *why* it should be so. It has come to baulk at the patience and long-suffering required to build a relationship which will last for a lifetime, privileging short-term thrills over long-term benefits. It focuses on the physical instead of the spiritual, the 'me' instead of the 'us'.

A problem of expectations

Let's delve a little further into this matter of expectations as it is quite important in understanding some of the problems marriage faces in society at large. We press forward in life with all kinds of expectations, some of them realistic, some of them not. In the case of marriage we bring expectations from what we witnessed from our own parents and those we know from other believers, expectations from the scriptures, and also expectations from peers and from the culture. The culture transmits various messages about relationships, many of which are not helpful. It privileges physical needs and techniques over a deeper emotional foundation. Similarly, fairy tales of handsome princes, true love's first kiss and happily ever after are cultural messages which are deeply embedded yet unrealistic. They are what they are: fairy tales, tales which never show Cinderella and Prince Charming doing the dishes or washing clothes the day after the ball, heading out to work with too little sleep after a night of feeding baby and changing nappies, or working out how they are going to afford this month's mortgage payment *and* take a family holiday.

The Cinderella story and others like it with which children are programmed has nothing to say about what will be needed in a strong marriage – it takes the story of marriage only to the point where the couple dance off into the moonlight, supposing that they know full well how to take it from there. In fact they often don't know anything of the sort; the popular culture has very little to say about that and we are simply supposed to 'know'. But we *don't* know – that's why the average marriage lasts only eleven years. We have reached the point where people typically keep their bank accounts longer than they keep their marriage partner.

Then there are expectations set by advertising and modern media: expectations of impossibly good looking forms who wouldn't even look that way in real life if the airbrush were taken away, expectations of ideal homes and idyllic holidays. Expectations of men who are smart, sophisticated, suave and strong – not to mention considerate, fun-loving, and, of course, *funny*. Expectations of women who look like models even when they are making breakfast, ever present for the needs of their husbands, yet also lovingly attending to the children while holding an intellectual conversation and simultaneously organising the local fund-raiser and plotting the next stage of their career as a marketing executive.

If we are caught up in these kind of daydreams and buy into these cultural projections for our partners, we may well find ourselves disillusioned when the realities of life dawn and what we end up with is something a whole lot messier. What is wrong in this case is our expectations, and it may be them rather than our partner which needs to change. Expectations and aspirations are on a much sounder footing when they are scripturally rather than culturally defined. We live in a culture which has come to worship the external, prioritising the gloss while ignoring the deeper attributes and needs within, yet it is those that need to be the first priority.

One way of summarising these challenges is to recognise that society is increasingly taking a 'consumer' approach to marriage – the view that marriage is about *me*, and what *I* can get to fulfil *my* needs (and what I am prepared to pay or invest in order to have those needs met). This is a fundamental mistake, and is totally different from the Bible's model for marriage which is based around the concept of a Godlike promise or covenant. We'll explore this much more thoroughly in chapter 17 about Samson, but for now we can merely note that if we take society's consumer approach then it's not surprising that many marriages don't last very long – if I'm not getting out just what I want from my marriage or I'm no longer prepared to pay the price for what I do get then why would I stay in the marriage? – and indeed, we are seeing that people don't; they vote with their feet. We live in a consumer society, and insofar as this has influenced our approach to relationships then it's not a surprise that there is a crisis. The consumer approach is good neither for the one who practises it nor for the partner or the children who must endure it; it leads only to emotional stress, turmoil, and potential bankruptcy.

The recipe

The good news, however, is that there *is* a recipe for getting it right. God knows both the physical and emotional ingredients of which we are made, the nature of our needs, and what is best for us. He hasn't locked this secret away in a hidden vault as if we were trying to reconstruct the recipe for Coca Cola but somehow lacked both the magic ingredient or the quantities required; He has recorded it right there for us in the pages of scripture. The first part of this book is therefore about rediscovering that recipe in Genesis (the next three chapters will be all about Genesis 1-3, the foundation for everything which follows); from there we shall look at the wonderful pattern it points to in Christ and his bride as disclosed in Ephesians 5. These two portions of scripture lock together beautifully and provide all the essential ingredients for God's teaching about marriage.

In the face of the confused expectations and cultural scripts we've been reflecting on, the Bible's recipe for marriage is both realistic and wonderfully grounding. By building its vision for marriage on a covenant model rather than a consumer model the Bible holds forth *promises* and *faithfulness* as being key. By doing this it is encouraging us to raise our game to the very highest level, to live aspirationally by striving to show the faithfulness to our partner that God has showed toward us. Faithfulness is an attribute of God Himself, and it is an attribute He has asked us to show in order that we may be like Him. We are to be covenant-makers as God is a covenant maker; we are to be one with our partner as God is one. What we are saying here then is that marriage is an opportunity for us to learn to be like God, an insight which can be transformational. Once we start to take this on board marriage will have reached its loftiest goal. There *is* no higher goal than the striving to be Godlike in one's behaviour and character.

The writer Selwyn Hughes put it like this: "Marriage teaches us more about the nature of the Almighty than perhaps any other human activity." To live in such close proximity to another human being – to share so much of one's outer and inner life with another person – provides an unparalleled opportunity to cultivate the fruits of the spirit, to learn tolerance, forbearance, self-sacrifice, forgiveness, patience, care, concern, empathy. Marriage teaches us to foster communication, common goals, support, constancy, faithfulness, and unity. These are the fruits of the spirit,[1] the very attributes that should be our life's goal.

---

1   Galatians 5:22; Ephesians 5:9.

2

Adam and Eve: same but different

Topics: Men and women: similarities and differences; Different sexes, different roles – same identity; Different perspectives in Genesis 1 & 2; Not good to be alone; Fellowship; The head and the side; Marriage is God's idea not man's; Unity – how a marriage can display the nature of God.

The reason why a marriage between a man and a woman can work at all is because of both similarity and difference. First, men and women are the same, two varieties of the same species with largely the same organs and faculties, beings sharing similar concerns, needs and hopes. In this sense marriage is about sharing an identity, sharing things which are held in common. But men and women are also different: different physically in terms of their sexuality and their muscular and skeletal structure, different emotionally and socially, and often different in their preferred communicating and thinking styles. These differences bring a fascinating complementarity to the picture which helps us get to grips with both the potential and challenge of marriage.

IF these differences between male and female are true at the generic level of gender they are true at the level of individual relationships also. One of the reasons my wife and I can have a reasonably successful relationship is because of what we have in common – our points of identity as human beings with similar hopes and needs, our common faith and the goals it entails, our common interests, likes and dislikes, certain common features of our personalities such as an appreciation of similar kinds of humour, and so on. But neither of us would want to be married to a clone of ourselves. The relationship also works because of our differences – whether they be physical, social, emotional, intellectual, educational, or genetic. These differences are an endless source of fascination (and of course sometimes frustration!), and they inexplicably draw us to one another perhaps as much as our similarities and points of identity. In our better moments when we appreciate our differences rather than attempt to quell them, we can see that there is a complementarity about the whole thing – a partnership in which the whole is stronger than the two of us simply added together.

We began, though, with the broader observation about 'same but different' with respect to men and women as two forms or genders of the same species. This is an interesting tension to consider particularly because for a good portion of the last century an extreme form of the feminist movement seemed to want to emphasise only the sameness of men and women, being in denial at least to some extent on the rather obvious points of difference between the two. After centuries of unwarranted female repression it seemed that the pendulum had finally swung for a short while to the other extreme: that it was politically incorrect to say anything that even hinted that there were anything other than physical differences between the genders. Nowadays Western society seems to have come back to a position where the differences between the sexes can be discussed and valued at least to some extent, helped along by the appearance of populist books such as *Men are from Mars, Women are from Venus* and *Why Men Don't Listen and Women Can't Read Maps* and the more in-depth works of professional psychology lying behind them. Whatever the deficiencies of such books they have at least helped enable an environment where the psychological, emotional and behavioural differences of males and females can be recognised and valued once more. Men and women are the same (we're all human beings, after all); men and women are different (and the genders *still* sometimes don't understand one another, despite all the explanation!).

Once we accept that there are significant differences between the genders – while simultaneously holding onto the concept of the identity that both male and female share as human beings – then it's no surprise that God's recipe for marriage would take account of the fact and ask different things in terms of roles and responsibilities of the two partners in a marriage. While they are meant to share an identity as a couple, husband and wife are not meant to be identical. This is made abundantly clear in Genesis. Since God made us male and female He would know what the right thing to ask of each of us would be, given the mental, emotional and psychological apparatus that He had given us – and we must trust Him on this point. There wouldn't be anything accidental about this; it would be the natural consequence of Him making us right for the roles He wanted us to fulfil and designing those roles so that they complement, enhance and complete what the other provides. It's no less than we would expect of such a Great Designer. We may find it difficult to specify precisely the nature of the differences between the genders and we may risk descending into caricature and stereotyping if we do try – but the fact is, we don't really need to engage in this exercise! All we need to do is recognise that there *are* differences, and that God knows what He is doing in making us this way.

Similarities and differences in Genesis
Turning to the Bible now we find both concepts of similarity and difference clearly taught. In key respects men and women are indeed the same – hence Paul could say "there is neither male nor female ... ye are all one in Christ Jesus". Sometimes, however, this is quoted as though this is *all* that Paul had to say – as though we could close our Bibles at that point knowing all we needed to know about man and woman in the sight of God (of course this isn't the case, a point we shall get to shortly). With respect to salvation and value in His sight we are indeed all the same – all sinners, all needing forgiveness through Christ, all fellowshipping in one need and finding in our Lord one way

of salvation. We are one in these respects despite our diversity; none is above another whether in regard to gender, nationality, socio-economic status, or anything else. The man and woman thus stand together before God in Genesis 1 and receive His blessing. Together, as a pair, they are told to have dominion over the rest of creation. We are the same, then, in these respects, and after the punishments have been handed out in Genesis 3 and God makes coats of skins to clothe their nakedness, the text says explicitly that God makes them for both the man *and* his wife. The need and mode of salvation is the same for both.

The differences, though, are equally apparent, and must be held in balanced tension with the points of identity. The Bible talks about *different* roles and responsibilities for the man and the woman within marriage and within the family, and it talks about *different* roles within the congregation of believers. In Genesis 2 God creates the man and the woman through quite different processes and He gives His commandment to the man before the woman is created. In Genesis 3 when the punishments are handed out these are quite distinct for the two genders and will have massive implications for their future roles and responsibilities. It is desperately important to realise that the basis for those differences in role and function described later in the scriptures is found in early Genesis, as we'll see in a bit more detail in two chapters' time.

As is the case for many key Bible truths, God's principles about marriage and the relationship between the sexes are laid out at the very beginning – right there in the book of Genesis. By the time we've reached the end of chapter 3 all the key elements are in place which will form the basis for the New Testament's more extensive teaching on the subject. When 1 Corinthians 14:34 discusses male and female roles in public worship and justifies its position with the phrase "as also says the law", it is referring back to early Genesis; when 1 Timothy 2:13-15 broaches a similar subject and talks about the deception of Eve, it is referring back to Genesis; when Paul elaborates on the Christ / bride model for marriage, he quotes Genesis again.

In fact, Genesis 2 ("for this cause shall a man leave his father and his mother ...") is quoted no less than four times in the New Testament, one of the most frequently used Old Testament passages in the New – that's how important it is. In properly laying the foundations for our subject it's critical therefore to get to grips with what Genesis has to say about man, woman and relationships. Understanding what Genesis teaches about gender (primarily this chapter) will help us with what it says about marriage (both this chapter and the next).

In our image

Let's start in Genesis 1 where the perspective is very much on the common identity of man and woman:

> "And God said, Let us make man in our image, after our likeness: and let them have dominion ... So God created man in his own image, in the image of God created he him; male and female created he them. And God blessed them, and God said unto them, Be fruitful, and multiply, and replenish the earth, and subdue it: and have dominion ..."
>
> (Genesis 1:26-28)

There is here no reference to the separate creation of Adam and Eve (we know of this only from Genesis 2): no breath of life, no rib, no marriage. Genesis 1 presents us with a 'top-down' account of creation: creation from God's perspective as the great Master and Commander, creation as a great system in subjection to Him. The creation of man spoken of in 1:26, therefore, is effectively the creation of human beings as we would say today. 1:26 is not man as opposed to woman, it is man(kind) as opposed to gorillas or fish. God creates two varieties of man(kind), two sorts of human beings: male and female. They are both 'man', and they are both in His image.

From the perspective of this passage, then, men and women are equal, two varieties or sexes of the same species. They are both equally in the image of God, they both receive His blessing, and together they are commanded to be fruitful and multiply, and to have dominion. Men and women are the same, and by their combined reproductive capacities there is the possibility that the earth can gradually be populated with similar creatures as they who will also have the potential to bear the image of God.

Not good

When we come to Genesis 2 (strictly speaking, 2:4 onwards), the perspective is different. Now we are looking at creation more from a 'bottom-up' perspective: creation as humans see and experience the world and their environment, the way in which the various elements of creation fit together in relation to humanity.

It is in this passage, then, that the details of the separate creation of man and woman are recorded, an aspect not relevant to the perspective of chapter 1. We now learn that God did not in fact create them both together as He seems to have made the other animals, but instead created the man initially on his own. He forms man from the dust of the ground, breathes into his nostrils the breath of life, and gives him various commands including the one about his diet and the tree of knowledge of good and evil.

And then this:

"And the LORD God said, It is not good that the man should be alone; I will make him an help meet for him. And out of the ground the LORD God formed every beast of the field, and every fowl of the air; and brought them unto Adam to see what he would call them ... And Adam gave names to all cattle ... But for Adam there was not found an help meet for him."
(Genesis 2:18-20)

It is tough to overemphasise the import of verse 18: God has created something which is *not good*! Six times in chapter 1 the constituent parts of the record concluded that "God saw that it was good". Every day began with the expression "Let there be ..." and concluded that it became so, and that it was good. When we reach the seventh day God looks at the totality of what He has made and pronounces it even better: *very* good (the whole being greater than the sum of the parts and the expression constituting the seventh and climactic statement of goodness). But now in chapter 2 – how can this be? – something which is "not good"!

Now of course God has not made a mistake. God deliberately forms the man alone for a specific purpose and then leads him through a process whereby he comes to appreciate both his uniqueness in comparison to the rest of the animals and also his loneliness. The animals form a procession before Adam and he is brought to consider each one, which is both an education about the world into which he has been brought and an education about himself. He notices that each animal seems to come in two varieties – each has its mate – and yet somehow he himself has none. Perhaps as the animals proceed by he will eventually spot one like himself? Yet they come and go, come and go, and there is nothing. He is truly alone, without a companion corresponding to him.

Why does God want him to appreciate this point? There may be several dimensions to it. For one thing it elevates Adam's sense of uniqueness and therefore responsibility. Second, it shows him his need of fellowship both natural and spiritual – it tells him there is something missing, something which will only be satisfied by the feeling of completion which he will get when he eventually meets his mate. This in turn speaks of a more ultimate spiritual need that will one day be met when he finds unity with his Maker through the Lord Jesus (one of the Bible's final images of unity and reconciliation between God and man is of a bride meeting her waiting husband). Third, Adam's wait forms the outline of a spiritual principle: first the bridegroom (Christ), then the bride.

The most immediately practical of all these factors is the simplest: that the process of deeply understanding one's loneliness makes one appreciate the wonder of companionship, partnership and wholeness when it finally comes. When Eve is eventually brought to Adam by God he *knows* as he could never have known otherwise that this is the one for him. He appreciates the wonder of God's provision and the wonder of the possibilities of marriage. As Proverbs says, "Whoever finds a wife finds a good thing and obtains favour from the Lord". God is showing the man in a way that hopefully he will never forget just how special the woman is. By doing so it gives everyone who is married a fresh opportunity to pause and reflect on just how wonderful it is to have someone to share one's life with, someone to confide in and walk with through life's journey. There might be times of frustration here and there, but if we truly appreciate what it means to have a companion rather than to be alone then this should meaningfully inform the way we treat our partner.

Side by side

What God specifically says He will make for Adam is a "help meet" for him, that is to say, a helper who will be appropriate for him, will match him, correspond to him, and be his counterpart. To help someone generally implies that a task has already been assigned, as is indeed the case here: God has already given instructions about tilling the ground to the man in the narrative of Genesis 2 and He has told him of the restriction in eating the tree of knowledge. Given that these tasks have just been assigned and God then speaks of a helper, it makes sense to assume that these are at least some of the tasks that she is to help with.

The actual process of the creation of woman we'll consider relatively briefly:

> "And the LORD God caused a deep sleep to fall upon Adam, and he slept: and he took one of his ribs, and closed up the flesh instead thereof; and the rib, which the LORD God had taken from man, made he a woman, and brought her unto the man."
>
> (Genesis 2:21,22)

There are obvious spiritual echoes here concerning Adam's 'death and resurrection' and the work of Christ but we'll focus instead on two other aspects. The first is that woman is created from Adam's side. As the rabbis used to point out she is not created from his head (as later passages will put it, the man is the head of the woman and together they form one body; a body with two heads is a monster – the spiritual pattern seems very much to be in view here: Christ is to be the head and the husband's headship is based on that pattern). Just as she is not created from his head, neither is she created from his foot so as to be used or downtrodden by him. She is created instead from his side so that the two of them will stand together side by side as true partners would – to complement and complete one another and to fulfil their joint role as human beings in God's sight. This reinforces the message of Genesis 1 in which the two of them stand side by side in the image of God as they receive His blessing and His command for fruitfulness, but it also takes it further by giving more specific information regarding the man-woman order.

The second point from this passage is that God fashions the woman and brings her to the man. This means that the woman is provided for the man by God; she is His gift, and the marriage state which ensues from this gift is also from God. Marriage is not Adam's idea even though he recognises its potential instantly as God presents the possibility. Marriage is *God's* idea. The more we can consider our marriage partner in this manner as *God's* provision for us rather than something which we select, just like Adam did, the more we are likely to have the right attitudes in our marriages and a fuller appreciation of what we have.

We cannot know the precise interactions of our own free choice and God's providence in the affairs that lead up to our getting married (more on this in chapter 11 on Boaz and Ruth), but it is a good principle, nevertheless, to think of our partner as a provision from God. It is something which is easy to believe on one's wedding day and on other occasions when everything is going well. The challenge is to continue to believe it later, through the trying times that may come. We may then start to hear little voices in our head whispering that perhaps we made a mistake or perhaps murmurs of blame towards our partner for having changed. When we are afflicted by these thoughts it can be very helpful to remember that our partner is God's provision for us and that it is God who has, as His son put it, "joined (us) together" (Matthew 19:6). There are times where it can take considerable faith to believe it, but faith has always been what God has been looking for from His people.

If we really believe that marriage is God's idea and that our partner is a gift from Him, then we shall not denigrate either marriage itself or the partner to whom we are married in the way that we speak about them. We shall not speak about marriage as if it is an encumbrance to us or something to be endured; we shall not treat His particular provision of a partner in our lives as though they are a nuisance, nor shall we imply that we might have been better off without them. Our very language and manner around the subject is one of the ways by which we can reveal our appreciation; it isn't good to be alone.

Fellowship and unity

The whole process God undertakes in Genesis 2 is to take something in His creation which is not complete – a man alone – and render it so. In doing this He is showing both Adam and all subsequent generations the power and the beauty of fellowship, not just between a man and a woman, but in a wider sense between humans at large, and, in a spiritual sense, between man(kind) and God. Adam gets to see what it means *not* to have someone to fellowship with, and then to experience the delight of the reverse. God *creates* fellowship in this very scene. In the most literal sense Adam didn't have anyone quite on his own wavelength to commune with prior to Eve's creation, but God enables that communion which will become so precious to him.

Not only does He create fellowship and communion, He also creates *unity*, another crucial spiritual virtue and objective. A half of something is not a unity, it is a half; it is when Adam receives his 'other half' that he is no longer alone and becomes instead a complete '(hu)man'. Adam thus receives an education not only in fellowship but also in oneness.

This principle of oneness is fundamental, and we shall return to it again and again throughout this book. Why is it fundamental? *Because God is one!* It is the most basic fact about

Him, the Shema – "Hear, O Israel: the LORD our God, the LORD is *one*". Bible principles don't get any more fundamental than this, and it is the very thing that God wants us to strive for in marriage.

What does it mean to be one? Why is it such a big deal? If we try being something other than one for a moment – if we try being a half, for instance, as Adam was forced to try – then we'll soon see. Adam got to experience the beauty of oneness-through-fellowship that is core to God's whole purpose. God is one intrinsically, by definition. But He wants to extend His unity and incorporate others into it, including ourselves. Right on day one (as it were) God showed Adam the power of one. There is one God and Father of all, one Lord, one spirit, one baptism – and so the list from Ephesians 4 goes on. Jesus' desire for his disciples in his moving prayer of John 17 was that his disciples should be one as he and his Father were. Is it any surprise then, that Malachi should say, concerning human marriage:

"Because the LORD hath been witness between thee and the wife of thy youth, against whom thou hast dealt treacherously: yet *is* she thy companion, and the wife of thy covenant. *And did not he make one?* Yet had he the residue of the spirit. And wherefore one? That he might seek a godly seed. Therefore take heed to your spirit, and let none deal treacherously against the wife of his youth. For the LORD, the God of Israel, saith that he hateth putting away ..."   (Malachi 2:14-16)

Malachi's dual-pronged attack on both divorce and marital unfaithfulness has as its pivot the foundational axiom that in marriage *God* (and not man) is creating oneness! We note, then, the centrality of oneness as the creative goal of marriage. Malachi's question is rhetorical: "And did not he make one?" Absolutely! Knowing Him as the one and only true God, how could He have done anything else?! In all marriages God gives believers this incredible opportunity of learning to be like He is – learning to be one. For all the connection we may feel with our partner we will not be 'intrinsically' one as He is, but He gives us the opportunity to come as close to it as we can get by learning oneness-through-fellowship during the course of our shared lives. This is more possible in marriage than in any other human relationship. It is an unparalleled opportunity.

The story so far …

Where has all this brought us, then, in our consideration of marriage so far? We've seen that marriages must operate and thrive through the virtues of both identity (what is common between the couple) and difference (what each partner brings to the party to complement the other). This very dialectic of identity and difference is basic not only to the individuals in a marriage but also to the wider similarities and differences between male and female, a feature essential to the Genesis account. While we haven't really explored the implications of the differences between men and women and the complementary roles they are asked to take in marriage yet (that comes in the next-but-one chapter), we've noticed that these differences are real and significant, and that they are the basis for the teaching in the rest of scripture concerning marriage and the roles of men and women. We have to keep in balance these two aspects – the things men and women share as members of the same species before God and within marriage, but also the way in which their differences complement one another and form the basis for God's 'recipe' for marriage.

In His deliberately separate creation of man and woman and the bringing of them together God created the possibility of a fellowship and unity unique in human experience and a fitting parable of even more important spiritual relationships between God, His Son and the bride of believers. By making Adam experience aloneness and incompleteness God taught him the power and importance of their wonderful opposites. God made the man and woman as perfect partners to one another, able to stand side by side in God's image, the one helping the other but both recipients of His blessing. It was God who instituted marriage, who created the woman and brought her to the man to correspond to him and to enable a mutuality between them. God is one, and fellowship with Him is divine; the more our marriages can approximate the splendour of that calling the closer they will be to the pattern God intended.

3 |

Adam and Eve: the Marriage

Topics: Defining marriage; Promises and commitment; Mother-in-law; Creating a new family unit; Love is a choice not a feeling; Infatuation and deeper love; Physical unity.

One can well imagine Adam's wonder at seeing his future wife for the first time at the end of Genesis 2 – her beauty unmarred by age and sin, the way in which she was similar and yet so intriguingly different from him, the way she corresponded to and completed him – and all this before they had even begun to talk! In this chapter we'll examine in some detail the pronouncement that Adam makes regarding marriage on meeting his wife because it contains all the essential ingredients we shall need for understanding what marriage means from God's perspective.

ONE can almost hear him catch his breath at the beauty of his bride-to-be before he speaks – the first time he has ever seen a woman! Then, pulling himself together and stepping ably into his role as head, he has this to say:

"(Adam:) This is now bone of my bones, and flesh of my flesh: she shall be called Woman, because she was taken out of Man. (God?:)[1] Therefore shall a man leave his father and his mother, and shall cleave unto his wife: and they shall be one flesh.

---

1 It is possible that these words are spoken by Adam but the New Testament seems to hint that they are in fact God's.

(Narrator:) And they were both naked, the man and his wife, and were not ashamed."   (Genesis 2:23-25)

The word 'pronouncement' feels right to catch the spirit of Adam's speech. There is something formal in the air as he announces to the world the significance of his discovery and the parameters around the institution of marriage. In fact, the passage is tremendously helpful as a *definition* of what marriage is, for it contains all the essential elements, Adam speaking aloud to make a formal proclamation as if in the presence of an audience. As it happens, there were no other humans around on this occasion to constitute an audience of witnesses, but every generation which has read these words since has effectively *become* the audience as they join the throng of witnesses to Adam and Eve's wedding. Human audience or no, God is always present as audience member number one; perhaps He was present in a very tangible way through His angel in the garden, responding to Adam's comment and recording for all posterity the divine perspective on marriage.

A marriage today, then, ought to have the same solemnity and sense of occasion that Adam creates here. It is a proclamation and promise made before witnesses who can testify that a promise has indeed been shared, the pronouncement nowadays also being made before the state or its representatives for legal reasons and reasons of social clarity. Most importantly, however, it is a promise and a covenant made before God. *He* was the witness at Adam and Eve's wedding, just as He should be at ours.

Bone of my bones

Marriage, then, is a statement and a commitment made before others, most particularly God. But Adam's words contain more than just this. Adam expresses *identity* with his wife – that they will now be *one* unit, for she is bone of his bones and flesh of his flesh. Independence is gone, but gone in glad surrender because of the fellowship, companionship and creative potential that will replace it.

When Adam speaks this way ("bone of my bones …") he
is also employing the language of *recognition* (after the long
sequence of animal-naming he has finally found what he might
be looking for: another human!), but his words also carry a sense
of being made of the same stuff, of being in it together, partakers
of the same nature. This *identity* Adam expresses speaks of
commonality and fellowship; it incorporates the notion that as
a couple they will have a similar set of problems and needs but
also a similar set of blessings as each other – there is a sense of
shared origins and shared destiny. Adam is emphasising at this
crucial moment the *similarity* in man and woman, the things in
which they are bound together within a marriage, whatever their
differences may be as individuals or as members of a different
sex.

He also puts focus on the fact that they will now be a
new *unit* since they are now one and the same, two parts of
the one whole. This means that to hurt one's partner is to hurt
oneself. Cruelty and mistreatment make no logical sense and are
implicitly excluded from the menu; they would be completely
counterproductive and out of place. Most importantly, Adam
proclaims oneness, that central principle which enables he and
his wife to experience a foretaste of the divine. Adam captures a
great deal in these few short words of his.

Leaving and cleaving

There is an important Biblical principle that God works through
families, the creation of a new family unit being the task on
which the man and his wife will now embark. This means leaving
behind one's parents, a point which is specifically picked out for
further elaboration. Neither Adam nor Eve had human parents,
so they didn't have in-law relationships to worry about – but it
seems as though the scriptures foresee that this might well be an
issue for others. Indeed it has been in many, many marriages; in
fact, it has been said that there is no other cultural stereotype as
powerful as that of mother-in-law.

Why is it that this in-law tension can arise? A common speculation is that a root cause can be insecurity (whether from the wife about whether she will be 'good enough' to 'replace' the man's mother in either his or his mother's opinion, or whether from the mother because she is 'losing' her role of care and nurture for her boy); sometimes it has been explained as culturally embedded competition for the male so that possessiveness rather than insecurity is the driver. But whatever the cause, there is clear direction in this passage about the right way to go: a man is to *leave* his father and his mother and to *cleave* to his wife. This means that if there is tension or interference from parents then it must be made plain, lovingly but clearly and firmly, that the new husband and wife are no longer under the authority of the parents but must make their own decisions and cleave together as a new family unit.

If the tension is between the wife and mother-in-law, then the husband may need to show the headship he has been given in his new family by addressing the matter with his parents. A husband or wife's highest loyalty and commitment is now not to either set of parents but to the spouse; loyalties and authorities have changed. This doesn't mean excluding parents and in-laws; far from it, since the command to honour one's parents remains in place throughout life and is not cancelled out by marriage. But one can honour and respectfully receive suggestions without being *obligated* any longer by parental authority. Parents can offer advice (though they should think smartly about how they do this!), but they are no longer responsible for direction and control, and they should take care not to interfere.

What's love got to do with it?

There is one very surprising detail about the speeches at Adam's wedding (if we might call them that) which is worth reflecting on: the complete absence of any reference to love. This is a very striking omission; even allowing for the fact that Adam can't say everything in this short verse-long speech, one would have thought that he would at least have said this! But no. How can this be?

It is not to say, first of all, that love isn't important or that partners should not love one another.[2] Love certainly has a critical place in marriage passages in the New Testament including Ephesians 5, the most important of all. But given that so many fundamentals of marriage are mentioned in this dense passage in Genesis, it remains conspicuous that love is absent.

Instead what is mentioned is leaving and cleaving and becoming one flesh. Perhaps what is important here is that these are supremely acts of *will*: you choose to leave, you choose to cleave, and you choose to become one flesh; none of these things happen by accident. Love can be an act of will too, but often we perceive it as a *feeling*, something passively experienced which either happens or doesn't and which we can't necessarily control. As a corollary to this it's often assumed in Western culture that if a loving feeling is not there any more then the marriage is over, or might as well be. But such a conclusion has no place in the concept of marriage Adam is putting forward here. We *choose* to leave and cleave, and when we marry this is precisely what we commit to; Adam is correctly focusing on what we must put *into* marriage in terms of promise, resolve and commitment (the active element), not what we may or may not get out of it in terms of our feelings at any particular time (the passive or recipient side). Marriage must be based on a covenant and a choice, not on a feeling.

---

2   It is interesting to note as an aside, however, that many cultures have managed to have marriages with a success rate at least as high as the West through arranged marriages rather than initially love-based marriages. This shows that marriage and even love may ultimately grow even when a couple aren't initially love-struck. Western culture does seem to have over-egged the pudding in its implicit claim that once you 'fall' or have 'that feeling' for someone there is nothing you can do but surrender to it. Vast swathes of human beings have managed to operate marriage at least as successfully and unsuccessfully under other assumptions, suggesting that Western obsession with love as a feeling under which you are helpless is misplaced. To be clear, this is merely an observation about the different ways marriage has worked (and also failed) in human culture through the years, not an argument for or against arranged marriage.

When you think about it, this makes a lot of sense. The basis of marriage cannot be a loving 'feeling', because what happens if that feeling goes away, as it almost inevitably does occasionally during the course of a marriage? What will happen then? Will the marriage just fizzle out and die, leaving us to pack our bags miserably and move on? This is, apparently, the conclusion that many in society have reached and why marriage as an institution has been in a state of some crisis for quite a while in modern life. Perhaps it is the very confusion over this issue, the jarring clash between 'what happens if I don't feel it any more?' and 'but I promised we'd be together until I die' which has led many in the world to choose to live together rather than deal with this issue, abandoning God's commands as they do so.

But there is only a dissonance here if our concept of marriage is based primarily upon *feelings*. We cannot promise we shall always *feel* this way or that; there will be times, hopefully only brief flashes (although it could last for months or even years) where we may *not* feel that way. But we have not promised to *feel*, we have promised to *be* something for our partner and to *do* something, something active which we *can* control: we have promised to leave, to cleave, and to be one. If we really commit to that promise and base our marriage upon it, then it is highly likely that loving feelings will come in tow as our partner responds to us and makes a similar commitment of their own.

Virtuous cycle
What, then, of those passages which *do* speak of love? They are massively important too, and none of the foregoing is meant to deny or downplay the importance of love in marriage. But those scriptures which do deal with love are speaking, I suggest, about *active* love, if we can call it that, rather than passive. They are not speaking of love as a feeling, something which either happens to us or doesn't and may come and go; instead they are speaking of love as an action, love as a conscious choice. This is something very different. Love as a feeling is important – almost everyone experiences it and knows its great power; popular music and

much of literature is virtually one continuous obsession over it – but it must lead to love as a commitment, love as an action.

If this happens – if love as a feeling as we're dating, let us say, grows into love as an action – then we find ourselves in a wonderful virtuous circle. Initial attraction (a feeling) may grow into love (also a feeling), ultimately culminating, if so we choose, in a commitment to marriage which is *more* than a feeling: it is now a promise of the kind that Adam makes in Genesis 2, a resolve of the mind and will, a covenant entered into that come what may we will cleave to our partner and love them by choice.

Those heady feelings of infatuation as a relationship really gets into gear are tremendously important in cementing a couple, but they are an *aspect* of – rather than the *essence* of – what builds a foundation for marriage. This rush of feeling is important and not to be dismissed by any means, but it will not of itself carry a marriage through forty years or more. Commitment and the promise of a cleaving and self-sacrificial love *also* brings wonderful feelings, feelings which develop in their sophistication, power and subtlety as a relationship deepens and grows. It is these feelings, put through the crucible of experience and trial, that enable us to look at our partner and say, 'Yes, it *was* worth it, even in those difficult times when it seemed there was nothing to cling on to *but* our vows. Because now I can say that I know you more and love you in richer hue and with deeper understanding than I ever could before'. Now there is a oneness with a fuller appreciation of what unity in difference really means, a oneness which is different from and yet in many ways more powerful than that initial rush of passion, that seemingly insatiable desire to be together, with which it all may have begun.

One flesh

Returning to the pronouncements at Adam's marriage, we now turn to the physical. The man and his wife are to cleave together not only emotionally, but also physically: they are to be one flesh. This, then, is a final, essential, and amazing component of the 'definition' of marriage at the close of Genesis 2. Sex has been cheapened and isolated from its proper context of marriage by society, but in its proper place it is one of God's most remarkable gifts, a wonderful expression of the spiritual as well as emotional unity that a husband and wife may share. This helps explain how the overtly and covertly sexual language of the Song of Songs can stand not only as a depiction of the potential of human love, but also of the spiritual union of Christ and his bride. Other passages like the Song and Proverbs wax more lyrical on the topic, but the brief reference here leaves us in no doubt of its importance. Sex *outside* marriage is a serious sin, as other scriptures make plain – sex is not the same thing as marriage or a sufficient definition for it, and nor is the desire for sex a sufficient reason to get married – but it is a key component of a scriptural definition of marriage; *within* a marriage it is the most wonderful and complete expression of the unity which God has gifted and enabled.

The narrator's final comment about the nakedness-without-shame that Adam and his wife experienced brings together the sexual, factual and emotional aspects of intimacy which are each to be shared within marriage, each a facet of the richness of unity that a husband and wife will know. They *know* things about each other that no one else knows but God: from physical details, to likes and dislikes, quirks and foibles, weaknesses and strengths. If the correct boundaries have been maintained, they share a physical unity that is shared with no one else in the whole world – a oneness which is a figure for fellowship with God and His Son and for which the scriptural idiom of a man 'knowing' his wife is such a beautiful expression. They share an emotional unity too, an understanding of where the other is coming from, a participating together in life's ups and downs, a shared experience of life lived in the sight of God.

The essence

These short verses at the end of Genesis 2 are thus utterly remarkable for the way in which they pack in so much information in such a brief compass about what marriage truly is from God's perspective. They capture the very essence of marriage – that it is fundamentally about unity and about fellowship, that it involves separation from one's old family, yes, but that it is separation for the purpose of the creation of something new: a new family unit and indeed a delightful encapsulation of the whole of God's purpose. The verses express both the emotional and physical unity which are central to marriage, the new identity a couple comes to share, and they centre marriage not in feelings but in a conscious choice, in promises made and in faithfulness shown. These things – and the love and fellowship which flow from them – are what marriage can and should be all about as God originally intended it.

Adam and Eve: the Fall

Topics: The sexes: order versus value, role versus status; Adam – bringer of sin and death; Male headship in worship and in the family; Eve deceived and punished; Male 'rule' and female 'desire'; Childbearing.

It's time now to tackle in more depth the differences between male and female and what these differences imply for roles and responsibilities within marriage. This takes us particularly into Genesis 3 where we shall need to examine the punishments on the man and woman in the Fall and their consequences for married life.

THE sins of the garden were more than simply a disobeying of God's command by eating forbidden fruit; there was also a breakdown of the Biblically mandated order of things. Genesis 2 reveals that despite the equal status and value of men and women as human beings in God's sight there was nevertheless a particular order and responsibility prescribed by God. God created the man first and gave to him the commandment which Adam is presumably expected to share with his family as its head.[1] This is all undone when Eve takes the initiative in breaking God's command and leading her husband into sin.

---

1 The language of headship is not used in Genesis 2, but it can be regarded as implicit because of the principle of order which is clearly present and is picked up in the New Testament ("For Adam was first formed, then Eve ...", 1 Timothy 2:13).

Order reversed

The point about order is made very elaborately in Genesis. In chapter 2 it works like this:

The divinely appointed order in Genesis 1 and 2 (read left to right, then down)

God   creates
Man   from whose side is created
Woman both of whom are given dominion over
Animals

There is a caveat here. While God is superior to man and woman and they in turn are superior to the animals in terms of faculties and importance, we must be careful how we interpret the man's priority over the woman. As we saw in the first chapter, there is an equality between the man and woman as members of the same species which is also stressed in Genesis, made in the image of God, blessed and commanded to have dominion by Him, thrust from the garden together and receiving the same coats of skins to clothe them. We have to hold that necessary concept ("neither male nor female ... all one in Christ Jesus") alongside Genesis 2's point that man is created first and given particular responsibilities. This is a delicate balance but an important one; the two principles cannot be allowed to be contradictory. We must not say that the man is more important than the woman; they stand equal in the sight of God with respect to salvation. But we can say that he is to be the spiritual head and has particular responsibilities as male without this compromising the previous point. She is to be a helper so that together they can accomplish the commandments of God that were given to Adam, but the term 'helper' doesn't necessarily imply inferiority because the term is elsewhere used of God Himself!

What we are dealing with is a question of *order* not of *value*, or, to put it another way, *role* rather than *status* (our twin concepts of similarity and difference with regard to the relationship of man and woman are helpful to bear in mind here since Genesis is teaching *both* of these: that which is the same about men and women in terms of their privilege and need, and that which is different in terms of their calling and function).

Having dealt with this preliminary, let's continue to explore the principle of order which now wends its way into Genesis 3. An important aspect of the Fall is an error about order in which the chain above (God – man / woman – animals) is completely reversed. Instead of having dominion over the animals Eve listens to and effectively obeys the suggestion of an animal that it would be a good idea to eat the fruit. The upshot of this is that through its suggestion the serpent ends up having dominion over her rather than the other way round. Next, the woman (who received the command of the Lord from her husband and was supposed to be helping him to keep it) now helps her husband into sin by giving him the fruit! What is happening is that she is taking the initiative by leading him into sin whereas he was meant to have been leading her towards salvation. Finally, there is another attempt to usurp the proper hierarchy as Adam and Eve take the fruit in the hope that they will become like God. This is a systematic, point by point reversal of the proper order established in Genesis 1, thus:

The reverse direction of the Fall
Animal   persuades
Woman   who takes the initiative over her
Man   as the pair try to be like
God

The Fall is a disobedience of God's command about fruit-eating, certainly, but it is also a refusal to recognise the principle of role and order that God had established.

It's no surprise, then, that when God comes to address His creatures for their sin He re-establishes the proper order He had instigated in chapter 2:

God   first questions
Man   and then turns to
Woman   and then turns to
Animal

The order is exactly the same as Genesis 2 and the inverse of what had been enacted in the Fall. Just as God first made the man and gave him His command to pass on to his wife, when that command is broken God goes correspondingly not to the woman who first broke the command in chronological time, nor to the serpent who suggested the idea. Instead He goes first to the man, the one to whom the command was given. This fact emphasises the man's role as spokesperson and responsible agent or representative for both his family and the wider world. He represents his family to the world and he represents God to his family since it was his duty to pass on God's commandments. In this he is a kind of interface; his work takes on a priestly dimension which chimes with the roles taken by male priests in the Old Testament and those which males are commanded to undertake during the communal worship of believers in the New Testament.

Back in Genesis, the serpent now functions as a fulcrum as God reverses direction and goes back up the chain as the punishments are handed out. In this way the order of the punishments will conform to the order in which the Fall took place, not the order of responsibility. Given the serpent's fundamentally different and inferior mental and moral apparatus God does not even question it; He simply goes right ahead and announces its punishment (3:15). This is then followed by the punishment on the woman (verse 16), and climactically by the punishment on the man (verse 19), the most devastating aspect of whose punishment, death, will impact *all* creation, not just man himself (in this respect, then, Adam can again be seen to bear responsibility for all creation as representative, just as Christ will finally reconcile all creation to God once more). Adam failed to carry out his task of ensuring that God's command was discharged in his family and in the world and the consequences of this are inherited by all humanity who succeed him (and perhaps all living creatures too). By expressing the punishments in this order the most important punishment of death is recounted in last and climactic place.

Adam's responsibility

It is intriguing that death is ascribed to Adam even though Eve was chronologically the first one who had eaten the fruit. Why should this be? The obvious answer, particularly in the light of the divinely appointed order we have just seen in Genesis 2, is that it is because Adam is the spiritual head of his family. We observed that the command not to eat the fruit was given to Adam and that it was his responsibility to ensure that it was carried out in his family. Thus, even though *Eve* is the first to sin, God first questions *Adam* about what has taken place and assigns to him the most serious punishment (notwithstanding the pains of childbirth, the punishment of universal death is unquestionably more serious; even though women will die as well as men, the scriptures are very clear in stipulating that death was a punishment for Adam and that it has come into the world because of man rather than because of woman).

This marries perfectly with the teaching of Romans. Paul says: "Wherefore, as by one *man* sin entered into the world, and death by sin; and so death passed upon all men, for that all have sinned" (Romans 5:12). Chronologically speaking it was by a woman that sin entered into the world, but chronology is clearly not the point at issue. The issue is instead one of responsibility, Adam's failure being not only his taking of the fruit but also the fact that he became a follower (into sin) rather than a spiritual leader in righteousness. In short, he failed to be a good spiritual head of his family. It is because of these responsibilities that God speaks to him first and it is because of these responsibilities that Adam receives the punishment of death.

1 Timothy casts further light on this when it explains that "Adam was not deceived, but Eve being deceived was in the transgression" (1 Timothy 2:13,14). As soon as we attempt to read this in harmony with Romans it becomes apparent that Paul cannot be saying that there was no transgression on Adam's part in the Fall. Clearly there was – the most fundamental transgression of all, the one that has brought death upon all as Romans explains. Instead, in Timothy Paul must be talking about

either a different sort of transgression or a different aspect of it. In the passage he is explaining the rationale for a woman's less public role in the formal worship of God amongst believers and in explanation of this we must look to her *deception* by the serpent (that is to say, the fact that the serpent tricked her into thinking that it was a good idea to take the fruit) coupled with the fact that Adam was first formed then Eve (whence his role and responsibility as spiritual head). These points entail that males should lead communal worship – the topic of the Timothy passage – partly because males have to put right what they got wrong (spiritual leadership) and females have to put right what *they* got wrong (leading into sin instead of helping in righteousness).

But what does this imply about the nature of the Fall and how can it help us understand Adam's role? It implies that the nature of Adam's sin was different from Eve's. If Eve was 'tricked' or 'deceived' by the serpent, Adam was not – the record says specifically that he was "not deceived". What, then, was the nature of his sin? If he was not deceived then he knew full well what he was doing – the sin was deliberate. In full knowledge and awareness that he was seriously contravening the commandments of God, Adam chose to join his wife by following her lead into sin rather than standing up for righteousness as spiritual head. The deliberate and blatant nature of his sin may therefore be a further aspect behind God's assigning him the role of 'death-bringer' – the one who brings sin into the world and death by sin.

Spiritual headship
But if that is one aspect, there is another. God had given His commandment to Adam rather than to Eve (who hadn't even been created at the time) and was therefore putting responsibility for the family's spiritual performance and health at his door. When the family falls one by one into sin it is only appropriate, therefore, that God should first speak to Adam about it to ask

him what has gone wrong in the family unit of which he was supposed to have been head.

Is there a modern day analogy to this which doesn't involve fruit and trees? Perhaps so. If in what is supposed to be a godly household spiritual topics are not brought up and discussed, if the Bible is not being read and prayer not offered, and if, instead, there is a preoccupation with self-seeking entertainment, say, or money-making to the exclusion of other more important matters, then God comes knocking, as it were, at the man's door first because he is not properly exercising his role as spiritual head. In such a scenario the modern day husband is not seeing to it that God's commands are practised in his family as he should, his sin starting to take on resemblances of Adam's failure all those years before. What is required here is not a heavy-handed humourless thumping of the Bible, but rather a gentle and 'smart' leading of the family in the ways of God with the word of God at the centre. And the great news is that he has his wife to help him in his essential task.

Does this notion of the husband's responsibility for the family remove the principle of individual responsibility? Does it mean that, because the man has the role of spiritual head of his family that the woman can get away scot-free behaving how she likes? Clearly not; that would make no sense, and the husband cannot be held responsible for the individual decisions the members of his family may make. She too must play her part, bearing responsibility for her own actions as helper, the influence she has on her husband, and her role as mother to any children she may have. The children also have increasingly to learn the independence to make their own decisions as well and thus to carry their share of responsibility. But it remains the case that the man bears primary responsibility for the spiritual health and direction of his family as a whole and the influences it is subject to, his wife by his side helping him in this crucial responsibility.

In sum, the teaching of Genesis concerning male headship finds its fulfilment in two aspects of modern life. One is the more public role males must play in ecclesial worship which is not the topic of this book. The other is the one we have been discussing: the role of the male as spiritual head in his family which will be enlarged on further in later chapters but in particular in Part 3 when we look at the role of husbands. In both of these aspects, congregation and family, public and private, what the man is now expected to do – as drawn out explicitly in New Testament passages like Ephesians 5, 1 Corinthians 14, 1 Timothy 2 and 5, etc. – is to see to it that he gets right the very things that went wrong in Genesis. He must be a spiritual leader where once he was a follower in sin; he must speak out God's word in his family and in his community as once he failed adequately to accomplish. For her part, the woman must help where once she hindered; she must look to her husband instead of leading him astray.

The punishment on the woman
We've thought about the punishment of death brought upon the man by his deliberate sin, but the scriptures also mention the curse on the ground for his sake and the sorrow of his labour and toil. This punishment of work (necessary in order to have food to eat) is assigned to the man not to the woman, so the pattern is evidently that he would share the fruits of his labours with his wife while at the same time bearing the sorrow of their hard toil. The passage does not say that the woman would not or should not work – and there is no other scripture that says so either – but it is clear at the very least that there is no *requirement* or *expectation* that she should do so. If she chooses to then she is entering into a burden and to a toil that is incremental or additional to the one that God has assigned her, a burden that she doesn't 'need' to take which will put her under more stress and pressure than God requires of her. She may choose to do this for one reason or another, but she should be aware that if she does so she is going 'above and beyond' what the scriptures require of her and is taking on an additional burden that from a spiritual perspective she does not need to take. Of course there may be exceptional circumstances in which there is a true economic need – though sometimes it may be more of a lifestyle

'want' than a real 'need' – or she may simply choose to do so for reasons of personal fulfilment. But this shouldn't get in the way of her scripturally mandated responsibilities towards her family (on which more later). If children are neglected in some way, for instance, because she is out at work, then she is leaving undone something that the scriptures do require of her in order to focus on something that they don't.

What, then, do the scriptures say to the woman, and what light does this cast on her role in marriage and in the family more broadly? Here is the requisite passage:

"Unto the woman he said, I will greatly multiply thy sorrow and thy conception; in sorrow thou shalt bring forth children; and thy desire shall be to thy husband, and he shall rule over thee."   (Genesis 3:16)

Let's first take the relationship with her husband – the 'desire' and the 'ruling'; after that we shall turn to her role as mother. The question immediately arises whether these words about desire and rule are prescriptive (men *ought* to rule over their wives) or whether they are descriptive, the passage stating what in practice would happen even though it should not, at least not in the cruel way that 'rule' is sometimes exercised through oppression (the passage thus prophesying and predicting the whole sorry history of male exploitation of the female). My suspicion is that there is an element of both prescription and prediction in the passage so that it carries a dual fulfilment and is true at both levels. At one level, then, men *ought* to exercise scriptural, self-sacrificial spiritual headship in their families which their wives should accept; this is what should be, after the manner of Ephesians 5 with Christ's self-sacrificial headship of the church the model for the husband's headship, not some warped notion of male power or supremacy. At another level, because of sin (the ignorance of God and a wrong model for leadership embedded into society) men will often rule over and oppress women in a way which is evil and not sanctioned in the scriptures at all, Biblical headship morphing into a cruel and exploitative control. This is a matter-of-fact consequence of sin, the scriptures descriptively telling us how it will be as the physically stronger exploit the physically weaker (incidentally the very opposite of what Peter calls for when he tells men to honour their wives as "the [physically] weaker vessel"). It isn't *right* that this kind of exploitative 'rule' should have so often been practised, any more than any other sin is right. But this doesn't change the fact that this is what all too often has been the case in cruel human history, the passage prophetically capturing this in a powerful way.

What God requires instead is the spiritual leadership of the male, a spiritual headship carried out in the spirit of Christ. As a result of this calling the man carries the responsibility for overall direction of the family (again, this is why Adam is questioned by God first) even though the two stand equal in status as sinners before God. Genesis 3:16 thus makes clear this subjection of the woman to the spiritual leadership of the man.

This concept of male headship (or 'rulership' as it is expressed here) can make us feel very uncomfortable in modern culture. It can be hard for a woman to accept, perhaps, but it may be equally hard for the man who may feel quite self-conscious and uncomfortable about it, perhaps feeling that if anything his wife is the more spiritual creature of the two of them. It is important to realise though that feelings of discomfort with this principle of male spiritual headship are culturally driven, and the culture – with the self-evident problems that it has generated with its 50% divorce rate and the crass sexualisation of women – ought not to be our guide in these matters in preference to the word of God. I was struck by the force of this cultural point when I was once on a flight back from South Africa. The passenger next to me was a businessman from Ghana, and we got to discussing our religious views. I mentioned that I was writing about marriage, and we chatted about male and female roles. It was interesting how, as someone from a completely different culture, he was unencumbered by any feelings of awkwardness about the topic of male headship. It seemed as natural to him as it might feel awkward to a Western believer trying to describe their views about the roles of man and woman within a Christian marriage to someone who has no Biblical perspective. What the culture says has nothing at all to do with what is right or wrong from God's perspective.

So much for the 'rulership' then (we shall be exploring what it means in practice in much more detail later in this book), what about the 'desire' of the woman being towards her husband? The basic meaning of this term 'desire' is 'turning' which seems to suggest the ideas of need and reliance. It might encompass sexual desire or economic reliance; it can be about more than both of these. She is to turn to her husband, to rely upon him rather than her friends, her parents, or her own ability to be independent. Again, there may be an element of both the prescriptive and the descriptive here. A woman *should* turn to her husband for his spiritual leadership and for other aspects of provision (rather than turning to other men or to any of the other sources we just enumerated); this will build a united family in which the two tend towards oneness as God requires. But the phrase may also describe and predict in a value-neutral way what would in fact transpire in the thousands of years of human history that have happened since. Whereas a man's sexual desires may easily be to any woman who he finds attractive (and he must therefore exercise strong self-discipline to control himself), a woman is more likely to turn for her needs to one to whom she is emotionally close (the idea being that this will be her husband). Similarly, it is a fact that for most of human history in most places in the world women have been economically dependent on men, as the passage may predict though not prescribe.

The other occurrences of the word 'desire' are interesting. In total the term is only used three times, another occurrence being in Genesis 4 which states that Abel's 'desire' or turning would remain towards Cain if Cain did the right thing – the background to this might be the spiritual leadership that Cain should have had as firstborn; if Cain offered a sacrifice to atone for his sin then perhaps he would retain his position as family priest (Abel's 'turning' towards him for this function would thus continue). If such a reading is correct, then it would suggest that there could be a spiritual dimension to the 'desire' of Genesis 3:16 also: a reference to the spiritual function that the man would fulfil as minister of the word of God and the leader of worship in his family (his wife would 'turn' to him to fulfil this function). The third passage where the term is used presents an interesting twist because it shows that the 'turning' between a man and a woman is not all one way – it is not just that the woman turns to the man for various needs while he has no needs of his own. In the Song the woman states that his desire (that is, her lover's desire) is towards her and that she is his. There is thus a reciprocal element to 'turning' and desire. Even if women have been 'dependent' on their husbands in various different ways throughout human history, in a good marriage patterned on Christ and his bride there will be a mutual element to the dependence.

Mother of all living

The other aspect that Genesis 3 brings out in the punishment of the woman is her role as child-bearer and mother. She will bring forth children in sorrow, just as man will sorrowfully bring forth food from the soil over which he toils. What is this sorrow of childbearing? At one level it is the physical pain of labour and the health dangers that childbirth has brought through much of history when medical technology was not what it is in the West today. But the sorrow also speaks of the emotional burden that a woman will carry for her children throughout her life, an area in which it might be easier for the average male to have a greater degree of emotional detachment not having carried the child in the womb or given birth himself.

While the punishment on the woman focuses on the sorrow of childbirth and motherhood, there is nevertheless a massive amount of potential joy in childbirth as well. Jesus picks this up in John 16:

"A woman when she is in travail hath sorrow, because her hour is come: but as soon as she is delivered of the child, she remembereth no more the anguish, for joy that a man is born into the world." (John 16:21)

Jesus' use of the expression "her hour is come" in relation to her labour suggests that these pains are almost a kind of death (the main use of this expression in the Gospels is for Jesus to speak about the sorrow of his own death). The whole principle of salvation is built on the idea of death giving birth to new life, and it could be that Jesus is suggesting a link with the childbirth metaphor in this. Jesus underwent the suffering of death when his hour was come in order to become the firstborn of the New Creation. A woman, similarly, suffers the travail of childbirth – her hour of death-like pain – in order to give birth to a new life. Correspondingly, human society as we know it must undergo a kind of 'death' at the end-time when its 'hour' is come in order to usher in the birth of God's kingdom (this is what the John passage is about, and it is also what Romans 8 is about, a passage which similarly uses the metaphor of travail and childbirth to talk about the troubles that will herald the advent of God's future kingdom). There is a pattern of spiritual things here then, enshrined in the natural things of childbirth. These spiritual things are enacted in parable every time a child is born.

Childbirth is thus a reminder of how God's whole plan of salvation will come about. We've examined how this works in general terms, but it works too in the specific details of Jesus' own birth. The birth of a new child is the ultimate symbol of hope. Only the verse before Eve's punishment God had foretold how one day her seed would crush the serpent's head – and now, immediately afterwards, God tells her of childbirth. It would be a painful process, but through her having children the hope would come of a solution to the serpent's legacy of sin and death. Adam had brought death into the world, but through the pain of her childbirth she would be the bringer of life, the mother of all living. From that point on, therefore, every time a child was born there would have been the theoretical hope that this child could be the one, the one that God had promised who would free men from sin and death. Those hopes were not fulfilled until Mary's child Jesus finally came, but still the hope was enshrined or re-enacted with every birth: the *possibility* of salvation was alluded to. And then at last it happened – Mary conceived by the Holy Spirit and God's plan came to fruition; he was indeed the "seed of the woman", a child born without the involvement of any man. Every birth that has happened since that time has similarly been a reminder – a re-enactment – of the way God chose to save men and women. This is what Paul is talking about when he speaks of women being "saved in childbearing" (1 Timothy 2:15). No woman other than Mary has given birth to God's *actual* Son, but in the birth of each human baby the possibility of a new start is enshrined. Meanwhile the woman's massive responsibility as mother of a new generation is re-emphasised through time as each and every child is born.

In all this Genesis 3 establishes the role of the woman as mother and carer for her family (she is interestingly called the mother of "all living", not just her own children which may allude to her wider empathetic capacities). This chimes perfectly with what the New Testament says about the role of women within marriage with respect to the family. We shall look more closely at the "keepers at home" and "guide the house" passages from the pastoral epistles later (chapter 33; cf. also chapter 19), for now merely noting the connection and the consistency of the message. The wife has a particular responsibility 'inwards' towards the home and her family, just as the husband has a particular responsibility to lead the family forwards in a spiritual direction and as he interfaces with the outside world through his role as worker, provider and spiritual head.

Just as we saw with the man, the teaching of Genesis 3 in the punishment of Eve forms the basis of the teaching elsewhere in scripture – particularly the New Testament – concerning the role women are asked to take both in public worship and in their role in the family and their relationship towards their husbands. Everything builds on the foundation of Genesis: in terms of the nature of their individual commissions as man and woman, the different nature of their respective sin, the breakdown of the order which God appointed, and the distinct punishment He allocated – each appropriate to their gender; we'll explore some of the practical outworking of what this might mean in the next chapter.

Christ and his Bride

Topics: Marriage is about Christ, not us; Living parables; Wives submit as if to Christ; Husbands love as much as Christ; A wife's need for her husband's love; What does 'submission' mean?; A husband's need for his wife's respect and validation.

In the last three chapters we have looked back at how marriage began in Genesis: its divine design and wonderful benefits, the principle of similarity and also the difference of order and role God has called for from men and women within marriage. In all this we have been thinking about the origins of God's marriage requirements and what they mean for marriage today. While this is an extremely useful exercise, marriages are not primarily to be built by looking backwards, informative though it is; instead they are to look forwards in an ambitious way to an even better pattern, one which was never marred by sin at least on one side – the example of Christ and his relationship with the body of believers. It is to this we now turn.

W E'LL address the topic from the angle of Ephesians 5, the most sustained New Testament exposition on marriage. What is supremely interesting about this passage is that it seems on first reading to be about *our* marriages, but Paul's whole point is really that our marriages are not really the subject at issue at all. They are not the real point – that is to say, they are not ends in themselves; instead what they are really about is Christ and his bride. It is *that* marriage which is the most important of all and our attention is turned to that fact by one of the smallest but most important of words...

The importance of 'as'

Dennis Gillett once wrote some articles called "Little Words, Big Meanings" (now included in the book, *Words and Weights*) which captured a most important point: sometimes the littlest words can capture the most important truths; these little words can be the keys to unlock some of scripture's 'Big Passages'. The same notion was captured in the title of another unrelated book: *The Little Big*.

One such 'big' passage is Ephesians 5, the scriptural 'recipe' for Christian marriage. There are a number of important words in the passage but one of the most significant and oft-repeated has merely two letters. It is the word 'as':

"Wives, submit yourselves unto your own husbands, *as* unto the Lord."   (verse 22)

"For the husband is the head of the wife, even *as* Christ is the head of the church."   (verse 23)

"Therefore *as* the church is subject unto Christ, so let the wives be to their own husbands."   (verse 24)

"Husbands, love your wives, even *as* Christ also loved the church and gave himself for it."   (verse 25)

"So ought men to love their wives *as* their own bodies."
                                                   (verse 28)

"For no man ever yet hated his own flesh; but nourisheth and cherisheth it, even *as* the Lord the church."   (verse 29)

"Nevertheless, let every one of you in particular so love his wife even *as* himself."   (verse 33)

There are seven occurrences here in all, six of them defining the marriage relationship of the man and his wife in terms of something else – something bigger than either of them – the relationship of Christ and the church. The one is to be shaped, patterned and defined by the other. The couple's marriage does not exist in its own right or for its own ends; instead it is to be *as* something else. It is to find its truest meaning and its highest goal in terms of another marriage, the marriage of Christ and his bride.

In a world which has so very much 'take' and a whole lot less 'give', this is revolutionary. The idea that my marriage might not be about *me* or even *us* (my wife and I) but about someone and something else is shocking. And yet, by his insistent repetition of this little word 'as', Paul drives home that the analogy really is what it's all about. The more we can re-conceive our relationships on this higher level, seeing them as a living parable of something else, the more we shall be relieved from the ever-present danger of self-seeking and sullen dissatisfaction. It will give us a glue and a reason beyond ourselves to stick together through fallow times.

When we think about the power of 'as', therefore, we can find real exhortation and real challenge to take our marriage relationships to a higher level. Let's consider how it will work from the perspective of each of the partners. As for wives, they are to love their husbands, submitting and respecting *as if* he were Christ. Now if they have any sense at all, both the wife and the husband will know that this is not in actual fact the case. In my own case my wife knows only too well all the ways in which I am *not* like Christ and fall short of his example. Yet she is asked to treat me as if I were, in spite of this glaring incongruity! *In the face of* my blatant falling short, she is asked to submit and honour my headship. A wife is to do this, not for what her husband is, *but for what Christ is*. When she does so, she not only honours her husband, but, much more importantly, she honours Christ who is the true head her husband but typifies. She does all this not because she thinks her husband is necessarily so great (hopefully he is doing his best, but no doubt he has many failings!) but because she thinks *Christ* is great, holding him in the highest regard.

When we turn to husbands, they are to love their wives and give to them their everything – for this is what Christ gave, even his very life for his bride's salvation. The husband is to love his wife *as* the Lord loved the church and gave himself for it. He is to be *that* kind of self-sacrificial head, one who did not lord it over God's heritage but as lord and master washed his disciples' feet. No human has shown greater love than this, and it is *this* which is to be the measure and definition of the husband's love, cherishing and nurturing his wife and family with that same self-giving love as Christ. If he does this there will be no problem about the notion of 'headship' as a power play; it simply cannot happen. 'As' is thus a measure-word: it is the measure of the nature of the wife's submission to and appreciation of Christ and it is the measure of the quantity and calibre of the husband's love.

Both roles, therefore – husband and wife – are incredibly difficult, ones which we shall not find ourselves able to carry out perfectly. But it is the aspirational nature of this ideal, the potential beauty of what we are called to strive to achieve in the daily comings and goings of life which is inspiring. The scriptures are full of images and parables, and God asks us to build our own living parable through the daily ups and downs of married life. It is an eloquent way of showing how much we appreciate what God has done for us in Christ and the extent of our love for him. With this as a foundation, therefore, we can turn to a closer examination of what Paul enjoins upon the husband and wife in their turn.

The husband

The husband receives more attention than the wife in terms of the number of instructional verses devoted to him (he gets nine, she gets three or four), and the insistent emphasis is very clear:

"Husbands, *love your wives*, even as Christ also loved the church ..."   (Ephesians 5:25)

"So ought men to *love their wives* as their own bodies ..."
                                              (verse 28)

"He that *loveth his wife* loveth himself."   (verse 28)

"Nevertheless let every one of you in particular so *love his wife* as himself ..."   (verse 33)

Four times, then, it is stated that he is to love her, the measure of his love being clearly delineated in the first passage as we have already seen: the ultimate, self-sacrificial love of Christ for the church, the greatest love possible in which a man lays down his life for his friends. It is the opposite of Abraham and Isaac's, "She is my sister" approach in which they were afraid to die for the sake of their wives. It is the opposite of Adam's joining his wife in sin rather than trying to save her, the opposite of Lot who would have sent out his daughters to the evil men of Sodom, or the Levite who sent out his concubine to be sacrificed to the lusts of an angry mob. The love of a man for his wife is to be modelled on the greatest love of all.

A second measure for the husband's love is that he should love her as he loves himself. Perhaps selfishness and pre-occupation comes more naturally to a man than to a woman, but if this be true and it is possible for a man to relate to what it means to love himself and take care of his own interests, then this is precisely the extent of the love he should bestow on his wife. "No man yet hated his own body", says Paul, "but loves it and cherishes it; even so should husbands love their wives as their own bodies." This point is made twice over in the passage to make sure that it has sunk in (5:28,33). Anything that you would do to take care of your own interests you should be looking to do for your wife.

It isn't just Ephesians that emphasises the imperative that love should issue from the man and that he should focus particularly on this aspect of his marriage, there are other passages as well. They may not necessarily use exactly the same language, but the point they seem to be getting at looks similar:

"Husbands *love your wives* and be not bitter against them ..."
(Colossians 3:19)

"Likewise, ye husbands ... *giv(e) honour unto the wife* ..."
(1 Peter 3:7)

There are a couple of fascinating things here. One is that the emphasis and repetition should be so insistent; why should Paul need to emphasise so many times that a man should love his wife? Isn't it obvious that this should be the case? Yet there it is: "Love her ... love her ... love her ... love her" in Ephesians 5. Second, how come Paul doesn't tell the wife to love her husband with the same repetition? In fact he hardly tells her at all, instead focusing on something quite different. Why should the husband be told to put such focus on love when it scarcely be mentioned for the wife?

There are perhaps two aspects, the first in terms of the husband's own nature and capabilities (what he will find difficult and therefore needs to give attention to), the second in terms of the wife's needs. Let's take the husband himself first of all. He needs telling to focus on showing love to his wife because it doesn't necessarily come easy to him to do so – he isn't naturally very good at it! A woman generally speaking does not need telling how to love or that she must focus on it in a relationship with someone she is close to. She has been pre-wired by God, we might say, to show concern, empathy and affection, to be emotionally engaged. A man, however, may need to focus actively on these things; he may be more inclined to be wrapped up in his own world, more concerned with the relationship of the family to the outside world. He is cautious, perhaps, of appearing 'soft' or 'vulnerable'; he may find it harder to show his love. It is a cliché and a stereotype, but it has become one because there is often truth in it – men can be somewhat 'emotionally constipated', finding it difficult to be aware of and to express their emotions in comparison to a woman.

But if this is at all the case, Paul insists that he must get over it: the husband is to love his wife, to love her, to love her and to love her. He mustn't take his focus off this aspect – he must make sure he is doing his divinely ordained duty as Christ loved the church, and he should ensure that his wife knows that she is loved. This isn't necessarily about saying 'I love you' at every conceivable moment; it is about making sure that his wife is assured of his love in whatever way she most appreciates it. He must make sure that if his wife were ever to be asked, 'Are you sure your husband loves you, and how do you know?' then she would have no hesitation in her reply. This is a great test, and a worthwhile question for husbands to ask their wives from time to time ('Do you feel sure that I love you, and is there any way I can demonstrate it better or make you feel more certain of it?') – with no defensiveness or push-back, just a simple desire to know whether or not we are doing our job properly, and whether there is any way we can improve in this fundamental responsibility. She – not him – must be the arbiter of whether or not what he is doing is working; it is no use for him to *claim* he loves her – it is only working if she feels it and knows it.

The second aspect to all of this arises from the wife's perspective. Love is not only something that might be difficult for the husband to show, it is also the thing that his wife most needs – she needs to *feel loved*. This is a very important point. Everyone has different emotional needs and these can vary over time, but one of the most fundamental needs for a woman in her marriage is to be confident in the love of her husband. It is supremely reassuring; it provides a foundation that can be relied upon as a constant, a resource that can be tapped no matter what else is going on. It helps her to feel safe, secure and special; it can be the life-force that helps her carry on.

What we are saying, then, is that Paul asks husbands to concentrate on that which might be most difficult for them, yet which paradoxically their wives may most need. There is something beautiful and apposite about this. A husband's communication with and passion for his wife is not something scripture allows to stop with courtship or the early years of marriage. A husband owes it to his wife and to his Lord that he pay conscious and constant attention to this critical aspect of his marriage. Would the church ever forget that Christ loved her? Would Christ ever stop showing his love? If the answer to these is 'No', then so it must be for a husband towards his wife. He must ensure that he shows his love and that his wife is assured of it. It is a crucial ingredient in God's recipe, and in a sense it is the single most powerful thing a husband can do to improve his marriage. If there are problems, what should he do?

Just love her. What if she doesn't respond right away? Just keep concentrating on loving her; this is what God has asked. What if she is suspicious or persists in her annoying behaviour? Same answer – love her and keep loving her. Of course issues have to be talked about and reasoned through; a husband is always going to be impacted by the behaviour and attitudes of his wife making his task easier or harder at any particular time. But his first responsibility is always to come back to Paul's fourfold dictum of Ephesians 5: "Husbands love your wives."

For most of us, whatever the difficulties, resentments or frustrations in our marriages, if the question came back to us, 'But have you really done the very best you possibly can in repeatedly and consistently showing your wife that you love her?' we would probably have to admit that there is more to be done. If that is at all the case, then that is what we should be doing. It is the very essence of the analogy between Christ and his bride: that the husband should strive above all else to illustrate the love of Christ in his relationship with his wife, imperfect as she is, because Christ loves us in spite of our faults. It's God's recipe, and He is the Master Chef.

The wife

Just as it was for the husband, so too for the wife. Ephesians 5 presents a challenge which is emphatically repeated. If she manages to achieve this she will have gone a long way down the path of fulfilling her role as representing the bride in the Christ-church parable. The command is the following:

"*Wives, submit yourselves* unto your own husbands as unto the Lord ..."   (verse 22)

"Therefore as the church is *subject unto* Christ, so let the *wives be* to their own husbands in everything ..."   (verse 24)

"... And the *wife* see that she *reverence* her husband."
                                                                (verse 33)

And to demonstrate this isn't a concept restricted to this passage, here are the other New Testament references to the same theme:

"*Wives, submit yourselves* unto your own husbands, as it is fit
in the Lord."   (Colossians 3:18)
"But I suffer not a woman to teach, *nor to usurp authority* over
the man …"   (1 Timothy 2:12)
"(Young women) be discreet, chaste, keepers at home, good,
obedient to their own husbands …"   (Titus 2:5)
"Likewise ye *wives, be in subjection* to your own husbands …"
                                                 (1 Peter 3:1,5)

The idea of submission carries almost entirely negative
overtones in modern culture. The long history of the oppression
and abuse of women at the hand of males has deserved this in
considerable degree of course, but it is important not to be swayed
into apologising for (or worse, denying) scriptural teaching on
this matter. With modern cultural norms pushing down on us
it is tempting to assume that submission must be something
negative and repressive and therefore to want to 'explain away',
minimise or sweep these passages under the carpet.

But we need to realise what we are doing if we take that
step. US pastor Voddie Baucham once pointed out that we are very
grateful to God for positioning the earth the precise distance that
it is from the sun (not too close so that we fry, nor too far so that
we freeze); we are thankful to Him for establishing the physical
constants of the universe, such as the gravitational constant,
exactly where they are (if any of these were infinitesimally
different life as we know it would be completely impossible). We
admire His skills in these areas, His artistry and power seen in
all aspects of creation. We are grateful to Him and don't debate
whether He knew what He was doing or whether He has done
the right thing in these matters; we trust that His competence
is infinitely greater than ours and allow Him space to be who
He is – God. Yet when it comes to the submission concept we
can be tempted to start doubting. We can begin to second guess
Him, to think that He must have been somehow mistaken or
that we have now become more enlightened than He. If we are
prepared to allow Him to be the Expert of the cosmos, whether
at the sub-atomic level or the level of stars and galaxies, why

would we not allow Him to be the Expert of relationships? If He made us and perfectly understands us then why wouldn't we trust Him to know how relationships stand the best chance of working effectively? His model is the model of male headship, and for this to be even remotely possible the wife has to practise submission.

In a way the very word 'submit' has become so loaded, so replete with the overtones of sexism and repression – almost a dirty word – that it might be better if we could find a different word entirely that didn't have these negative connotations. One way of paraphrasing, perhaps, when Paul says "Wives submit to your husbands" is to understand the phrase in the sense of 'Wives, allow your husband (space) to be the spiritual head'. This means not competing with him for that role but instead helping him to fulfil it. A creature that has two heads is a monster, and a relationship that tries to function that way can end up looking very much the same.

There is a crucial point to note here. A husband can only become the spiritual head that God asks him to be if the wife allows him to be it – if she gives him the space and the support. If she fights him for it there will instead be either strife or else one of the parties will retreat in frustrated silence for the sake of a quiet life. What is the man to do if his wife will not allow him this space? Arm-wrestle her for it? The very concept is ludicrous, but it illustrates powerfully that the headship of the male is not something that he can take by force but rather something which is in *her gift*. If he attempts to take it by force – by imposing his will in some way upon the family – then we shall have something horrible, not like the Christ-parable at all. The very idea of the man attempting to force his will takes us back into the era of repression and risks causing severe harm to all in the family; that's clearly not what Paul has in mind and would not be in the spirit of Christ. But if the wife is not prepared to allow him to learn spiritual headship by giving him the space to step into that role we shall also have something which is not in the spirit of Christ, a marriage not made according to God's recipe. Spiritual headship is in the gift of the wife – she must create space for her husband to grow into what Adam failed to be; it is her job to help him and support him in that task, treating him with respect as she would respect her Lord Jesus Christ. This is how he will grow to become the spiritual man that God wants him to be.

This term *respect* is critical in all this. Three times in Ephesians 5 Paul talks about submission, but in the final reference to this idea, right towards the very end of the chapter, Paul talks about the wife's reverence or respect for her husband. To respect one's husband means to give space and worth to his opinions; it means to speak highly of him and it means to *think* highly of him in one's heart (remember Sarah who called Abraham "lord" even when he wasn't present). This isn't easy. A wife will be very aware that some of the things her husband thinks, says and does are selfish, others are idiosyncratic (perhaps in a vaguely charming way!) and yet other things he thinks are perhaps downright foolish. He is a sinner, after all, just like she is, and it can be easy to get into the habit of seeing one's partner through negative spectacles and zooming in on these aspects as though they are representative of the whole package. But to reverence one's husband is to do the opposite of this.

Now why is this matter of respect so important? It is just as we saw with the husband. It is a real challenge for him consistently to express his love to his wife in a way that will make her feel nurtured and appreciated, yet it is one of her deepest needs in the relationship. Similarly, it is a real challenge for the wife, through all her husband's quirks and foibles, to show him respect in public, in private, and in her heart – and to give him the space to be the spiritual head when at times she may well feel she would do a better job. But he *needs* that respect and validation just as much as she needs the love we spoke about earlier. This isn't to say that she doesn't value being respected also or that he has no need for love; at some level these are universal needs for all human beings. Generally speaking, however, the feeling of being loved will be more important to her, and the feeling of being respected will be more important to him. We can link this to a man's ego and speculate about what it is in the male psyche that makes him like this, but it is probably better simply to recognise that it is broadly true. A man seems to find this validation from his wife an important part of feeling good about himself; for him one of the key ways in which he feels loved by his wife is by feeling that both he as a person and the views that he holds are respected even where they are not always agreed with. It can be useful for a wife to ask her husband whether he feels that he does have her respect in this way – it is not whether *she* claims she is or isn't respecting him that counts here, it is whether *he* feels it which is key because this is something that he needs in the relationship and which God has asked her to supply.

There is a wonderful mutuality about the template God mandates and which Paul puts before us in Ephesians 5. It is aspirational and idealistic in the best of senses, and it has the power to transform married life. To each of the partners in the marriage God asks what is difficult but also what is supremely valuable in developing our own character and meeting the needs of the other. If a man truly takes his example of headship from his Lord and focuses on loving his wife in the fullest, most sacrificial way possible as Christ loved the church, then it will be entirely natural and appropriate for his wife to submit to his spiritual leadership and the greater husband he prefigures in the great marriage parable. This submission will not be about kowtowing on her part or a power-trip on his but rather a giving of space for him to grow to be like his Lord, a respect and validation that makes him aspire to be his best. Her 'submission' and the help she will bring will have nothing to do with subservience or the suppression of her own personality and interests but everything to do with embracing her divinely mandated responsibilities towards the family, the development of godly virtues that He seeks from the bride of believers as a whole, and the enabling of her husband to aspire to become the man she treats him as. Her respect fuels his love, and his love increases her respect in one virtuous circle which has Christ at its centre for both partners. It is a surprising model – most likely not one we would have either thought of or chosen if left to our own devices and certainly not one which harmonises well with the voice of the culture – but it is *God's* model. The question is whether or not we trust Him to know what is best.

Part 2
Finding the right partner

Introduction:
the right match

Topics: A crucial choice; Reasons to date – good and bad; What to look for – external versus internal; Knowing oneself; Is this the one?; Talk, talk, talk.

NOTE: Many readers will already be married and therefore wonder whether there is any point wading through several chapters on choosing a partner and dating. By all means skip this part in that case. Some of the scriptural case studies we shall examine (chapters 7 to 11) may still be relevant and interesting for married and unmarried alike.

THE scriptures do not really give dating advice; in fact there isn't even a category of 'dating' from a Biblical perspective: you are either single, betrothed, or married. Nor do we know a lot about how men and women would meet and how marriages were agreed in Biblical times. Isaac's marriage to Rebekah is an example of an arranged marriage; Samson's marriage to his Philistine wife takes place after he sees the woman and believes he is in love, dispatching his parents to go and take care of the details; Shechem's hoped-for marriage to Dinah is sought after the two had met and fraternised, a meeting of the families then being necessary to work out whether or not a marriage could be agreed. There are several other examples here and there, but details are scant and it would not really be possible to construct a scriptural 'model' for how marriages are meant to come about from this dataset. In contrast to the very clear passages setting out the scriptural pattern for marriage there are very few details about what comes before. This suggests that the process through which a couple agrees to marry is less important; it appears that God is content to let this be to some extent culturally determined – it is what happens when and after the couple decides to marry rather than how they get to that point which appears to be the more critical point.

This does not mean that 'anything goes' beforehand, however. There are some very clear passages that mandate that sexual relations are only for within marriage (to be discussed in chapter 28), and there are clear examples of bad marriage choices which provide stern warning. The right approach is to consider what scriptural principles are in play in the decision of whether and who to marry and also in the matter of how to conduct oneself in a relationship while that decision is being made.

No one walking this earth is likely to have a greater impact on our spiritual well-being and potential than our marriage partner, should we choose to marry. That is how important it is. I once remember an older brother saying to me (in a particularly thick northern British accent): "You want to know what a nightmare is? It's being married to a woman you can't stand." He had a point – we simply don't want to get this one wrong. To make a wrong or bad choice here will have terrible emotional and possibly spiritual consequences; it can make life thoroughly miserable and worse. Dating is an opportunity to do our utmost to make sure we don't make that mistake. Or, to put it positively, it is an opportunity to work out whether a person we are attracted to is the right person from a spiritual, emotional and practical perspective for us to build a home with, to create a shared life together, and to be one with in the sight of God.

Lesser motives
Once we see it in this way then it gives the lie to other potential motives we might have in dating. Dating is not for self-indulgence, for simply 'having a good time' by trying out as many

different potential partners as we possibly can and obtaining the maximum physical gratification that we can or dare. Our lives are lived before God, and our aim in dating as in everything else in life is that our bodies should be a temple for Him and that we should give Him glory by the way that we behave.

It is also unhealthy and even dangerous to date from a position of emotional neediness. People sometimes speak of making mistakes when dating 'on the rebound' after another relationship has broken down, so this may be a time to exercise particular restraint. Similarly it is good to be secure in who you are yourself and in your relationship with God first, before looking to another person for fulfilment or to obtain a sense of identity from them. Some people move from relationship to relationship, each new partner allegedly 'the one', yet none of them ever really lasting more than a few weeks or months. Such people seem to have a deep emotional need to have to be with someone in order to be legitimised as a person, but this isn't healthy and the attempt to fill an emotional void or make up for an insecurity through one's relationship with another person is not wise. We shall be much more likely to make good decisions about who to be with if we are already somewhat grounded and settled as a person in our own right and confident in our relationship with God – the most important relationship of all.

Sometimes young people can feel pressure to date because their friends and peers are doing so and seem to talk about nothing else – but this isn't a good reason either. While one of the wonderful things about finding the right partner is the sense of completion that it brings, we still need to have some sense of who we are as a person in our own right rather than dating to fill a hole. It's best not to operate from a deficit – as though we need someone on our arm to validate our existence – but instead to be in a secure place where we do not need a boyfriend or girlfriend to make us feel safe, needed, significant or affirmed. If we are in a solid position – safe and calm in our relationship with God, family and peers, then if the right relationship comes we shall be in a far better place to evaluate its worth.

What to look for

What should we look for in someone that we might date? If we want to seek first the kingdom of God and if we appreciate the primacy of our relationship with Him then we shall want to be with someone who feels the same way. This should be our first objective. If we can find someone who loves God even more than they love us then we shall potentially be onto something. Conversely, if spiritual topics don't naturally come up and get discussed with our potential partner then we would want to think about why that is, and whether it's partly our problem (and if something therefore needs fixing about that) or whether it's our partner who changes the subject, glazes over, or has nothing to say. This doesn't mean that we should expect our partner to be able to recite the order of the kings of Judah backwards or that their interest has to be a studious or intellectual one, but we might hope that there is a draw for them towards spiritual things and that they have some passion for (or, if they are new to such things, an openness to) the things of God, things which include practical qualities and actions as well as knowledge and doctrine. If someone isn't showing the fruit of the spirit now, or is not listening now (for example), why would they start later? They might, but that may not be a great bet to take.

In a sense it all comes down to the question, 'What is the most important thing in your life?' If the answer to that has God in it then you will want to look for someone who will take you to a higher spiritual place rather than a lower one. It is all about building on the right foundation; Jesus told a parable about a house founded upon a rock which is quite applicable to the concept of building a home in marriage.

All of the Biblical character studies in the next few chapters of this section will be exploring the question of what to look for (and what to avoid or not be distracted by) in a potential marriage partner. In these studies we shall find ourselves constantly face to face with the notion of God's perspective versus man's. It is the habit of human beings to look on the outside – whether in terms of the beauty and figure of a woman or the more rugged physique of a man, or whether we think of other 'outward' factors such as money, status, educational accomplishment, social background and other trappings. God, however, looks on the heart and it is self-evident that ultimately it is these inner virtues of character such as patience, compassion, fellow-feeling, selflessness and the ability to forgive which will have far more creative power in a marriage than anything else. Whether a person is kind, open and forgiving is far more important to a marriage than whether they would win a prize in a fashion show, bodybuilding or beauty contest.

The same principle can be extended into the question of *when* to marry. The quality of a relationship is more important than having a 'perfect life' that comes out of a picture in a magazine. To refuse to consider marriage until you or your partner has a job that pays three times the national average, a new house in an idyllic neighbourhood and two flash cars standing in the driveway is quite simply to prioritise the wrong things, severely to limit one's potential options, and perhaps to set oneself up for considerable disappointment. There can be a joy in marriage being a bit of a struggle at first from an economic or lifestyle perspective, in everything not being quite ideal but in gradually working together perhaps to add some of those external aspects over time, if it is God's will. That way there can be a sense of shared accomplishment and enjoyment from some of those external blessings if they do come along. We should think deeply about what is truly important in marriage and relationships, not on the surface.

Learning who we are

One of the challenges of dating in one's earlier years is that as a young person you haven't necessarily made up your mind what you are looking for – you may not even know quite who you are yourself and who you want to be at this crucial stage of development. The teenage years bring massive change: physical, sexual, educational, emotional and relational. A young person moves from being thought of as primarily the subordinate child of his or her parents to being increasingly a person in their own right with ever-growing independence: the ability to make their own choices, craft their own lives, and grow up into who they choose to be. While these processes of change never stop, they are at their most intense in these crucial years, most likely the very years in which a young person will start to be interested in the opposite sex and begin to date. Again, how can you know who you should date and what sort of a partner to look for when you are still very much in the process of working out who you are in your own right?

There's no need for over-much alarm on this point: God evidently designed our bodies to go through these developmental changes and the evidence regarding when our sexual and physical attributes reach their peak suggests that it is indeed quite appropriate for these two spheres of increasing personal independence and dating to coincide. This suggests that it is quite possible (and hence a reasonable expectation) for an individual to be still in the process of working out their own identity, as it were, while they start engaging with the opposite sex. That said, the more emotionally mature and sure of his or her own identity and direction a person is (particularly where spiritual and emotional matters are concerned) the less likely it is that grave mistakes will be made and that there will be unnecessary emotional trauma. It suggests that it is smart as a young person to think carefully and deeply about who you want to be and what you want longer term out of life before you begin to date in any serious way. It suggests that if you are a parent, friend or confidant of someone who is considering dating that you help them to think through these issues.

The emotions and physical feelings that can be unleashed in a relationship can be extremely strong and the wise course is to keep these in step with (rather than racing ahead of) the individuals' emotional maturity and the 'seriousness' of the relationship. To do otherwise is to risk a lot of emotional pain and the possibility of actions and decisions that can be regretted for the rest of one's life. It's not wise to use dating as a way of finding out who you are as though it were an experimental tool of some kind that we should test out as often as we can and in as many different ways as possible. Far better to be secure in who you are and your own values as much as you can; then it will be possible to make choices you will be able to respect later and that will be true to who you want to be.

Although it may sound boring and rather old-fashioned when compared to the current culture, a little effort to know who you are yourself in order to date wisely will lead to the conclusion that it's usually better to go slower rather than faster in dating, and that generally speaking it might be better to err on the side of older rather than younger when thinking about whether to start a serious relationship. If a person already has a lot of emotional maturity and has set a clear spiritual course for themselves then this may be less of a concern, but not all of us are in that position or get to it so quickly. In the meantime there is plenty of time for friendships, both male and female, without the complexity of romance. These give plenty of opportunity to learn about oneself and about the opposite sex without all the emotional entanglement that dating adds to the mix.

Is this the one?

There are lots of other practical matters that might be addressed regarding dating and we'll pick up a number of these in the concluding chapter of this section (chapter 12), plus there is the important question of marriage and dating non-believers which we'll discuss in chapter 10. One final topic for this chapter, however: how do we know when we have found the right person? How shall we answer the question, 'Is this the person I should marry?'

Clearly it's not a question with one right answer, but it's a question worth reflecting seriously upon. First of all it is a matter for sharing with God. The whole course of a relationship should be brought to God in prayer – from the start through to these culminating moments of decision-making. For some, the marriage question will simply not be a question at all; it will be so supremely obvious that the answer is 'Yes!' that all that needs to be done is to check that a good spiritual and practical choice is being made as well as a good emotional or romantic one – the head and the spirit should be in step with the heart.

Some people know instinctively while others agonise interminably and struggle to come to a decision; yet others fall somewhere in between. There isn't a right or wrong way to reach a decision; we are all different with respect to our decision-making processes and on top of that every relationship is unique and will impact us and our thought process in a distinctive way. It is right to engage our brains as well as to listen to our emotions – marriage is an active choice, a commitment of will and an act of covenant-making that we choose to undertake. It is vital for the spiritual and practical implications of our choices to be at the forefront, and the main yardstick we should use is the spiritual one. If two people both have the same spiritual goals and priorities an awful lot of difficulties can be overcome; there is a common approach and set of values that will pervade the whole marriage.

For some people the question is rather less 'Can I live with this person for the rest of my life?' and rather more 'Can I live without them?' If the answer to the latter is 'No!' or 'Not easily!' then this might be a helpful indication – assuming that the foundation is right. For some it might be more difficult – perhaps a more cerebral process – and this is okay too. It can be useful to think about the benefits of marriage and to weigh them against the drawbacks or limitations it imposes (again, in general and in particular). It might not sound like a very romantic exercise, but if it helps you come to a decision then why not? Think about what the longer term future with this person might be like, the qualities and attributes they have or don't have that will be a source of enjoyment and support. What about if you have children together or when you are in your fifties, say, or in old age – what do you think life with them will look like then? Can you imagine growing old together, and would the sort of life you envisage be good for both you and them? It can also be very valuable to ask for counsel from parents and friends, but it's important to be wise in who to take into one's confidence – it's possible to get so many opinions that all it does is create more confusion. At the end of the day this is a decision only the person involved can make.

Other good questions to think about might include the following:

- Do I respect this person's character? What is that character truly like?
- What spiritual attributes do they have?
- How do they talk to and interact with others – children, young people, adults, old people? How do they engage with family and friends?
- How are they when they are stressed, annoyed, disappointed, or in a crisis?
- How are your core values similar and different?
- Would you be happy for them to be the mother or father of your children?
- Do you know the whole person? What different situations and environments have you seen them in?
- How do they cope with change? How do they cope with the humdrum?
- How are they in everyday life, not just when washed, brushed and ready to go out?

The more you know about your partner the easier it will be to make a decision and the greater likelihood you will have of making a good one. The secret here is 'talk, talk, talk!' Talk about everything – expectations, hopes, values, views about money, children, education, sex, work, balance in life, responsibilities towards God, family, what's happening in the world ... the list is endless and if you and your partner are really in love your mutual sharing of opinions and your exploration of all these topics will be fascinating. Of course this doesn't mean asking them how many children they would like to have on your first date(!), but over time, as the depth of the relationship renders it appropriate, there will be more and more to talk about and discover about each other. Not everything has to be perfect and you don't have to agree on everything, but you do need to be able to understand each other and where you are both coming from at least in some measure – there has to be a mutual respect for the other's views. By the time you come towards the point of making a decision about whether this person is the right one for you to strive to build a home with in God's presence, if you have talked extensively you will already know a huge amount about each other and your compatibility. You will be in a great position to make a decision which, with God's blessing, will be a source of strength and comfort for the rest of your life together.

Solomon and the Thousand

Topics: Looking for the wrong thing; Blinded by the external; Choices for wrong reasons.

Solomon's experience of partner-selection and marriage, attempted an astonishing one thousand times, has a lot to teach about how misguided it is possible to be when looking for a partner.

THERE is an intriguing passage in Ecclesiastes all about looking for a companion which reads like this:
"Behold, this have I found, saith the Preacher, counting one by one, to find out the account: which yet my soul seeketh, but I find not; one man among a thousand have I found; but a woman among all those have I not found. Lo, this only have I found, that God hath made man upright; but they have sought out many inventions."   (Ecclesiastes 7:27-29)
          Solomon's measure of success here is not very impressive whether it be women *or* men that he is looking for: one in a thousand men is not much of a hit-rate (whether Solomon is looking for court officials or friends), and the failure to find any women whatsoever (perhaps for a companion or wife) seems even worse. Just occasionally – about one time in a thousand, perhaps – he met a man engaged in the same search as he, someone with whom he was on a similar spiritual wavelength. But he never met

a woman like that. All he met was the bitter woman with "hands as bands" – again and again.

So what does the passage really mean? What *sort* of man or woman is Solomon seeking, and to what end? And what bearing might this have for a man seeking a woman or a woman a man today?

A great search

We can first note that the verses revolve around the idea of *finding*: "This have I *found* … Counting to *find* out the account … My soul *seeketh* … I *find* not … one man have I *found* … a woman have I not *found* … this only have I *found* … men have *sought out* many inventions."

So Solomon is certainly looking, but what is he looking *for*? Paradoxically, in the first sentence of the passage he does not tell us. The effect is highly ironic: "Behold, this have I found …" (this is the 'eureka' moment where we expect the nature of the discovery to be disclosed, but we are left hanging: what exactly he has found is not said) "… counting to find … seeking …" (and now the punchline:) "… *but I find not*". So perhaps what he has found – the very thing we are asked to behold – is that he hasn't found anything and that his quest has failed. Perhaps Solomon has been so busy counting one by one, accounting and seeking, that he has lost himself in the search, forgetting, perhaps, even what it was he was looking for. Along the way he manages to pick up a thousand wives and concubines, but what he was actually supposed to be seeking he does not find.

The irony of this is both delicious and likely deliberate. It is a little parable about life: we get so busy pursuing a certain course, pre-occupied by the intensity of the search or the minutiae of this or that, but somehow on the way we forget what we were looking for, the direction in which we were supposed to have been headed. At the most literal level, who hasn't had the experience of going into a room to pick something up only to forget what it was we intended to find? Shockingly the counterpart to this can even be found in looking for a partner or the acquiring of friends.

We can know the sort of person we *ought* to be looking for yet somehow get distracted into looking at or spending time with all sorts of other people who don't really fit the pattern at all.

A thousand wives and concubines

Now is Solomon's 1 in 1,000 hit-rate for men and 0 in 1,000 for women because men are more spiritual than women even if just by a whisker? This is probably unlikely. Perhaps more likely is that Solomon got *distracted* by other things about women which attracted him and forgot to look for the spiritual qualities he should have been seeking. In fact we do know that this is precisely what happened in his case because the historical records of Kings and Chronicles tell us and in doing so they warn us that we too, when searching for a marriage partner, need to be very clear and very careful about what we are looking for. Physical attraction will likely happen without us having to pay it a huge amount of attention, but finding a person who is a good spiritual match will require more thought and effort on our part.

Solomon didn't find one woman in a thousand because he was blinded by a thousand other women who were not like that. In that context, then, it's fascinating that the very number of wives and concubines Solomon had (1,000) marries up perfectly with the number of good women that he failed to find – the missing woman in a thousand. While finding a spiritual person of either gender is a rare find and one of unspeakable value, it is an awful lot harder if you are looking for or distracted by the wrong thing. The passage is about what Solomon failed to *find*, not what women (or men) necessarily *are*. Perhaps it was because he wasn't attracted by the physical attributes of men as he was for women that he was able to be more discerning and – very, very occasionally – to find one on the right spiritual wavelength.

Solomon should have known better. In trying out a thousand women and not managing to find a spiritual soulmate amongst them all he is almost a parody of himself. Can it be possible to be *so* distracted from what is right, and to repeat the mistake so many times? Can it be that one can know what one should be looking for and what would be truly helpful in a spiritual partnership but then deliberately choose something completely different? Well yes, it is quite possible, so we must be on our guard. We must pray that God will save us from ourselves if there is anything of the Solomon in us in this respect. The historical books tell that his wives turned away his heart from the Lord, the very opposite of the help that they should have been giving. He was pulled in so many different directions by all these women there was no wonder he got off track and forgot what he was looking for – not one of them was the right one.

What does Solomon's misadventure, mistake and misfortune teach? Though we may not be as wise as Solomon we have to think smarter than he in this respect. The choices he made, with his women at least, were made for the wrong reasons – for outward appearance perhaps, for sexual thrills, for political expediency, to express his status or his power and virility, for variety so as to try something new, or simply for habit (using his power to collect wives as someone else might collect fridge magnets). Not one of these was a good or sufficient reason. While polygamy itself isn't generally the issue nowadays, making an unwise choice in a marriage partner certainly can be; Solomon's example provides a very telling warning. We have to know what we are looking for and the reasons why – the spiritual qualities that can sustain a relationship, the virtues that will last and grow when outward appearance has passed its best – and it would be as well to be aware of the propensity to be distracted and to forget just quite what it was that we were supposed to be seeking. Fortunately God is rather better at finding and providing than we are, and it's a great comfort that we can pray to Him for assistance in these matters. In the end physical beauty only goes in one direction as we age (and it's not up!); this isn't to say it isn't important to find your partner attractive, that beauty isn't a breathtaking feature and that looks aren't a powerful force. But Solomon found all those things, no doubt, yet failed to find the things that were more important. In this respect the wisest of men proved himself a fool. Outward appearance may be an important factor in our thinking, but if we want to avoid Solomon's repeated failure it must not be the most important.

There is a flip side to Solomon's discussion of finding a woman and his personal failure to do so, despite all the resources at his disposal. Another verse of his, from Proverbs this time, declares that "Whoso findeth a wife findeth a good thing, and obtaineth favour of the LORD" (Proverbs 18:22). This passage is not talking of the kind of wife that Solomon found, but one who would be a true spiritual partner, a helper on the quest for a life guided by the wisdom which Solomon loved so much but somehow lost along the way in this key aspect of his life.

Samson and Delilah

Topics: You're not as strong as you think; Superficial 'wants'; Serving two masters; Putting a stop to destructive behaviour; Nagging works only at a cost; Games people play.

There is no evidence that Samson and Delilah were ever married but the dynamic of their relationship is sufficiently bizarre that it merits our attention if only as a prime example of a relationship that ought not to have been. As an example of what *not* to do, Samson is highly symbolic, his name meaning something like 'little sun' or 'sunny boy' and hers being an obvious sound play with the Hebrew for 'night' ('laylah' which is pronounced so as to rhyme with the '-lilah' of 'De-lilah'). Their relationship is indeed an example of darkness overcoming the light when the one in the light thought it never would. The price Samson paid was both the literal quenching of the light of his eyes as they were put out, plus his slavery in the darkness of the prison house, rich in symbol as both of these are. The scriptures leave us in no doubt how serious Samson's mistake was, even if he ultimately finds redemption as he dies.

SOME of the lessons from Samson and Delilah are obvious: you shouldn't get into or persist in alliances with people who have the power to lead you astray, and you shouldn't overestimate your ability to withstand. Samson falls into temptation thinking he is strong enough to resist, only to find he has fooled no one but himself as the darkness overcomes the light. His attraction to Delilah seems to be primarily physical and despite the irrefutable evidence that she is trying to trap and harm him, played out over and over, he persists in the relationship. Why does he do this? Either because he enjoys the game – enjoys flirting with temptation in a kind of spiritual brinkmanship, wrongly thinking that ultimately he'll be able to draw the line and walk away – or because his amorous feelings are so strong that he can't resist being with her despite the massive warning signs.

Unequally yoked

The relationship is doomed from the start because it is an unequal one in which both partners want completely different things: she wants the money that she will be paid for successfully betraying him, and he wants her. Needless to say, neither seem to want the spiritual good of the other. There is something very contemporary about her desire for money and his desire for her (that is to say, his focus on her appearance and where that takes him), because these are exactly the two things men and women are said to care most about as their number one priorities in mate-seeking today. According to evidence from surveys and analysis of online dating sites and the like the thing that men focus on most is the looks of their women while women focus on the money-generating ability of their men. While this may sound disappointingly hollow (surely we're better and more sophisticated than this?!) it seems that the sexes have figured out the other's requirements, actively marketing themselves to these goals. Men are highly likely to inflate their earnings on dating sites; women highly likely to over-hype their appearance. Then the advertising industry and the media step in to exacerbate the matter and the whole thing feeds itself in a vicious cycle where these things become ever more important while other qualities become sidelined.

Samson's case shows the imperative to be honest with ourselves about why we like someone and whether or not those reasons are a good basis for a partnership, a meeting of mind or spirit rather than merely body. The temptation to underestimate temptation is always there, and we are almost always wrong when we 'think we can handle it'. There should be no place in the disciple's life for spiritual brinkmanship, for wanting to get as close to the line as possible in a relationship with someone who is just not right for us. Why would we want to do this if our hearts are truly set on following our Lord? The prize of the mark of the high calling of Christ is what we should be aiming for, not the line that takes us as close as we can get to selfishness and sin.

Many of those who have ended up in relationships with unbelievers which have become too entwined will attest to their having overestimated their ability to control their feelings and not take such a relationship beyond a certain point – a very similar mistake to the one Samson makes. Where marriage has followed many will admit the frequent clash of objectives and mindset that it entails. Life will be difficult and in certain respects even dysfunctional, just as we shall observe for Samson and Delilah.

Being able to say 'No'

It's important to have the courage to get out of a relationship that is going in the wrong direction or simply isn't going anywhere at all. It is rarely easy to do so – powerful feelings are involved – but it is important both from the perspective of liberating you and your partner for other more suitable relationships and to avoid deeper hurt and counterproductive effects further down the road.

Why would you need to make such a choice? It could be about spiritual compatibility as we've seen with Samson and Delilah – you learn that you and your partner simply aren't heading in the same spiritual direction and don't share the same spiritual values. But there are plenty of other reasons also. Perhaps it turns out that you just don't have much in common in other areas of your life; perhaps you tend to irritate each other too often and bring out negative aspects of your personalities rather than the positive; perhaps you find that the physical side of your relationship isn't really working or that you just don't really care enough about each other to put in the work required to sustain and nurture the relationship.

Samson and Delilah's case shows the worst of these: spiritual incompatibility and destructive and dysfunctional patterns of behaviour. It's sometimes the case that people persist in relationships like this because they're scared to get out, because they can't face being alone and single again, or even because they have failed to see clearly just how unhealthy the relationship is. What is needed is an honesty about whether a relationship is really working or not, and if it isn't – or if it is going in a poor direction – the courage to move on. Bad relationships are unlikely to correct themselves; they're more likely to end up in disaster like Samson and Delilah's did.

Persistence

While we've now drawn out the obvious lessons from Samson and Delilah with respect to dating it's worth making a closer analysis to observe some further points about relationship dynamics. One of the things we see which is not particularly pleasant is the effectiveness of persistency and the power of nagging. Samson had already experienced this with his first wife and he should have learned his lesson; instead he again falls headlong into the same trap:

> "And she said to him, 'How can you say, "I love you", when your heart is not with me? You have mocked me these three times, and you have not told me where your great strength lies.' And when she pressed him hard with her words day after day, and urged him, his soul was vexed to death. And he told her all his heart, and said to her. 'A razor has never come upon my head, for I have been a Nazirite to God from my mother's womb. If my head is shaved, then my strength will leave me, and I shall become weak and be like any other man.'"
>
> (Judges 16:15-17, ESV)

Now nagging is not a pleasant method of communication as everyone knows, the words chosen here ("she pressed him hard with her words day after day, and urged him") culminating in his soul being "vexed to death"! But even though nagging is unpleasant to the point of making a husband's life not worth living, it can still work – the husband, if he is a certain type of person, grudgingly falling in line for the sake of a quiet life. It works at a steep cost (the misery of the husband and the deterioration of the relationship), but in Delilah's case what would she care? She wanted Samson betrayed and captured in any case, and it was hardly likely the Philistines were going to value Samson's life any more than she did.

Strange bedfellows

Samson and Delilah's relationship can't possibly work because both partners want different things and are pulling in different directions: she is serving the 'master' of the Philistines and he is (presumably) serving the 'master' of his own lust. Serving two masters isn't possible and the only thing they have in common is their physical attraction to each other (and we don't really know for sure that Delilah has even this or whether she is just pretending).

The two of them seem to be playing a weird game within the relationship: "Please tell me where your great strength lies, and how you might be bound, that one could subdue you", she asks (16:6, ESV). What kind of a question is this, and who would want to ask it of a partner they are supposedly in love with? Can it even be asked with a straight face, as if she is just so fascinated and obsessed with him that she simply can't get enough information about his great strength? Or is there actually not even an attempt at pretence here, Delilah simply being blunt and up-front about what it is that she wants, and he so convinced that she won't get it that he plays along?

Later it descends into pantomime as the Philistines jump out of the closet on top of him once more and she says again, "The Philistines are upon you, Samson!" Surely it must be obvious to him that she is using the information he provides to try to get the Philistines to overcome him, yet still he persists in playing the game. If this is the case then Samson either doesn't care or he assumes that his strength is so great that it cannot be undone, that God's Nazirite can come to no harm.

But it will get you in the end, Samson. You think you're strong enough – you always have been before – until you suddenly find you aren't. What you needed to have done was to stop the destructive pattern of the relationship while you had the chance.

Influence and dysfunction

Perhaps there can be an analogy to this within a modern marriage. It may be that one partner is pulling the pair or the family in a particular direction that is not to the good of the whole. Such an influence or objective can be stated and explicit or it can be covert and implicit – perhaps not even realised. It may be something seemingly innocuous like a hobby or interest over-zealously and disproportionately pursued; it may even be something 'good' or something pursued or sought for good motives but which somehow distorts the proper, proportionate objectives the household should have. Samson's extreme example highlights that it can be dangerous to think that we are necessarily strong enough either to withstand or counteract this. If there is an influence which is taking the family in the wrong direction then we may need to stand up and do what's right by addressing the issue.

Quite apart from the specifics of their particular relationship, Samson and Delilah's is also a first-rate example of just how twisted and counterproductive relationships can sometimes get. Dysfunction of all kinds can exist in the freak show of human relationships: one partner may routinely humiliate another (there are all kinds of ways in which this can happen), or may threaten or suggest break-up or infidelity to manipulate or control the other. A couple may 'play' at aggressively arguing and making up or can 'joke' at each other's expense which can undermine confidence in a way which is far from funny ... and so the list could go on. None of these things is healthy; the challenge is to get outside oneself and the relationship, to see these destructive and dangerous behaviours for what they are and to take appropriate action.

What we can see from this *particular* example of dysfunction is that it should have been spotted and stopped much earlier, one or other party standing up to say, 'This is not right and it needs to stop'. The way Samson and Delilah were treating each other was bizarre and doomed to failure, something which we can see easily as outside observers not emotionally involved. But while it's clear to us that it wasn't healthy and was never going to work, why was it not clear to them? Unfortunately it can be much harder to see such things from the inside of a relationship. But if we *do* see it – if we can spot patterns of behaviour between us which are harmful, demeaning or destructive – then we need to call time on them now; in the end Samson paid a very full price for his failure to do so.

The mighty fallen

Samson's eventual capture is somewhat reminiscent of a bullfight: Samson the great strong bull of a man who should have been strong enough eventually exhausted and brought down by tiny darts thrown by the Delilah matador prancing around in fancy garments and more wily than he. Despite the massive strength of the bull, he is brought low by the matador just like Samson.

The text describes Delilah making Samson go to sleep on her knees (16:19) and shaving off the seven locks of his head symbolising his Nazirite vow (the word 'vow' has affinity with the number seven in Hebrew). Samson had gone to sleep; he thought he could get up, as at other times, and shake himself – but he didn't know the Lord had left him (verse 20). What a pathetic figure he would look now, perhaps attempting to lunge and heave about in combat as he would have done previously – but this time nothing happens as he exerts himself, for his strength has departed and it is all too late.

What he needed to have done was to wake up earlier, before it was too late, to refuse to allow an objective to be pursued that would ultimately destroy both him and his relationship. Given the potential for aspects of dysfunction in human relationships both before and within marriage there are times when we might need to do the same.

David and Michal (1)

Topics: Good on paper but not in practice; Being 'on the same page'; When feelings change; Basing a relationship on promises not feelings; Figuring out who you and your partner really are; Being honest and not deluding oneself.

It had all the makings of a fairy-tale wedding: she the king's youngest daughter, he the new all-star hero: musician, giant-slayer, poet and gentleman. Her love for David was strong (the text twice mentions it: 1 Samuel 18:20,28), and her sense of loyalty towards him acute. When Saul begins to hunt David's life she correctly leaves her father and mother and cleaves to her husband, saving his life by letting him down through a window and manufacturing a fake David in the bed to fool her father. But for all these wonderful beginnings, the relationship certainly didn't end well. We'll discuss their argument and how it ended in chapter 30, but here the focus will be on the way in which there seems to have been a deep underlying incompatibility or lack of connection which imperiled their relationship even though it appeared to start so well. This is a potent reminder that even if many things in a relationship seem good we must be careful about pressing ahead if there is a basic underlying lack of unity or failure to connect.

WHILE David and Michal's relationship looked great on paper there was a deep underlying problem because they were not truly 'on the same page' in one crucial respect: their spiritual perspective and the source of their deepest concern. No doubt there was a backstory to all this that the scriptures do not reveal but in the single-event snapshot we do possess the disharmony between them which effectively marks the termination of their relationship as man and wife can be plainly seen. The incident in question is David's second and successful attempt to bring the ark of God to Zion, a spiritual high for the king as the procession triumphantly ascends the streets of the Holy City:

> "And as the ark of the LORD came into the city of David, Michal Saul's daughter looked through a window, and saw king David leaping and dancing before the LORD; and she despised him in her heart."   (2 Samuel 6:16; 1 Chronicles 15:29)

The contrast between the couple here is exquisite and captures their lack of unity: David's outward extravagance, her inward thoughts; his positive self-expression, her negativity; his in-the-moment oneness with his Lord, her dark and disloyal thoughts towards her husband. We might even ask why she was not with him at his side on this, one of the most important days of his life, but is instead disdainfully observing him from her window. As she sees it, David has turned into a freak: crazily leaping and dancing like some lunatic with no sense of proportion or social decorum. Religion was all very well, she might have thought, but not if it led to this kind of behaviour. Where was David's self-control, dignity and self-respect? This was no behaviour for a king, and she would tell him so.

Once she had indeed loved David (twice the text had said it), yet now she despises him in her heart (twice, again, it is said: once in Samuel, once in Chronicles). The feelings of her heart have changed from loving to despising. How can this happen in this or any relationship? What has gone wrong?

Feelings change, promises don't

In Michal's particular case things are extremely complicated; it could be, for instance, that she still harbours resentment for the way in which she has been treated like an emotional football by the key men in her life, forcibly separated from her first husband by Saul and then from her second by her first (2 Samuel 3:13-16); it could be very difficult for her fully to give her love and wholeheartedly support a man again after these experiences. While we cannot know Michal's feelings and motives unless the text tells us, we can stop to consider the wider issue however. What happens if, for whatever reason, we no longer feel the same way towards our partner as once we did – or they towards us, for that matter? People can change; hearts and feelings can change as they did for Michal – so what can be done? In such a world of flux, can marriage survive? We'll temporarily leave the case of David and Michal to one side to consider this broader question.

The fact is that marriage *must* survive. Although it is true that people do change as they age and as they pass through different life experiences, marriage is a commitment to choose to love our partners through *all* the changing scenes of life – for better, for worse; in sickness and in health. While people may change their interests, their attitudes – even aspects of their personality and the way they respond to things – the marriage commitment must transcend these changes; that's what the promise is about: 'in all these circumstances, whatever they might be, predictable or otherwise, I will love and cherish you.'

But what, specifically, of feelings? Michal no longer feels the way about David that she once did which brings to light an important point: marriage cannot merely be based on feelings, as it unfortunately often is in the current age. If we marry only because we have a loving 'feeling' towards our partner (we are overcome by infatuation) then we are essentially taking a self-centred approach. What happens when we no longer feel that way about them, when, instead, we feel cross with them, or the feeling of infatuation has worn off? If some physical feeling has been the main basis of my union – such that it all revolves around *me* and what I *feel* – then I am going to want to move on. I will have lost 'that loving feeling' and will be inclined to start looking for it elsewhere.

Instead of being based predominantly around 'my feeling', marriage should be built on a choice, a promise, a commitment. We love because we *choose* to love, not just because we feel like it. Feelings may come and, from time to time, they may go; they may or may not be sufficient to hold us through. Love and marriage must be built on more than this; they must be built on a commitment, a conscious choice which we deliberately make and to which we dedicate ourselves, come what may – the very thing that Adam's 'leaving and cleaving' in Genesis 2:24 was all about.

Change of heart

Returning to the particulars of Michal and David, there is perhaps a hint that she has never really understood what David is truly about – in particular the primacy and all-consuming nature of his relationship with God. She probably thinks that David has changed ('the man I fell for would never have done that ridiculous dancing!'); but if there is one thing we know about David it is that his fervour for God never changes. Perhaps what she was in love with was not the most important thing about David or else she would have better understood his need for God and the way in which everything else (including social convention, self-respect, and, yes, even his feelings for her) must be secondary. She may have been more in love with the fairy tale: the swashbuckling and chivalrous David sweeping the princess off her feet and their happily-ever-after marriage. But the real David is the one who loves the Lord his God with all his heart, strength and mind, and is not afraid to show it. It seems that with respect to their attitude towards God and the question of His primacy in one's life they were never really on the same page. This is a key insight and it shows that even if many aspects of a relationship seem right, if we are not at one with our partner on the most fundamental issues it can lead to very serious problems as it did for David and Michal.

If this reading is correct then it highlights the importance of truly finding the right person when we are considering potential partners, not to mention the importance of encouraging our children and young people to do the same. We must make sure we use the opportunity dating affords to get to know our partner to work out if we are indeed on the same page, sharing the same outlook on the key issues of life. It is not good enough to leave this to chance or to be so wrapped up in the emotional high of being in love that we pass off such matters as being something to worry about another day. David and Michal's experience painfully shows where that kind of failure to connect can ultimately lead.

With the force of physical attraction upon us it can be possible to delude ourselves or overlook the true personality or interests of our partner. We can create or fall for an illusion of what they are (whether that illusion is created by them or us), rather than seeing the reality. If we want to put God first in our lives, then we shall want to take a good hard look at our potential mate to ensure that our spiritual objectives are shared. If they are not then we had better prepare for a life of tension, frustration, or conforming to the lowest common denominator. We can't be too honest with ourselves in these matters. If Michal had truly cared for the Lord as much as her husband, it is doubtful that she would have reacted quite the way she did. In that case this argument, so fatal to the emotional and physical oneness of their relationship, would never have happened. It's impossible to take these issues too seriously.

Lot and his wife

Topics: One marriage, two fates; Marrying an unbeliever, being unequally yoked; Dating an unbeliever.

It was difficult for both of them. Despite the grotesque nature of the scene the night before in which the men of Sodom had sought to gang rape the angels who had visited him, Lot still lingered in the city. How bad does it have to be in order for us to be persuaded of the evil in the world and to leave it behind? But even though he found it hard, he managed to do it while his wife ultimately did not. This complete discrepancy in their fates can be a foil for thinking about the implications of marriage to an unbeliever and also give us pause to consider the related question of whether or not believers should get into serious relationships with those who are not.

GOD'S command to leave Sodom is issued to Lot as the spiritual head of his house; he in turn is expected to share it with his family, all of them then having responsibility for its keeping. This was exactly the pattern set in the Garden all those years before when God had issued His command not to eat of the fruit to Adam and he had then shared it with his wife. Lot did as he should have done, but still none of the family wanted to leave, including him. The angel has to instill a sense of urgency in the lethargic Lot who seems to be still rubbing sleep from his eyes the following morning. Still he lingers, the angels being forced physically to grab him, his wife and his two daughters to get them under way. His enforced deportation, though it might have seemed rough and heavy-handed was actually a kindness:

> "And while he lingered, the men laid hold upon his hand, and upon the hand of his wife, and upon the hand of his two daughters; the LORD being merciful unto him: and they brought him forth, and set him without the city."
>
> (Genesis 19:16)

The mountain or the plain

Outside the city the angels repeat their urgent message to the family that they should escape to the distant mountains, but Lot is still dragging his feet and seeking a concession, his plaintive words pitiable and almost amusing in their pathos ("is it not a little one?" he says of the tiny city of Zoar (i.e., 'it can't be so wicked when it is so small, can it? – surely you can allow me to escape there and not have to travel so far!', verses 17-22) – anything to avoid the greater and scarier challenge of heading to the mountains proposed by the angels. His reluctance to climb a mountain perhaps symbolises his lack of spiritual conviction and bravery, his preparedness to compromise and underachieve rather than to go for the higher goal. These feelings of his are thoroughly understandable, but of course they are not how we should strive to be.

Still, the angels are prepared to make a concession to Lot's weakness, allowing him the lesser separation of fleeing to the little city of Zoar. His departure is more reluctant and less fulsome than ideal but he is at least broadly going in the right direction and prepared to follow a diluted version of the angel's initial instructions. It is a comfort that the Lord is prepared to make allowances for our weaknesses even though He would rather we followed Him more faithfully.

Up to this point his family have followed on behind, content for him to be their spokesman and negotiate with the angel as they follow, even if with some dilution of purpose. Now though their fates diverge.

Pillar of salt

Let's allow the passage to speak for itself:

> "The sun was risen upon the earth when Lot entered into Zoar. Then the LORD rained upon Sodom and upon Gomorrah brimstone and fire from the LORD out of heaven; and he overthrew those cities, and all the plain, and all the inhabitants of the cities, and that which grew upon the ground. But his wife looked back from behind him, and she became a pillar of salt."   (verses 23-26)

It was a new day marked by the sun's rising and Lot and his family should have been heading to a new place to make a new beginning. But at this crucial moment his wife looks back. It is not in intrigue that she looks to see the spectacle of the destruction, but in longing, harking back to the life she had left behind. It is this that is unacceptable – after all the tolerance of the angels at the family's slow departure, after the compromise over the destination of their flight. None of it is enough for her; this is not about making allowances for personal weakness such as Lot had negotiated, it is about turning back with the desire to be back as part of the world, even when you know it is so evil. She wants her old life and looks back in longing and desire for what she has left behind.

It is not, then, that she makes a quick backward glance. It is what her looking back represents. Lot is going in one direction (albeit reluctantly), and she wants to go in another, preferring to belong in that city even with the destruction it entails than to reach for the new and the better.

While we don't really know anything about the internal dynamics of Lot's relationship with his wife, we do learn in a very stark way from their example what happens when one partner goes in one spiritual direction and the other goes the opposite way: their two directions have completely different ends. You can't be in two places at once; you can't serve two masters. You

can't be going back to Sodom and at the same time be pressing
forward for something better. You can't be in the kingdom
and not be in the kingdom at the same time, and if you marry
someone who chooses human society and values rather than
the kingdom of God that is where they will be and this is how
the relationship will end. It's an unpleasant and a painful truth,
but it remains a truth nevertheless. There can be no oneness if
the two partners are seeking to go in two completely different
directions.

If this situation arises for an already established couple
(if one of them becomes a believer while the other remains
unconverted, for example), then the situation has to be lived
through as best it can unless the unbelieving partner decides
to leave (1 Corinthians 7:15). It will be challenging, but the
situation must be accommodated, and there is the wonderful
potential of the sanctifying power of the believer (verse 14)
and the possibility that the unbeliever may be won over by the
Christlike conduct of the believer (1 Peter 3:1; 1 Corinthians
7:16).

It is another matter, however, to choose to marry into
such a situation when there is no necessity to do so. Marrying
out of the faith is a serious matter and its implications and
consequences have to be thought through. Paul puts it like this
in no uncertain terms:

"Be ye not unequally yoked together with unbelievers: for
what fellowship hath righteousness with unrighteousness?
and what communion hath light with darkness? And what
concord hath Christ with Belial? or what part hath he
that believeth with an infidel? And what agreement hath
the temple of God with idols? for ye are the temple of
the living God; as God hath said, I will dwell in them, and
walk in them; and I will be their God, and they shall be my
people. Wherefore come out from among them, and be ye
separate, saith the Lord, and touch not the unclean thing;
and I will receive you, and will be a Father unto you, and ye

shall be my sons and daughters, saith the Lord Almighty."
(2 Corinthians 6:14-18)

There is no mincing of words here. We can attempt to cover it over by speaking of the deep love a couple may share, but Paul remains quite clear. The divergence in the fates of Lot and his wife is similarly striking: they are bitterly and bluntly pictured in the tragic end of this marriage. Of course while both partners are living there is the hope that they will both come to know the Lord. Peter talks about the possibility of the unbelieving husband being won over by the Christlike behaviour of his wife as we've mentioned, and there are examples of this having occurred. But the opposite is also possible: sometimes unbelieving wives and husbands have pulled their once-faithful partners back to Sodom and have ended up turning them both into pillars of salt.

The striking thing about the Lot account is its sheer brevity – she looked back and she was turned into a pillar of salt, and that is all – end of story. The text shows her no pity; she has made her choice. It offers no exploration of her motives, only the path she chose and the brutal reality of its consequence. There is no veneer that can be applied to it, no words that can sugar-coat its truth. But in that terseness lies its power. Jesus' reference is just as terse, "Remember Lot's wife!" (Luke 17:32). This is the bottom line: to choose to marry an unbeliever is to break God's command and to risk this same division of fates that Lot and his wife experienced.

Relationships with unbelievers

While there is no doubting the clarity of Paul's words with respect to marriage, does that mean that one shouldn't date someone who is an unbeliever or unbaptized? We need to walk a fine line here between appreciating the potential dangers of doing so on the one hand (after all, Paul's "unequally yoked" language could be interpreted to refer to lesser relationships than marriage), and not imposing rules and burdens upon people which are over and above what the scriptures mandate (the "unequally yoked" passage might only exclude marriage while providing a guiding principle for other areas of life, and there are perhaps no other passages which would condemn dating unbelievers).

At a practical level there are examples positive and negative. There are many, many examples of believers who have taught their partners the faith and have gone on to enjoy wonderful marriages. From this perspective what greater gift could there be than sharing the truth about God with someone that you are attracted to and then to see them respond in the right spirit? Conversely, there are examples where a believer has failed to make any impression on their partner's unbelief and where they have instead found themselves drawn away into apathy or unbelief; on other occasions unbelieving partners have expressed interest or even 'converted', but the interest has been short-lived or feigned for the sake of the objective of marriage.

If we want to be maximally safe then we could make a rule for ourselves not to date someone at all unless they have already shown a serious commitment to God (and some would go even further than this). Having said that, it's worth remembering that just because someone is a believer this by itself is no guarantee of the level of their commitment, nor does it ensure that 'everything will be OK'. None of this is a 'tick the box exercise'; it's always about really getting to know someone, so perhaps there are limits to the extent rules can protect us.

If a believer does have a relationship with somebody who doesn't believe there are a number of good principles to bear in mind. First, don't overestimate how strong you are (like Samson did), and don't underestimate how strong romantic feelings can be. Many of those who have eventually lost their commitment through becoming entwined with an unbeliever would have vehemently denied this would ever have happened to them if you'd asked them towards the start of their relationship. What happened was that they overestimated their immunity and eventually re-wrote their priorities. Second, make it clear to the person you're dating exactly who you are, what is important to you and the things which you believe from the outset; there is no reason why your partner shouldn't already know all of this before you start dating. To reveal later on how important a part of your life it is, if you haven't made it clear at the beginning, will come over as strange and perhaps dishonest. Third, go slowly with the relationship, slower than you perhaps might with a believer. That reduces the risk of emotional entanglement when oneness does not yet exist in key areas of life, it gives you an easier 'out' if your partner turns out to have little interest, and it gives them time to get to know you, your faith and your God before everything gets too serious. Finally, pray about it all – the golden rule for any relationship.

Boaz and Ruth

Topics: Unlikely relationships can happen and succeed; Ruth's diligence and risk-taking; Boaz' character and spiritual qualities; Learning about your partner's values; Noticing and complementing others' virtues; 'Coincidences' – divine design and human choice.

The last few chapters have discussed a sequence of negative examples of relationships – Solomon and his wives, Samson and Delilah, David and Michal, Lot and his wife – all of which serve to emphasise powerfully the dangers of getting it wrong. But the Bible also has many, many examples of wonderfully positive relationships which are a great source of encouragement. One of these – Boaz and Ruth – speaks particularly to the topic of finding the right partner. It is perhaps the most famous love story in the Bible, the unlikely nature of the pairing contributing powerfully to the sense of narrative drama. She is a Moabitess, her very presence in Bethlehem an anomaly and a testament to her unusual faith; he is likely a much older and wealthier man, part of the institutional fabric of his community – one never would have expected their relationship even to begin, let alone work; far less that they should become the ancestors of Israel's most famous king.

THERE is much to admire in the individual characters of both Boaz and Ruth, attributes which stand them in good stead for their relationship. We'll begin by looking at each of them as individuals before an examination of how they came to be together.

A virtuous woman

The most important point about Ruth is probably her faith and courage. She was not brought up as a believer – most likely she was schooled in idolatry of one kind or another – but when she discovers the Truth she is absolutely committed and there is no going back. Refusing to leave her mother-in-law to return to her own people she comes, as Boaz so beautifully puts it, to trust in the shadow of the wings of the Lord (Ruth 2:12). She has commitment and staying power; she has faith and courage to go with Naomi to build a new life as part of a new culture despite the suspicious stares and whispers that would no doubt have taken place. She forges a new allegiance, leaving her father and mother to be married as it were to Israel and to the Lord. Risk-taker that she is, it is after this crucial step in demonstrating her faith in God that He orchestrates events to provide a new husband for her. First she establishes her relationship with God; after that her relationship with the right sort of husband can be established; this is the right way round.

Later on in the story Ruth proves herself diligent and hard-working as she gleans in the fields all day long to support her small family (a plan that she herself instigates: 2:2, illustrating her proactivity once again). She has a sense of her place as a foreigner in this scene as throughout the narrative, and when she speaks her language is always measured and deeply respectful. She well understands the kindness Boaz shows her, so when her mother-in-law proposes she approach him to be a kinsman-redeemer and husband she recognises this is a good (if risky) course of action and is ready to act. The nocturnal visit to the threshing floor would probably have sounded like a bizarre and dangerous thing to do from the perspective of her own culture (much as it sounds from the unfamiliar perspective of today) but she appears not to hesitate when Naomi suggests it. She has implicit trust in her mother-in-law and a level of bravery that would put most to shame (3:5: "And Ruth said to Naomi: 'All that thou sayest unto me I will do'"). Once again Ruth shows herself to be wonderfully proactive, trusting others enough to follow their counsel (Naomi), but also by being willing to risk looking to others for support (Boaz) when along with that risk comes the possibility of rejection. There is a life to be lived and Ruth faithfully seizes her opportunities with both hands. If you want something good in life, whether in terms of a relationship or more broadly, you have to be willing to put yourself out there, taking considered risks for reasons which are well-grounded and thought through; opportunities and relationships of the kind Ruth comes to benefit from are not often available to cowards.

There is a fascinating verse in that threshing floor scene in which Boaz says to her:

"Blessed be thou of the LORD, my daughter: for thou hast shewed more kindness in the latter end than at the beginning, inasmuch as thou followedst not young men, whether poor or rich."   (3:10)

The fact that Boaz is an older man is brought out not only here but also in the set of references to her as 'my daughter' (2:8; 3:10,11). His praise of her seems to imply that she could well have 'played the field' for a younger and more superficially attractive husband if she had chosen to do so; in those respects she might have been considered by superficial society as being in a different league from him. He takes her request not as a desperate seeking for protection or an heir but as a wonderful gesture of the giving of herself to him – by implication she is a beautiful and desirable woman as well as being a spiritual giant. She offers herself to him, a man who perhaps had long passed hope that he would meet someone so special. If this is right it makes his response to the discernment of her choice and her willingness to give herself to him particularly poignant. She risks everything – being taken advantage of, being made a spectacle in some way, or simply being rejected (as painful as that would be); he well knows what she has done, and he is overcome.[1]

---

[1] This interpretation is perhaps strengthened by the expression, "thou hast shewed more kindness in the latter end *than at the beginning*". Evidently he regards her current seeking of his protection as a 'kindness' (an interesting perspective of itself – it can be kind to our partners to allow them to be needed by us rather than

Boaz the provider

Turning to Boaz now, his very name ('in him is strength') aptly characterises his status as "a mighty man of wealth", yet his riches are not what truly define him. Rather it is his willingness to provide and protect, the joy and satisfaction he seems to find in taking care of others. In the opening scene in which he and his servants greet one another there seems to be a warmth in their reciprocation – the scriptures perhaps bothering to recount this seemingly insignificant mutual greeting (insignificant to the overall plot-development, that is) because it captures the warmth and sense of inclusion that defined Boaz (Ruth 2:4).

On seeing Ruth he takes an immediate personal interest (more on which later), making a point of seeing she is more than well provided for by personally reaching her food and ensuring that she is undisturbed while she gleans. He acts behind the scenes when she is not present also (verse 15), a true testament to how much someone really cares for another and a nice contrast to the practice of being nice to someone's face and then griping about them when they are gone. He recognises and publicly praises her great faith and the sacrifice she has made (verse 11); he is a man who has a taste for spiritual things and when he sees them he is quick to point it out. He appreciates and understands what her faith and loyalty means given her position as an outsider (verse 12), and it is he who makes one of the loveliest statements in the book when he says, "all the city of my people doth know that thou art a virtuous woman". In doing so he provides the platform for Solomon's later exposition on the Virtuous Woman in Proverbs 31; Ruth was a living prototype of what it was all about, and Boaz rightly admires and respects her for it. Boaz recognises all these things, but he does not keep

our seeking to be independent or self-sufficient), but what is Ruth's kindness "at the beginning"? Perhaps it is her persistence in only gleaning in his field – being content to receive his gracious provision rather than looking over into the next field for something better. It suggests *his* appreciation of *her* appreciation of his kindness. Again, it's nice to be needed.

them to himself; he is a master of the compliment, of making the effort to express his appreciation of the good he sees in others.

Boaz is also a man of great diligence with the ability to prioritise. When Ruth discloses her wish for a more permanent relationship with Boaz he has to acknowledge that there is another relative who has a potential prior claim to serve as the "near kinsman". As he sends her away with six measures of barley (a rather tricky task while it is still dark and you are attempting not to wake anyone up!) his deep wish to get the matter resolved and to provide for her is again made clear. Naomi perhaps sums up his character best when she tells Ruth:

"The man will not be in rest until he hath finished the thing."
(3:18)

Establishing a relationship

Having explored the characters of the two protagonists in some detail it becomes apparent how suited they are for one another and what a solid spiritual basis their relationship would have. He appreciates her keen spiritual sense, her courage and her strong faith and he tells her so. That in turn shows her what his values are, and why he is prepared to share and give as the Lord has given him – why he wants to provide and protect both naturally and spiritually, why he is glad to become her husband. In her turning to him we see how a woman should be able to turn to and depend upon her husband for strength and support. In his repeated praise of her virtues we see a man who appreciates not only what is on the surface but more importantly the spiritual and personal qualities which are so valuable in building a great marriage.

It doesn't matter, then, that 'everyone (already) knows' that she is a virtuous woman – he wants to tell her both in the interests of being kind, to let her see how her example has been powerful to others, and to show her that he cares about who she is and what she has done. Many good things that might be said often go unspoken – whether taken for granted, unnoticed, or because we are too shy, too thoughtless or too tired to bother to say them. Boaz doesn't make this mistake – he goes right out and tells her how wonderful her faith, courage and virtue have been.

All this being said, we still haven't really explored the delicacies of how the happy couple first met and began to have feelings for one another. The first step of this is introduced in chapter 2 when Ruth goes out to glean:

"And her hap was to light on a part of the field belonging unto Boaz."   (2:3)

This raises an intriguing question. Is it *really* a coincidence, a 'hap'? Do things like this just 'happen'? Well, sometimes they do (there are good matches in the world too, and some of them seem to happen by coincidence), and sometimes they don't – one cannot know for sure, a fact which remains the case whether the matter in question is a Biblical one whose cause is not stated or whether it is an event in modern life; things that 'happen' do not usually come with labels on them explaining their origin, whether it be divine or human. We do know, however, that the angels in heaven have a role in the orchestration of God's purpose so the possibility that they were involved in this 'coincidence' is a very real one. The choice of wording by using the term 'hap' is thus delicious – is it a true 'hap' or one of those 'coincidences' that is really nothing of the sort? God has ways of bringing people together if He so chooses, and while it must remain their choice rather than His, He may create the potential, a potential that sometimes we may never have *begun* to consider were it not for His intervention.

Since one cannot know in any given case whether or not this is so there is nothing for it but to proceed faithfully on the basis of 'best endeavours'. This is exactly what Ruth does – she is open to possibilities and she has courage in exploring them. The possibility of a relationship with Boaz seemed to pass a spiritual and emotional 'sense check' for her, so she steps bravely forward to see how things will proceed, not knowing the end of the story as we do.

Even if we think that her marriage to Boaz is God's idea, that didn't mean she could simply sit back and wait for it to happen automatically as something 'written in the stars'. No, she had a huge role to play, with God looking for her to be proactively involved as indeed she was. Conversely, the fact that she 'happened' upon Boaz and his field doesn't mean that she should have gone ahead whatever kind of person he seemed or turned out to be; it can sometimes be tempting to take things that happen as 'signs' from heaven – that we should proceed with a relationship as something that was 'meant to be' just because someone we might date happens to arrive on the scene at a convenient moment. We simply must not do this if it defies spiritual logic, because God might just as easily be testing us to see whether we will show ourselves truly to value what He values or not, whether we can be discerning and choose not to pursue something which will likely take us away from God rather than towards Him. We shall meet all sorts of people in life, and we have a responsibility for the choices we make. It would be foolish to date or worse marry someone against wisdom and common sense simply because you'd 'happened' to meet them and you thought it was 'meant to be'. We have to remember that we are not forced into any relationship and that God expects us to exercise our free will and discretion and make good choices with our lives.

There are no easy answers here then. For Ruth there was what 'happened' (possibly though not certainly something that was in the divine blueprint), *plus* her spiritual discernment and choice about whether Boaz would be a good partner, *plus* her proactive stance, *plus* his response. All these came together to enable a wonderful relationship, but take any one of them away and there may well have been nothing. We have to make proactive choices, using spiritual values to measure and define our choices in dating and relationships rather than simply getting together with whoever comes along just because they did. But it is worth also bearing in mind the possibility that God can have a wider view of things than our own, and something that might appear 'out of the question' from a human point of view may not necessarily be so from the divine.

On seeing her for the first time Boaz asks, "Whose damsel is this?" and when he finds out he makes a point of engaging her in conversation, a conversation which neither of them (he especially) seems in any hurry to end. The narrative is too delicate to say whether he has begun to fall for her at first sight or whether his interest is purely based on curiosity or philanthropy, but his favouring of her – whatever the cause – is beyond any doubt. Their dialogue (2:7-14) contains no less than six exchanges, one of the longest conversations between a man and a woman recorded in the scriptures, its length perhaps lightly suggesting that heady feeling when two people who like each other find themselves wrapped in a conversation that neither of them wants to exit. Perhaps the attraction is more from his side at this point; perhaps it comes from both; or perhaps attraction isn't really the point as a material item on the agenda at this stage. If the text hints at their attraction (even that is a debatable point) it is done with a light touch which suggests that while attraction can be a wonderful thing, a good relationship is built out of more. It is the deep spiritual qualities of these two that stand out and make them such a great match. If as individuals we can concentrate on developing the kind of characteristics that Boaz and Ruth evidently had in their pre-existing separate lives, then it will be of massive benefit in strengthening our relationships with our partners, whatever the starting point or 'hap' might be.

Postscript: dating – some practical thoughts

Topics: Being honest about yourself and your partner; Setting standards; Different types of date; The physical side – how far, how fast?; Ending a relationship; Being single.

This chapter is a miscellany of practical points and thoughts about dating which didn't easily fit into the preceding chapters. We'll take six particular topics as summarised below.

1. The importance of being honest in how you represent yourself and in the conclusions that you draw about your partner;
2. The need to set standards around how you want to be treated in a relationship;
3. The value of different types of dates;
4. Some thoughts on the physical side of dating;
5. Ending a relationship;
6. Surviving and thriving when you're single.

Being honest

Honesty is particularly important with respect to two aspects of dating. The first is that it is very important to give a fair representation of who you really are and want to be rather than a projection of who you think your partner might want you to be. That way you can be yourself (which is always easier!) and your partner has a fair chance of making a sensible decision about whether or not you are the one they want to be with on a more permanent basis.

We're not talking here of making no effort regarding your appearance or paying no attention to your choice of words or etiquette; we all make an extra effort with our appearance or perhaps put on more make-up or aftershave when we are trying to impress another, and there is nothing wrong with this. The more important point is that it is dishonest and counter-productive to pretend you're something you're not or to feign interests you don't have. Imagine an (admittedly bizarre) situation where a man says nothing about his passion for supporting his local football team while he is dating, but once he is married he shows her his season ticket and tells her not to expect him to be around on Saturday afternoons whenever there is a game on. He has misrepresented who he is, what his interests are, what is important to him, and significant aspects of his behavioural patterns. For her part she feels defrauded: that he has been dishonest and that she hasn't had a fair basis on which to make a decision. An even more serious situation can result if someone pretends an interest in spiritual matters that they don't really have. Since you can't keep up an act every day for the rest of your life when you're married it's far better to be honest from the outset.

A second area where honesty is very important is when you reflect on and draw conclusions about your partner and the potential of your relationship. Every relationship will have its positives and negatives and sometimes it's tempting to cover over the negatives, minimising or ignoring them in the interests of the positive. Sometimes we can kid ourselves that glaring issues in a relationship are not really there at all or can be compensated for or managed in one way or another, or that particular traits or deficiencies in our partner's character are not really there. We can pretend to ourselves, for instance, that someone has a greater interest in serving God than the evidence clearly shows, or that someone's mean streak or volatile temper will not be an issue when there are some pretty strong signs to the contrary. We can project onto our partner attributes that, when seen in the cold light of day, they clearly do not possess. It's important to be able to recognise what a situation is with honesty, to evaluate it – and then to make an informed and honest decision about how to proceed. What we're saying here is not that we should only continue in a relationship if our partner is absolutely perfect – of course no one is – but instead that we should be honest about a situation and whether we can make allowances and live with it for the rest of our lives or not. This is far better than lying to ourselves only to find out later that we have a major issue on our hands.

Setting standards

It's important to set standards about how you want and expect to be treated in the relationship as this sets a pattern which, should you decide to marry, can inform and benchmark behaviours which may remain in place for the rest of your lives. Such patterns become ingrained and can be very hard to modify once they are set. Let's take a couple of examples to make this a bit more concrete. Suppose you, as a young man, have a girlfriend who has a tendency to flirt with other men when you are in public. You may not want to make an issue of it; you may try to tell yourself it is not a big deal, that it doesn't really upset you or that it will change when you are married – and yet, aside from the question of whether the behaviour is appropriate in an absolute sense, there is every chance that over time the impact of it will gnaw away at you and harm the relationship. If she behaves like this now when still in the flush of the early stages of love, is it likely that it will lessen when you are married and your physical presence is rather more old hat to her than it is today?

We could just as easily take an example in the opposite direction. Let's imagine you are a girl or young woman whose boyfriend treats her unreasonably when he has had a bad day at work or at college, taking his frustrations out on her in some way by being cruel or bad-tempered. What do you do in this situation? If you just accept it as a price you pay for being with him then you effectively legitimise the behaviour. By your tacit acceptance of it you tell him that it is okay for him to treat you like this as some kind of emotional punchbag; the behaviour can very easily become ingrained. What's needed here is to clearly yet calmly and pleasantly explain the dynamic you've noticed: that although you'd love to help him feel better when he's had a bad day, it isn't fair for him to treat you unreasonably just because everything didn't all go his way for a short period of time. It is important, then, to set the standards and to make it clear how you expect to be treated.

Couples can together fall into patterns of behaviour which are not particularly productive or helpful. A couple can help each other to move together to a higher standard by simply being observant of such things. You might fall into the pattern of indulging in gossip about other believers when you meet, for instance – if this is the case one of you can take the initiative by observing the trend, owning the problem, and suggesting that together you try to do better. This point about owning the problem (or your part in it) is key here – it's all too easy to observe relationship dynamics and then turn the blame entirely on your partner for their occurrence. Even if it is primarily their fault (as you see it) the examples of Daniel, Moses and Jeremiah in taking the sins of the people upon themselves and asking for forgiveness provide a great example.

Different types of dates

In order to make a good decision about your marriage partner you'll want to know as much about them as you possibly can and that involves seeing them in as many different circumstances as possible. If your average date consists in taking a helicopter tour around Manhattan or dining at the Ritz then of course your dates will be fun and you'll likely see your partner in a good light. Most of us will not have the financial resources to allow our courting to be quite like that, but even on a more mundane level if all our dates are primarily about having fun (eating out, making trips to new places, watching a movie) then we may well have a good time but there will be an awful lot about the relationship and about our partner that we shall be leaving undiscovered. While it's great to enjoy ourselves and have fun, these activities on their own are not representative of everyday life. A lot of life is mundane (making dinner, paying bills, getting ready for work ...), and we need to find out if we enjoy doing everyday activities together, seeing our partner in as many different circumstances as possible.

Is your partner someone who is prepared to make sacrifices to help others, someone who is considerate, someone who doesn't mind hard work when it is required? How do they respond when there is disappointment and frustration or when things don't go as planned? What are they like when not in their Sunday best or dressed to go out? What are they like in difficult circumstances or when they are ill or have had a bad day? How are they early in the morning – are they the sort of person that you should only risk speaking to after 11 am? You may be perfectly prepared to tolerate this for their wonderful qualities at other times of day, but it would be wise at least to know this sort of thing so that you can make an informed decision. Different types of dates that involve seeing your partner in different surroundings and situations will reveal a lot about both them, yourself, and how the two of you interact.

Knowing whether you work well together as a team is particularly important, because marriage relies heavily upon this. 'Service dates' where you do some activity of service together (a preaching activity, sick visiting, fixing up the hall, some kind of DIY, babysitting a younger brother or sister, running errands, and so on) can all be wonderful opportunities to see each other in 'everyday life' contexts and the otherwise humdrum tasks can be fun because you are doing them together. You will be learning a lot more about each other in the process than if all your dates are purely self-indulgent.

The physical side

Let's turn now to the physical side of dating. Sex is a wonderful gift of God but it is a gift to be enjoyed only within the particular context of marriage. In chapter 28 we look specifically at the question of sex before marriage and why it matters to God; we won't go over the same material here. If we accept, however, that a dating or engaged couple should not sleep together before marriage it still leaves open the question of how far it is appropriate to go in terms of physical intimacy before marriage. While there are few if any specifics on this question in the scriptures there are principles both spiritual and practical worth considering.

The first one is that our bodies are meant to be a temple for God; we are supposed to be giving glory to Him in the way we live our lives. If our approach is instead to indulge ourselves as much as possible, to go as far as we can while stopping short of full sex then we shall have missed the point. When Paul pointed out that our bodies are "not for fornication but for the Lord" he was admittedly talking about a slightly different issue, but if our approach is to seek as many physical thrills as we can, and to push the boundaries as far as we dare – to play brinkmanship with God's command, as it were – then his admonition will certainly have its relevance for us.

Let us be quite clear: if we are in a relationship which is at all serious (and probably even if it isn't), one physical thing will tend to lead to another and we will *want* to sleep with our partner. There is an entirely natural feeling / instinct that God has wired us with, and the chances are that most people who have ever dated seriously will have felt that way on some occasions. But God has also given us brains and the ability to exercise self-control; He has asked us to "possess our vessels" or to be in control of our urges and wait till the time is appropriate and the context right. This isn't easy, but it is very possible, and thousands of believers through the ages have done it. It can be tempting to think the feeling is just so strong that it can't be resisted – we may even be naive enough to think that we are the only ones who have ever experienced it with quite this intensity when this clearly cannot be the case. But we can help ourselves by not making the temptation harder than it need be. If we spend a lot of time alone in private with our partner then it is going to be more difficult. If our dates often end up in our or our partner's bedroom then it is going to be more difficult. We have to think smart about such matters.

It's possible to think of the physical expression of love in terms of a spectrum which ranges from a mere look (with no physical touch) or holding hands at one end to intercourse at the other. Different people might define the spectrum slightly differently in terms of where they would put a particular activity on that scale of intimacy, but there's not much doubt about the two end extremes. Clearly the Bible has forbidden one end, whereas most (though not all) would consider that it is okay to go further than the 'holding hands' end at the other.

The question is, how far does one go along that spectrum in terms of expressing intimacy? This is a very personal question that has to be worked out between a dating couple. There are a number of principles to point out, however. If our approach is to go as far as we can to our perception of the 'line' of what God has forbidden without technically crossing it, then it is doubtful that we shall be acting within the spirit of God's command. We are not meant to play brinkmanship with God's rules, extracting the maximum possible that we can without technically breaching a rule. Instead we are meant to be giving glory to God by showing the spirit of Christ in all aspects of life including this one. By contrast, others may feel that it is good to impose what most would regard as very strict rules upon themselves. If this is agreed and done for good spiritual reasons to avoid temptation then this is perfectly acceptable. What we should avoid is writing and imposing rules upon other couples which are not scripturally mandated – this would be an example of loading "burdens grievous to be borne" upon others.

How far to go along our imaginary spectrum will and probably should vary during the course of a relationship – it would seem appropriate for a couple to seek greater physical intimacy as an expression of their greater emotional connection as a relationship deepens. There is great merit, then, in going relatively slowly at the start of a relationship. This is entirely contrary to the culture which wants to jump into bed at the earliest opportunity, but there is great wisdom to it for several reasons. First, it means that you'll be less likely to do something which you'll regret later. Second, going slowly gives you chance to appreciate and savour each wonderful stage of intimacy that God has enabled – if you rush in all at once then a great deal can be missed or go under-appreciated. While it may be looked down on by society as being excessively 'tame', there is something absolutely wonderful about just holding hands, for example – so it is good to enjoy and take time to appreciate it for the wonderful thing that it is! Third, if you become deeply physically involved early on in a relationship (while still avoiding sex), where can you go if the relationship becomes more serious and your mutual attraction and emotional connection significantly grows? You can end up with no way of expressing your growing unity in a physical way because you already did all of that on your second date – this can lead to disappointment and frustration and the temptation to go further than you should. Far better to keep the physical side of the relationship in pace with the emotional side so that you can express your growing intimacy in physical but appropriate ways should you both be comfortable in doing so. Fourth, the more physical a relationship becomes the more emotionally entwined you become and the more traumatic it can be to end it should it turn out not to be heading in the direction of marriage. These physical feelings can be very powerful and can make it harder to make a rational decision about whether the relationship has a future or not, and it can make the ending of the relationship more messy and emotionally draining should this be necessary (it can also make it more awkward if and when you interact with that person in the future – not impossible amongst a relatively small community of believers).

Finally, it's important to be sensitive to your partner's feelings about what is and isn't appropriate. To use our imaginary spectrum again, be sensitive to where you and your partner are on this scale and be content to go only as far as the more 'conservative' one of you feels comfortable (where is the affection or love in forcing your partner to do something they are not comfortable with or feel is not appropriate? to do so is merely selfish and inconsiderate). There should be no mocking or blaming of our partner (stated or otherwise) if they are not comfortable going as far as we – in fact, their's may very well be the more spiritual path. Similarly, if we are mocked or pressured to go further than we are comfortable with because of our partner's 'needs', then that tells us something we need to know about their attitude and their (lack of) concern for our feelings in this sensitive area. Ultimately selflessness will be a key to a successful marriage and this is a good time to start practising it and to ensure that one's partner is capable of it.

Ending a relationship

Every relationship is different so there are few absolute rules with respect to how to end a relationship, but again there are principles. Christlike behaviour is to be the order of the day, and that mandates kindness and consideration of the feelings of the other. An announcement to the world on Twitter or getting a friend to pass on the bad news is not the way for our partner to learn we are through. The code of Christlikeness should impact both the things we say and the manner and timing of them: there is a more Christlike way to finish with someone and there is a more thoughtless or selfish way. What constitutes 'kindness' will vary according to the dynamics of every individual relationship, but it needs to be thought about beforehand. We owe it to our partner and to God to do the task thoughtfully and well, tricky though it might be.

While we should avoid being cruel at all costs, we also need to be honest. It isn't kind and it isn't truthful to hold out hope to our partner of a continuation or resumption of a relationship if there is no such hope from our perspective. Better to be clear and firm (if necessary) while at the same time being kind in the words we choose. Similarly it is not kind or wise to prolong a relationship that won't ultimately work because there is no one better around at the moment and we don't want to be without anyone. We owe it to our partner to set them free if they are not the one for us.

If we still want to be in the relationship but our partner doesn't and is seeking to end it there is also a responsibility for Christlike behaviour. While we shall potentially be extremely upset and our sadness may last for months it isn't helpful or right to attempt to blackmail our partner emotionally into continuing something against their wish, and neither is it right to try to extract revenge on them in some way because they have broken our heart. Marriage is about unity, and if the partners in a dating relationship are not unified in their desire to progress it then it is best for it to end sooner rather than later and minimise the emotional hurt.

Ending a relationship in the best way possible is important not only because it's the right thing to do from a godly perspective but also because within a small community of believers it is quite likely we shall see the person again and may very well have to interact with them, perhaps with some frequency. The easier it is to look each other in the eye knowing that we have both behaved appropriately even though the conclusion may not have been the one that both parties wanted, the easier it will be to interact afterwards.

If a relationship is ended in a Christlike way it can still have been a success even if it did not end in marriage. The two individuals have undertaken a journey together, have learned a significant amount about each other but also a significant amount about themselves and hopefully about spiritual things as well. Such a relationship is not a 'failure' but rather a great learning experience that God has blessed us with on our walk to the kingdom.

Surviving and thriving when you're single

Although this is a book about marriage rather than about being single, it is worth a few brief comments on the attitude we should have when we are not dating whether through our own choice or because we simply can't seem to find the right person at the moment.

If you would like to be with someone but aren't it is important to be patient. Certainly you should talk to God about your feelings and ask for His help, but you should not lower your standards to make poor spiritual choices because you are lonely. There are many examples of those who thought they would never meet someone and then did and found themselves happily married against all expectation.

One of the beauties of faith is that it provides a spiritual family. While this is clearly not the same as being married, having children of one's own or being part of a physical family (it would be both naive and insensitive to claim otherwise), it is nevertheless an enormous blessing which has very special rewards and can relieve at least some of the pain of loneliness. It can beget a sense of partnership and shared destiny between us that is not available for others who are single; it enables relationships and support-work with children, for instance, which can be wonderful; it can be the source of meaningful friendships across all age groups which would be hard to achieve elsewhere.

A good attitude here is to focus on spiritually preparing oneself to be the best person we can be within a marriage (or without!) should God ultimately provide the right person for us. Think about what you can prepare yourself to give to others rather than what you will take or what you are missing out on by being single. Ask God to prepare you for whatever role might come next in your life and trust that He will provide according to His will whatever is right for you.

Conversely you may have no desire to date, and you may not wish to marry. This is of course perfectly acceptable and both the Lord Jesus and the Apostle Paul spoke highly of such a commitment and the potential it brings.

Whether by choice or otherwise, then, there are significant upsides from being single which can be appreciated and made use of while in that state. Paul spoke about this in 1 Corinthians:

"But I would have you without carefulness. He that is unmarried careth for the things that belong to the Lord, how he may please the Lord: but he that is married careth for the things that are of the world, how he may please his wife. There is difference also between a wife and a virgin. The unmarried woman careth for the things of the Lord, that she may be holy both in body and in spirit: but she that is married careth for the things of the world, how she may please her husband."

(1 Corinthians 7:32-34)

The state of singleness confers upon a believer the freedom to be even more dedicated in their affections and service to their God, the possibility of a level of commitment and practical involvement which is challenging or even impossible for someone with family responsibilities. This presents a great opportunity – a calling to be highly esteemed.

Part 3
The husband

Introduction: on being male – masculinity in crisis?

Topics: What does it mean to be male?; A Biblical model for maleness; What is male headship about?; Different aspects of spiritual leadership.

What does it mean to be male? Sixty to a hundred years ago the answer to this question used to be so obvious that it wasn't really a question at all. Being a man meant being the main breadwinner and provider for the family and usually a job that was primarily *physical* in nature, an area where the larger male skeletal structure and bigger muscles carried obvious advantages. Men felt assured of their place in the home and in the family too, they were 'in charge' in some sense (at least, it felt to them that way!) and they were fed and clothed by their wives for their efforts. Rarely, if ever, did they venture into the kitchen or carry out domestic chores; they laid pipes, worked in fields, built bridges – that sort of thing. But how things have changed!

A MAN with such attitudes and expectations would be regarded as hopelessly out of date and perhaps chauvinistic in the West today. The nature of working life has radically changed so that the majority of men now have sedentary lifestyles in which a man's physical distinctions are no longer any advantage to him and women have taken on many of the roles and expectations that formerly would have purely been the preserve of males. For their part the men now assume part share of the domestic tasks, once the domain of the female.

The implications of this societal shift are significant for both men and women: we used to know what it meant to be male, but now society is not so sure. Indeed, the critic Anthony Clare made the point effectively in a newspaper article back in 2000:

"Now the whole issue of men – the point of them, their purpose, their value, their justification – is a matter for public debate. Serious commentators declare that men are redundant, that women do not need them and children would be better off without them. At the beginning of the twenty-first century it is difficult to avoid the conclusion that men are in serious trouble. Throughout the world, developed and developing, antisocial behaviour is essentially male. Violence, sexual abuse of children, illicit drug use, alcohol misuse, gambling all are overwhelmingly male activities. The courts and prisons bulge with men. When it comes to aggression, delinquent behaviour, risk taking and social mayhem, men win gold."

He continues:

"There is hardly anything to be done in today's society that cannot be done by women. 'So what!' say women, not unreasonably, given the age it has taken to establish such a state of affairs. So what, indeed. The problem is one for men and particularly for those men – and they have been the majority – who have defined their lives, their identities, the very essence of their masculinity in terms of professional and occupational achievement and have prided themselves on the work that only they as men could do. My father's generation prided themselves on being providers – for their spouses, families and themselves. Today, providing seems no longer required …" (Anthony Clare: "On Men: Masculinity in Crisis", www.guardian.co.uk, September 25, 2000)

Clare has put his finger on something quite intriguing here, identifying a 'crisis' of masculinity in which it can seem that there is very little for men to do which is specifically male other

than the occasional washing of the car or connecting up a new
washing machine. Where men used to go out and dig ditches,
now they sit around sipping lattes, instead finding expression
for their maleness in (depending on their income levels and
social background): loutish behaviour, sport, go-karting or
paintballing, and potentially DIY. There is nothing wrong with
most of these activities, but none of them could be considered
truly *important*. Are the things that make a man male now only
expressed through recreation and self-indulgence?

It seems that society hasn't really got any answers to this
conundrum, but the Bible certainly has. The Bible has always
seen a role for the male within both family and ecclesial life,
and it is a role of massive significance for which he will need
concentration, effort, discipline and dedication. For this work
real men are needed, men of both conviction and compassion,
men of spiritual insight and endurance. One writer castigated
many modern males for being little more than 'boys who shave'
– self-centred individuals content to have a good time whenever
possible and unwilling to take on seriously the mantle the Bible
asks them to shoulder. For any such the Bible's calling is to grow
up and embrace the responsibility and privilege that maleness
brings from a scriptural perspective.

Aside, then, from the practical aspects of the curse of work
we've considered in Genesis 3 the Bible lays at the male door
the responsibility of spiritual leadership. This isn't a role that
comes easily or naturally; it requires preparation and dedication,
humility and perseverance. Let's consider what it is all about.

Male headship – what does it mean?
A radio DJ once recounted that when he and his wife got married
thirty years earlier they had made an agreement that while she
would make the day-to-day decisions of marriage, he would make
the big strategic decisions. However, after the passage of thirty
years he had come to realise that there didn't seem to have been
any big decisions!

What, then, does male headship mean? It must involve greater hands-on, practical influence than the DJ's big-decisions-that-were-never-required; on the other hand it must mean something other than a triviality such that the husband gets to wield the TV remote and have first call on family viewing.

It's somewhat easier, then, to say what male headship does *not* mean than to say what it does. It is not about creating an environment for the male ego to run amok as will be seen in the hideous examples of the overgrown egos of Haman and Lamech in the following chapters. Male headship of the spiritual variety is not about the exercise of power and showing who's boss; it is something which must flow out of our *submission* to Christ not from the ego.

What is needed is leadership, not dictatorship; this must not be a power play; human history is littered with the debris of what male dominance *can* mean when human nature gets the upper hand – in abuse, in treating women as objects or as a group who are primarily there to service male needs. Wherever there has been power in human history there has been abuse of that power, men having used their superior physical strength to achieve it – but while maleness can be a route to evil, it does not need to be; it can be noble and honourable. What is needed is a different model of leadership, a leadership in which Christ must be the pattern. Once male headship is centred in Christ's headship and once leadership is about leading like Christ then it ceases to be a dangerous concept and transforms into something beautiful and empowering for the whole family.

But leadership *in what*? Here are some ideas:

Leading in example. If the husband is to represent Christ, then there is no alternative but to lead by example. The last thing we should be is hypocritical husbands and fathers, professing one thing but doing another. To set a consistent, positive example in our households requires study, determination, grit, perseverance, and sheer hard work. Paul exhorted Titus to show himself as a "pattern of good works" in the ecclesia (Titus 2:7) – this is what being a real man is about: leading in deed by *showing* the way of

Christ as well as merely talking about it, illustrating by example the high standards he espouses.

Leading in love. The husband is to love his wife as Christ loved the church, and since there is no greater love than this Paul's command will require *leadership* in love; setting the standard and showing by example. We are talking about the sort of love which gives itself in sacrifice, putting itself out again and again for the needs and well-being of the other. This is tremendously important – the main thing Paul exhorts husbands to focus on in Ephesians 5 (discussed in chapter 5) and something which doesn't necessarily come naturally for men yet which their wives deeply need. Husbands are to love after the pattern of Christ's self-sacrificial love – a lifetime's study but one more productive than any study of science, technology or sport will ever be. This love originates in the divine ("not that we loved God but that he loved us", 1 John 4:10) and in a marriage it can be initiated by the husband since he is the one who represents Christ. 'You want to know what maleness is about?' says Paul in effect back in Ephesians, 'then just concentrate on loving your wife like Christ – this will be one of the most worthwhile endeavours you could ever undertake'.

Leading in forgiveness and reconciliation. The pride and ego of the male can be easily bruised yet Christ's work centres on forgiveness and reconciliation, a stark contrast. If the husband's work is to follow the spirit of Christ, then he should look for reconciliation in times of conflict with his wife; he should be ready to forgive and able to take the initiative in saying sorry. This is no affront to his masculinity; instead it is a Christlike demonstration of our desire to be one with our partner, as he is with his Father. If it is right to set pride and discord aside, then why would the man not show the initiative and go and do it – this is good spiritual leadership, illustrating and enacting from the front line what is important in the marriage.

Leading in the scriptures. The priests in the Old Testament were all males and the husband performs a priestly role in the family just as the males are called to do in the public worship of believers. We saw this pattern when we looked at the early chapters of Genesis – God gave His command to Adam before Eve was created as his helper, and it was then Adam's responsibility to share it with his family and ensure that it was carried out. Of course he failed to do this so God explicitly specified it as part of his role for future generations, ensuring he put right what he failed to achieve in the garden. This responsibility has nothing to do with brain size or aptitude, it has to do with God asking the different genders to take on different responsibilities in the family and public worship. The male doesn't come pre-programmed with more knowledge of the scriptures so that he can better take on this role; his ability to execute it well will depend on how willing he is to put in the effort – whether he cares enough about God's word and will to learn it for himself so that he can share it with his family. This does not require him to accomplish great intellectual feats; just a simple love of God's word and a desire to share it practically and as powerfully as possible with his family will be all that is required.

Leading in worship, prayer and praise. Generally speaking he is to lead the family in prayer. An interesting passage is 1 Timothy 2:1-8 which both begins and ends with the man's role in prayer and contains in between a list of all the things and people that are to be prayed for. Fascinatingly this passage is immediately adjacent to the one which talks about women's responsibility towards the household and the children. If those are the things a woman should concentrate on, then a man should concentrate on prayer, a priestly aspect of his role. It might not come easily to him (his wife may be much more 'naturally spiritual' if we can call it that, much more attuned to this method of communicating with the Father than he), but the scriptures ask him to give it his special concentration. What about worship and praise? We perhaps don't normally think of a father leading these things in his family, but perhaps we should – why would it be any more abnormal for a family to sing a hymn together to God than it would for them to offer a prayer or read the Bible? The man might not be musical, of course, but he can delegate; he can see that the job gets done and that he values the activity through his participation. He doesn't have to become a musical genius but he can show his family that he cares about worshipping God by the way in which he joins in with public hymns, by encouraging his children to join in the hymns, and perhaps by showing an interest in music CDs which offer praise to God and which can invigorate the worship-life of a family.

Leading in provision. This one may seem to hark back to 'old-fashioned' gender stereotypes, but there is plenty of scriptural support for it. 1 Timothy 5:8 speaks of a man providing for his household, and if he is able to do so, what a wonderful blessing both to him and to the family. It is a huge task to give yourself day after day, year after year to a job that you may not even particularly enjoy, to cope with all the irritations and disappointments it brings, to find the energy to keep delivering. It needs resilience and strength, and it is part of the punishment that God has laid upon men. Their acceptance of it and their resolve in carrying it out shows their compliance to God's decree and their humble acceptance of His righteousness – in this way one's daily graft becomes a spiritual exercise as well as an economic one.

Leading in chivalry. The Lord Jesus Christ girded himself with a towel and washed his disciples' feet – this was the sort of leadership that he practised. Peter speaks of 'honouring' one's wife, an effect achieved both through words of tenderness, consideration and respect, and also through deeds of kindness, thoughtfulness and self-sacrifice. Honouring someone is about making them feel special, important, valued and appreciated; it needs to be something husbands remind themselves to do, not leaving this duty as a relic from a past world of dating. J. B. Phillips' translation runs as follows: "You husbands should try to understand the wives you live with, honouring them as physically weaker yet heirs with you of the grace of life" (1 Peter 3:7). While fully understanding one's wife may be a lifetime's study, Peter encourages husbands not to give up on the task. It's only if we understand our partners in a measure that we can truly serve them and meet their needs.

Leading in salvation. Paul speaks of the husband "seeking above all things" the salvation of his wife. This is a superlative – "above *all* things" – which really brings to the fore the extent to which the man is meant to be modelling Christ in the relationship. It is a tremendously powerful question for husbands to ask themselves, 'What can I do that will help lead to the salvation of my wife? What can I do that will make it easier for her to get to God's kingdom?' Usually it won't be by arguing with her or lecturing her (as though we had somehow got there already), by expressing frustrations at her shortcomings, or by ignoring her. It will instead be by giving more of ourselves, by giving physical help and freeing up more time and space for her, by encouragement, by well-timed conversations and reflections on godly things, by setting an example for the children and gently and kindly teaching them God's ways. It's a lifetime study of giving oneself for another, of transforming the male ego into the spirit of Christ.

Leading by setting the family's spiritual course. In our Genesis studies earlier in the book we looked at the way in which Adam bore responsibility for the spiritual health of the family. When Joshua was able to say, "As for me and my house, we will serve the Lord!" (Joshua 24:15) he was expressing spiritual leadership of his family in exactly the way a man should. This is good leadership of the sort that God is looking for, and if it is genuine and un-hypocritical the family members will generally respond to it, seeing the difference it makes in the husband's life and the power of his example. It is his job to see the big picture in terms of the spiritual health of the family: where it is, where it needs to get to and how it needs to change. Of course he will discuss this with his wife and she will help him with the analysis, but it is his responsibility to be strong, to carry on despite setbacks, weakness and frustration, to establish the baseline of what the family stands for and to set the course for its future travel. Spiritual headship is a Big Calling.

Leadership transformed

All of this is transformational as a concept of leadership and as a sense of what it means to endeavour to be a 'man of God' in the family context. It is no easy role, and there is no time for lazing around on the sofa while drinks are served. This is a calling to be striven for, the transformation of leadership from an ego-driven power play into something beautiful, creative and worthwhile. This is what we can be aiming for when we strive to be a man like Christ; maleness is redeemed from all uncertainty and doubt and elevated to its highest calling. This is our opportunity, as males, to change from being 'boys who shave' to grow towards the measure of the stature of the fulness of Christ.

Of course, none of the aspects of spiritual leadership we have mentioned is the exclusive domain of the husband. Love, forgiveness and worship are undoubtedly required of *both* partners in a marriage. But they are areas that a husband can concentrate on particularly in order to focus his headship role. It's not that he has to do these things all by himself; his wife is there by his side to help him and delegation is perfectly reasonable in some aspects of the marriage. But he needs to see that these aspects of family life are taken care of in the family over which God has appointed him head. He must take a keen role in executing them or in seeing that they are carried out, and he will do this not by barking orders but by his loving example. It is his job to strive to set the spiritual tone and direction for the family.

With this in mind it's time now to turn to some Biblical examples for further reflection on the role of the husband. In this particular section all the examples are negative – devastatingly so in the case of the Levite and his concubine, but things are hardly much improved in the case of Haman, Lamech or Samson and their wives. While this might seem one-sidedly negative, writing as a male primarily to other males in these chapters, I reckon we can toughen up and take it! It's not that there are no positive role models in the scriptures – there are plenty (Jesus, Joseph, Abraham, Boaz ...), and we shall be looking at them at other points in this book. But the ones that stood out to me particularly in respect to the question of what it means to be head in a world where leadership and maleness have been so abused turned out to be predominantly negative. There is a lot to be learned from thinking about what we ought *not* to be; it is often a very helpful foil for thinking about its opposite and for seeing the beauty of Christ.

The Levite and his concubine

Topics: What happens when everyone does their own thing; Big problems can have little beginnings; Male bonding and the dangers of selfishness; Ignoring the other's needs.

Perhaps the most harrowing account in the entire Biblical corpus, the narrative of the slaughtered concubine sits in final and climactic place in the book of Judges. Morning light betrays the horror of the night before: a body raped and abused by the men of Gibeah, the corpse butchered into twelve pieces and a portion sent to each of the tribes of Israel to martial them to battle against this Benjamin atrocity. From whence this hideous barbarism? How can it be that God's chosen people are brought so low? In fact the sin did not begin with the men of Benjamin though it finds its cruelest expression there. There were problems even in the couple's own relationship which whispered long before the ominous threat of a horrifying conclusion.

THE refrain of the closing chapters of Judges, found on no less than five occasions is that "every man did that which was right in his own eyes", a self-seeking approach focusing on what suited a person's own particular interests with scant regard for anyone else. It impacted relationships too, a point which is easy to miss until the culmination of the story (the rape and the slaughter) is appreciated. The clues to the underlying problem are there in the text right in the opening verses:

"And it came to pass in those days, when there was no king in Israel, that there was a certain Levite sojourning on the side of mount Ephraim, who took to him a concubine out of Bethlehem-judah. And his concubine played the whore against him, and went away from him unto her father's house to Bethlehem-judah, and was there four whole months. And her husband arose, and went after her, to speak friendly unto her, and to bring her again, having his servant with him, and a couple of asses: and she brought him into her father's house: and when the father of the damsel saw him, he rejoiced to meet him. And his father in law, the damsel's father, retained him; and he abode with him three days: so they did eat and drink, and lodged there."   (Judges 19:1-4)

These verses describe a climate in which people do as they please in relationships with scant regard for others. The concubine felt herself to be in that position so she goes off to 'play the whore' with other men for a while, seemingly using her father's home as a base. The account is so matter of fact in its description as though this behaviour is the most natural thing in the world: if you felt like it, why wouldn't you? No point sticking in a relationship where you're not fulfilled if there's adventure to be had elsewhere, if you can find someone you like better or who gives you more financial support. The narrative is starting to sound very modern.

Whatever you feel like

Her behaviour is an example of what happens when people do what they feel like. The environment that she is in (in which everyone is doing just that) takes its toll, making it seem so much more reasonable to behave that way herself. It is just the same today. When people break faith all around us and the truly permanent relationship starts to feel like a rare thing it is hard not to assume it as the norm, just 'what one does', a symptom, perhaps, of the modern frenetic world. 'Hang on a minute,' one might say to oneself, '*I'm* not that fulfilled either when I come to think about it. Maybe there's somebody more compatible for me out there too?' The tragic ending of the story, however, reminds us that if she had adopted a different attitude and never left home in the first place none of the awful things which unfold later in the story would have happened. While she appears much, much less to blame than her husband for the ultimate tragedy (and he less to blame than the men of Gibeah), it is her dissatisfaction which kicks off the whole sorry chain of events.

And what of the Levite himself? His delay of four months before he goes to seek his concubine seems a bizarre detail but one the text draws our attention to by inserting the emphatic word "whole" into the description: "she was (in her father's house) four *whole* months." It seems as though *he* is not particularly desperate to go and find her if he can wait four whole months before he bothers to do so. He'll go when he feels like it – there is no urgency here; it doesn't really matter that much. When he gets round to it, then he'll go – when it is right in his own eyes.

The final character in this part of the story is the girl's father. His behaviour is somewhat odd also, his joy at seeing the Levite seemingly disproportionate ("when the father of the damsel saw him, he rejoiced to meet him"). Maybe he is just glad to see his daughter back in a respectable relationship; this could certainly be the case. But the previous narrative of Micah and the children of Dan which had all the characters fawning over a Levite as if a personal Levitical connection could have a talismanic effect, suggests that the reason for the father's exuberance may be because his daughter's 'husband' was a *Levite*. If this is the case, then his motive is essentially self-seeking also, his gladness but a reflection of his desire for status in his community. The sum of the matter so far is that *all* the characters are thinking primarily of themselves – everyone is doing that which is right in their own eyes.

A heartless reunion

The eventual reuniting of the couple is told matter-of-factly, their reconciliation as (un)natural as their separation in the way it is told: they split up, they get back together – so what? It's as if she opens the door with an 'Oh it's you; I wondered if you might show up at some point. Well, you'd better come in', and the relationship picks up where it had left off.

This isn't anywhere near being healthy, so it would seem. There appears to be no real connection between the couple, no oneness, and the chapter now recounts a strange sequence in which the Levite repeatedly tries to leave but is constrained by his father-in-law with insistent use of an expression which refers to the Levite's *heart*:

> "(The father-in-law is speaking:) 'Strengthen your *heart* with a morsel of bread, and after that you may go.' So the two of them sat and ate and drank together. And the girl's father said to the man, 'Be pleased to spend the night, and let your *heart* be merry.' And when the man rose up to go, his father-in-law pressed him, till he spent the night there again. And on the fifth day he arose early in the morning to depart. And the girl's father said, 'Strengthen your *heart* and wait until the day declines.' So they ate both of them. And when the man and his concubine and his servant rose up to depart, his father-in-law, the girl's father, said to him, 'Behold, now the day has waned towards evening. Please, spend the night. Behold, the day draws to its close. Lodge here and let your *heart* be merry; and tomorrow you shall arise early in the morning for your journey, and go home.'"   (verses 5-9, ESV)

This is not the only occurrence of the idea of the men's hearts being merry, a further reference appearing when the Levite arrives in Gibeah:

> "As they were making their *hearts* merry, behold, the men of the city, worthless fellows, surrounded the house, beating on the door ..."   (verse 22, ESV)

What is the point of the drum-beat repetition of the men's hearts and the mysterious sequence of the man wanting to leave and being compelled to stay another day for some further drinking celebrations?

The answer comes when we notice who it is whose hearts are merry – it is the *men's* hearts, "the two of them" as the narrative puts it, *with absolutely no mention of the woman at all*! The woman is completely marginalised by their activities. To be sure, the Levite is back with her again, but that fact immediately becomes a sideshow as the two men concentrate on having a good time with each other, a farcical, over-the-top caricature of male-bonding with neither of them really sharing fellowship because they actually *like* the other (the Levite keeps wanting to leave and the father-in-law probably wants to detain him more because he is a Levite than because he is his friend). The father-in-law, so desperate to retain the Levite in his company, keeps him there as they continue their empty 'rejoicing' of their hearts, raising their glasses one more time.

This complete inattention to and ignoring of the concubine perhaps goes some way towards explaining why she may have left in the first place, so completely oblivious the men in her life appear to be to her needs and feelings. The Levite had gone to "speak to the woman's *heart*" (that is the literal form of the expression "to speak friendly unto her"), but the men had wound up thinking only of their own hearts, completely marginalising her in their hollow celebrations.

Selfishness

As is often the case in marriage difficulties, there are faults on both sides. Her departure from her husband to "go and play the whore" is clearly and absolutely wrong, an action not to be defended. But when we look more closely at the way *he* behaves we find that this is clearly inadequate also. In fact, it is the Levite's behaviour that is the more interesting to consider: although it is less overt than hers in its error, it too undermines the whole relationship, ultimately leading to the devastating conclusion of her slaughter. This is not an exaggeration – it eventually kills her, as we shall see. He has no awareness of her thoughts or feelings; he does not see it as his responsibility to care for and share with her. Instead it is all about *his* agenda. She is sacrificed on the altar of his self-interest and lack of concern.

What of the modern analogy? When either partner is ignored so that the other can pursue *their* goals, whatever they may be, there is danger. We do not marry someone in order to ignore them, whether it is by investing so much of ourselves in our career that we never see them, whether it is by staying up until the small hours idly browsing on the internet (isn't this the biggest potential time-sink of all in the modern age?), or whether it is being absent from family life by doing things with our peers as if we were free agents, as we might have when we were single. Those examples were given with a male in mind, but females can also be susceptible to the danger of over-investment in career at the expense of husband and family. Husbands can also be neglected by wives pursuing fitness goals and community or social goals – or even goals with the children – all fine in themselves, but dangerous if allowed to grow to a point where they start to have a detrimental impact on the marriage relationship. Particularly in the early years of child-rearing it can also be difficult for a mother, exhausted by the new workload, to find time for her husband. A husband needs to understand and make allowances for this, reassuring himself that it will not always be this way for his wife, but it's a good idea for the wife to be aware of the danger of being so wrapped up in the lives of the children (and so exhausted!) that she loses sight of her man. The fact is that whether we are male or female our partners need us, and we them: we neglect them at our peril and at the peril of our relationships.

We can also ignore our partners when we are right there present with them, not paying attention to what they are saying, not giving eye contact, not caring about how they feel, not sharing in their load. All of these undermine our relationship and speak preoccupation with self and a failure to understand what it means to be one as a couple in the Lord. We must not allow familiarity to breed either contempt, emotional isolationism, or indifference.

Disaster

The consequences of the Levite's attitudes could not be writ larger by the Judges text. We may seem only to be dealing with a relatively humdrum and common problem of inattention to one's partner in a marriage at this point in the Judges narrative – but look where it ends up for the Levite! It is because of his procrastination and his focus on the rejoicing of male hearts to the exclusion of the female that the homeward journey becomes dangerously delayed and they find themselves in the fateful streets of Gibeah. His apparent complete unawareness of her needs and feelings comes out even more strongly in their final interaction. The horrifying scene takes place with the pair now in Gibeah, an evil mob surrounding the house and beating upon the door. The master of the house says to the mob:

"'Behold, here are my virgin daughter and his concubine. Let me bring them out now. Violate them and do with them what seems good to you, but against this man do not do this outrageous thing.' But the men would not listen to him. So the man seized his concubine and made her go out to them. And they knew her and abused her all night until the morning."

(verses 24,25, ESV)

What we've got here is the inverse of male chivalry, a man sacrificing his wife to save his own skin, the inverse of what Christ did for his bride. If one had asked the Levite in a less pressured moment what he would think of someone who would do such a thing to his partner he would be as categoric as we in his denunciation. But perhaps the point of the narrative is that if you care about your partner so little as to treat her in the way that he has, then this is effectively where it can end up under the wrong set of circumstances. This is the horrific conclusion of self-interest if the stakes are high enough, as he pushes her out of the door, a sacrificial offering for the protection of the great Himself. Similarly as he comes out of the door the following morning he greets her prostrated and abused body with a brusque, "Up, let us be going". But none answered (verse 28).

Marriage is not about this, not about the interests of one's own heart. It is about self sacrifice and the needs of the other, as Christ has definitively shown.

Haman and Zeresh

Topics: Controlling the male ego and the inner child; Male headship gone awry; The dangers of being self-absorbed; Earning loyalty.

It is said by those who study such things that men and women are approximately as likely as one another to tell lies, the distinction residing not in the frequency of the lying but in its purpose. Whereas a woman will often lie to protect others (so it is said), a man is apparently eight times more likely than a woman to lie for purposes of self-inflation, to make himself look better than the facts permit. Why should this be? Why this drive to push himself forward, to say 'Look how great I am!'? Welcome to the male ego – a notoriously thorny topic which has unleashed on the world all manner of psychological speculation. Fortunately, however, we are not left to speculate in abstract fashion because we have a worked example in the scriptures portrayed by an inspired writer. Who better to illustrate to us the problem of the male ego run amok than Haman?

WE start with Haman returning home in ebullient mood after being invited to Esther's private banquet with the king:

"When Haman came home, he sent and called for his friends, and Zeresh his wife. And Haman told them of the glory of his riches, and the multitude of his children, and all the things wherein the king had promoted him, and how he had advanced him above the princes and servants of the king. Haman said moreover, Yea, Esther the queen did let no man come in with the king unto the banquet that she had prepared but myself; and tomorrow am I invited unto her also with the king ..."   (Esther 5:10-12)

Haman doesn't simply go and visit his friends if he wants to talk to them as most normal people would; nor does he go home and talk with his wife, casually mentioning his good fortune that day in the course of the conversation. No, he goes home and *calls* for his friends and his wife to come to see him. He is issuing a summons, as it were, for them to appear before him. He treats them as if they were a fan club or appreciation society at his beck and call; in his own mind he is already playing at being king.

Egotist
The content of what he says is even more monstrous. He tells them first of the glory of his riches, a detail there's a good chance they're already familiar with (this may of course be why they *are* his wife and 'friends'!). Next he tells them of the multitude of his children – a bizarre fact to recount, for if there is one thing that his wife does not need to be told it is the number of his children! She carried them inside her, after all, and having given birth to them she knew in only too vivid a fashion how many there had been! That's not the point in Haman's mind, though, because he thinks of them only as *his* children rather than hers; that's why he reminds her and his friends just what a potent fellow he is to produce such a vast brood.

Haman's boasting is capped off in the narrative by an actual quotation from him, so blatant in its self-satisfaction that its childishness can readily be seen: "Yea, Esther the queen did let no man come in with the king unto the banquet that she had prepared but myself; and tomorrow am I invited unto her also with the king!" So much pride in being invited to a tea party!

In psychologist-speak we are hearing a lot of Haman's inner child here. There's way too much 'Mummy loves me more than you', 'My dad's car is faster than your dad's', 'Pick me, pick me!' in what Haman is saying. When we become men we do not necessarily put away the childish things that we should.

No grown-up wants to be considered a child, but that is what Haman is when he behaves like this. A child is self-centred and dependent – it has to be in order to survive. But Haman has no such excuse any more, his deep neediness showing that he has never really grown up. He wants to be liked, loved and admired, as most people do – but he overcompensates with all his boasting and in doing so he betrays a deep sense of insecurity.[1]

Caricature

Haman's boasting is an example of astonishing hubris, captured exquisitely in this passage in just a few sentences. Could anyone really be so self-obsessed, such an egomaniac? The text is mocking Haman, to be sure, but in doing so it makes a serious point. When self-obsession is writ this large it is easy to see it for what it is: it is comical; a caricature. But in less exaggerated forms it is not necessarily uncommon. Strip away a few layers of social veneer and we may find the same force raging inside ourselves. A man's capacity for self-centredness and for self-promotion is a dangerous well to draw from.

It was true that Haman *was* rich, he did have a lot of children, and the king had indeed advanced him – but that doesn't mean he has to tell everyone about it, least of all those who already know! But people do exactly that sort of thing in less blatant form in conversation all the time: gently placing little clues and reminders about how wealthy, influential or smart they are, about how they were right while others were wrong, or how

---

1   Haman's childishness is also seen when he doesn't get his own way – first when Mordecai refuses to bow (Haman's 'tantrum' is effectively his plan to exterminate the Jews), and again when Mordecai is exalted by the king (he returns home to sulk, mourning and having his head covered). Such examples of childish behaviour can also sometimes be seen in marriages when partners do not get their own way; that inner child can be a real problem if he doesn't grow up!

colourful and interesting the life is that they lead – all this to ensure that others have an appropriately elevated opinion of who they are, placing them in the correct box of success along with others also worthy to be admired. Alternatively, we may talk in over-indulgent detail about things going on in our lives, moving the conversation swiftly back to ourselves or our own perspectives when someone else has the temerity to move the conversation elsewhere, or (perish the thought!) to talk about *them*selves.

How, then, should a man keep these propensities in check and control his ego? He must insist on interest in others over himself, reminding himself that the world does not revolve around him and that he does not have to prove himself constantly to be worthy of a place within it. Whatever place he does have has been granted to him by virtue of the grace of God, so any leadership role that he has should be patterned on the sacrificial leadership of Christ, not on any intrinsic merit he may possess. He must be aware of his shortcomings, his needs, and of his status in God's sight. He must ask God to help him so that he can find his identity and sense of self in his relationship with God rather than by beating his chest.

Ego in marriage

What happens when you bring an ego like Haman's into a marriage? We can explore this by thinking about the two scenes in which Zeresh his wife appears. These two scenes are so vivid and brilliantly drawn that they reveal much in the few details they contain. The first one, already considered, was not a pretty sight. Haman puffs and preens himself in front of his wife; his implicit assumption is that she is there to listen to him, and it is hard to imagine him coming home from his day at the court to ask how she has managed with the children or some other facet of her life. This is because he has no interest in her as a person in her own right, her function being merely as a sounding board for his ego, a mirror in which he can see his own reflection. He is completely self-absorbed, the marriage's only purpose being for his benefit. Haman's ego is so large there is no room for anyone else.

The grotesqueness of Haman's behaviour warns us just what can happen if we don't get a grip here. One-sided marriages like Haman's are no good. They are not what partnership is about. Self-centredness and self-absorption must be avoided at all costs, a man guarding against being overly wrapped up in his own world and too focused on himself. There may be a lot going on in his life – particularly if he has a demanding job where pace and stress are high; it is easy to get caught up in the corporate race and in the unfolding of business plans and office politics. Ecclesial demands (and sometimes, unfortunately, ecclesial politics) can add to this whirlwind and, sometimes, they can engender an inappropriate self-importance and self-absorption.

Marriage is an excellent forum for a man to display proper control of his ego. If he is in a marriage relationship where he determines to care for and take a deep interest in his wife and family, sacrificing himself on their behalf as the scripture commands, then there is a half-decent chance he'll be able to avoid turning into a Haman.

It's also helpful if a wife realises that ego and self-image can be a big deal for a man. He needs to feel respected and (hopefully!) admired, and if this kind of appreciation and validation is present from his wife in a natural way (rather than in the charade we see here) then he will be less likely to feel the need to puff and strut quite so much because his need for this affirmation will already have been met by his wife, the person he cares about the most. When we think about what has gone wrong for Haman we can start to get a sense of how great this need can be and how it can hurt when a wife puts her husband down and makes him feel small; a judicious wife can really help her husband bring out the positives and eliminate the negatives that his ego and competitiveness can present.

Supportive … for now

For the time being, when things are on the up for Haman, his wife and friends are willing to tolerate him, as the first of the two passages which reference Haman's marriage shows:

"Then said Zeresh his wife and all his friends unto him, Let a gallows be made of fifty cubits high, and tomorrow speak thou unto the king that Mordecai may be hanged thereon: then go thou in merrily with the king unto the banquet. And the thing pleased Haman; and he caused the gallows to be made."

(verse 14)

But the support offered here by wife and friends turns out not to last for long. The second encounter between Haman and his wife takes place in a very different context after Haman is forced to lead his arch-enemy Mordecai around the city on the king's steed. This time Haman's return home is not so triumphant:

"But Haman hasted to his house mourning, and having his head covered. And Haman told Zeresh his wife and all his friends everything that had befallen him. Then said his wise men and Zeresh his wife unto him, If Mordecai be of the seed of the Jews, before whom thou hast begun to fall, thou shalt not prevail against him, but shalt surely fall before him."

(6:12,13)

Haman's switch from ebullience to despair has a touch of the manic about it. His mood is too driven by circumstance – too excited when things are going his way, too cast down when they are not – there is no consistency or stability about him. In these extremities of mood he allows himself to be dictated to and controlled by external factors.

But the key thing to note at this point is the behaviour of his wife and friends. How they have changed: from supporters in one scene to woe-mongers in the next! What turncoats they are, so quick to rush to his support one moment, so quick to pronounce his doom when his fortune turns! Why this change of heart? Why this sudden reversal in their support for him? No explanation is given, but a moment's reflection suggests that the reason may be this: they have no loyalty to Haman now his chips are down because his behaviour *merited* no loyalty from them. If you behave in a self-obsessed way where the only purpose of others such as your marriage partner is as a sounding board for your own ego then you can *expect* no loyalty. This is exactly what

Haman discovered. His wife and friends were prepared to suffer him while they had to or while he was (perhaps) a generous host and provider; but a relationship built on this will turn out to be shallow and one-sided. In the end it seems as though his wife and friends didn't really care about Haman because he didn't care about them; he was only interested in himself. In the end you reap what you sow; if you want a partnership you have to be a partner.

Lamech, Adah and Zillah

Topics: Polygamy and its problems; Children's achievements – prioritising what's important; The male ego (again!); Insecurity.

Lamech was, as far as the Biblical record is concerned, the first polygamist. Adam had spoken of a man leaving his father and his mother and being joined to his wife – but for Lamech one wife was not enough; he wanted two. God had given, but he would take not one but two. In doing so he set in motion a pattern of behaviour that would influence the line of Shem also, the many Old Testament examples of polygamy often involving the faithful. While this isn't explicitly commented upon within the Old Testament the consequences were rarely if ever positive (think of Abraham, Jacob, Solomon, Elkanah, debatably David); putting this data together we may detect an implicit criticism in the Biblical narrative, even if it is not explicit.

LAMECH'S taking two wives seems to be an illustration of the principle of man not being content with God's gifts but always wanting more. It's like someone being invited to take a chocolate but instead greedily taking two or more without asking. While polygamy may now be outlawed in most of the West, man's inability to be satisfied lives on as healthily as ever.

Lamech's polygamy is also an example of the way in which men as males would exploit and pervert their authority in the family. Male headship should never have been about power and dominance, yet we find it is always the male who decides he will take two wives and never the female that she will have two husbands. The practice of polygamy, kicked off here by Lamech, is but one example of the male's abuse of the responsibility of headship. It morphs so quickly and becomes distorted into a power play: taking because one can.

Talented children

The account of Lamech and his family begins like this:

> "And Lamech took unto him two wives: the name of the one was Adah, and the name of the other Zillah. And Adah bare Jabal: he was the father of such as dwell in tents, and of such as have cattle. And his brother's name was Jubal: he was the father of all such as handle the harp and organ. And Zillah, she also bare Tubal-cain, an instructor of every artificer in brass and iron: and the sister of Tubal-cain was Naamah."
>
> (Genesis 4:19-22)

We know little of the two women who become Lamech's wives, but given the achievements of their offspring we might at least conclude that the genetic material from both themselves and Lamech was of high quality. We might also conclude that the education and stimulating environment the two mothers provided their growing boys was powerful: they were good mothers as far as developing the talents of their offspring was concerned. Through their instruction the natural curiosity of the lads was awakened and fed, the achievements to which it gave rise significant both from an agricultural and economic perspective and also from an emotional and aesthetic one. These were boys who shaped history and they did so in part because of the mothers who raised them.

There is, though, no mention of the spiritual in their accomplishments. Adah and Zillah would have no doubt been immensely proud of their children's achievements – as any modern parent would be proud of their child's musical, educational or creative prowess. But ultimately it is spiritual development which will count for more and therefore spiritual stimulation and the begetting of spiritual curiosity which a parent must place first. If our children turn out to be as talented as Adah and Zillah's we may even make our own mark on history through our children as they did – but what will it really matter, even if such a surprising thing were to come about if God is not put first? It is our standing in God's sight that is more important than our standing in man's.

And it is here where Lamech and his family seem to fall short. The real tragedy of the passage is that Lamech is the seventh from Adam, the worldly counterpart to the spiritual Enoch who was translated and also the seventh from Adam. Lamech's genealogy is terminated at this point of the Biblical record so that space can be dedicated to what really counts in God's sight – the spiritual line through Shem. It is alignment with this line that counts, not whether our children are good at baseball or the clarinet. In the very busy lives that modern parents lead it can often be worth doing a quick sanity check: how does the effort we put in to giving our children extra-curricular opportunities in music, sports or other areas compare with the effort we are putting in to making them spiritually curious and ambitious?

Hear my voice
The children having been described, the narrative moves on to consider one more aspect of Lamech's character and his relationship with his wives. It is a surprising snapshot to include at first reading but one carefully selected because of what it shows about the kind of man he was and the quality of his interpersonal relationships:

> "And Lamech said to his wives, Adah and Zillah, Hear my voice; ye wives of Lamech, hearken unto my speech: for I have slain a man to my wounding, and a young man to my hurt. If Cain shall be avenged sevenfold, truly Lamech seventy and sevenfold."   (verses 23,24)

First let's look at what he says, and then its context and motivation.

What he says takes the form of a poem or lyric – an artful composition with strong use of parallelism and various other devices of Hebrew poetry (evidently the children took some of their talents from their father). But look at the content! The words are violent and evil. In fact, the nearest equivalent that we might be aware of from modern life are the offensive, violent and misogynistic words of some (lots?) of rap music. It would not be too much of a stretch given the nature of the lyrics here in both form and content to cast Lamech not only as the first polygamist but also as the forefather of the modern day rapper.

Let's look at the lyrics more closely:

"Adah and Zillah, Hear my voice;
Ye wives of Lamech, hearken unto my speech."

Parallelism in Hebrew poetry usually involves intensification in the second line of the two-line verse, and if that is the case here then what Lamech most believes about his wives is that they are *his* property. The key fact about them is not their own identity (as two women named Adah and Zillah), but that they are the wives *of Lamech*; they belong to him, and what's more, they ought to listen to him!

The lyric continues:

"I have slain a man to my wounding
A young man to my hurt."

This is about escalation, and the force of it is best seen when it is rendered slightly differently, for instance this from Hebrew literary scholar Robert Alter:

"For a man have I slain for my wound,
a boy for my bruising.
For sevenfold Cain is avenged,
and Lamech seventy and seven."

What Lamech is saying is that if anyone so much as wounds him, he will escalate the violence and take that person's life – in fact he boasts that he has already done so. What's more (and again, it is the second, intensified line that reveals the true awfulness of the sentiment), even if it is only a boy – and if that boy only so much as *bruises* Lamech – he will take even his life also. These are despicable sentiments showing escalation and retribution bereft of all proportion. Lamech's boast is that in defending himself he can best even God's ability to defend Cain, for he is at least seventy times more important, seventy times more vengeful, and seventy times more powerful.[1]

Seeking an audience

The crassness of what Lamech is saying is only heightened by the audience to which he chooses to announce it. He does not announce it to the world at large; no, he gathers his wives and announces it to them! Why he does this we don't know. Perhaps he is all talk and wouldn't actually dare say any of this outside his own four walls, but he can at least pretend he is tough to his wives. Perhaps his neighbours have all moved away out of fear of one of them putting a foot wrong and falling victim to his anger, or perhaps they are simply tired of his aggressive sentiments and self-absorbed boasting.

But his poor wives have no such option. They are trapped there inside the house (it's hard to imagine they would genuinely *enjoy* or be impressed by this sort of posturing from their mate), and all they can do is sit down and patiently humour another of his self-aggrandising postures.

His sentiments are not even redeemed by chivalry. Lamech's point is not even 'if anyone should as much as lay a finger on *you*, my wives, then rest assured this is how I'll take revenge …' No, Lamech boasts to them only of his determination to take vengeance on any wrong done to himself! One might well think that if any harm were to come to his wives the only reason why Lamech would care would be because it would be a slight on him!

There is something at once deeply pathetic and deeply disturbing about the whole thing. How can it be that he cannot

---

1　Jesus deliberately subverts Lamech's evil by telling Peter that he should forgive his brother not seven times but seventy times seven.

step outside himself and see the lunacy of this scene he has manufactured? Like a strutting peacock he prances before his wives telling them of his exploits and might – how can it be that he cannot see how silly he looks? So big in his own mind, yet so small that the only people he can get to listen to his boasts are the wives who are forced to live with him. Could it *possibly* be that there is anything, no matter how small, in our own behaviour that remotely resembles this, because if there is, once we have seen Lamech we will surely want to get rid of it!

Insecure

We must be careful about psychologising too much from what is admittedly a small sample of data about Lamech, but it seems reasonable to think that perhaps there lies in his heart a deep sense of insecurity. Perhaps he is not really sure about who he is, whether he is big enough, whether anyone cares enough about him to stand up in his defence. Because of this insecurity perhaps he overcompensates through the monstrous display we have before us. No doubt he craves the admiration and respect of his wives, but he has absolutely no idea about how to earn it!

We might think too, about what sort of headship it is that Lamech would exercise in his family. In fact we scarcely need to ask the question because we know instantly that it would be the wrong sort. As he struts about before his wives telling of his exploits and of his power we know only too well that his would be the sergeant-major model of headship, a headship so full of itself, so dominant, and so sure that it is right in every circumstance that what we are left with is a grotesque perversion of what ought to be the case; a head so big and so horrifically distorted that there is no room for a body – a mouth speaking great and terrible things but with no ears or eyes to relate to anyone else. With the help of this parody of maleness gone wrong may the Lord grant all husbands who seek Him to lay aside self-obsession and seek instead the protection and the well-being of others.

Samson and his wife

Topics: Being ruled by one's body and instincts; Selfishness and lack of trust; The problem of part-time husbands; The consumer approach to marriage and why it's destined to fail.

Samson's weakness with women is well known. One after another he falls for those he ought not, deluding himself that he is stronger than he really is. In this chapter we'll look at his relationship with his Philistine wife, drawing some further lessons about the problem of self.

THE scriptures record Samson's relationships with three different women, none of which are founded on a good spiritual platform. The first two accounts begin in a parallel manner:

"Samson *went* down to Timnah, and at Timnah he *saw* one of the daughters of the Philistines." (Judges 14:1, ESV)

"Samson *went* to Gaza, and there he *saw* a prostitute, and he went in to her." (16:1, ESV)

He sees, he wants, and he gets – but in time he pays the price. Getting what we want is not always the best thing, particularly when the first things that strike our fancy are often superficial and external, that which pleases the flesh rather than the spirit. The sight of the eyes has always been a problem for men where women are concerned; this is an episode where we can learn the consequences of what happens if this is all we pay attention to. Samson gets what he wants, but he isn't wise enough to want what is good for him.

There is something very contemporary about Samson's 'go getter' attitude, the directness of his words and actions. He is the sort of person who might be admired in the current culture: strong, decisive, a man who knows what he wants and has the follow-through to go and get it. Seeing this woman, he doesn't even appear to prevaricate so as to debate with his conscience about whether or not it is a good idea. In the case of the prostitute he simply goes in to her (the record is notably matter-of-fact); in the case of the Philistine girl he abruptly commands his parents:

> "I *saw* one of the daughters of the Philistines at Timnah. Now *get her* for me as my wife."   (14:2, ESV)

This is doubly ominous in the original, a more literal rendering being as follows: "Get her for me, for she is right in my eyes" which echoes that terrible refrain which characterises the end of the book of Judges: "Everyone did what was right in his own eyes" (this expression occurs multiple times in chapters 17-21, the devastating conclusion to the book). The fact that God was working to provoke a quarrel with the Philistines through Samson's choices doesn't make those choices any wiser.

Wedding gone awry

Despite the remonstrations of his parents Samson insists on the match and soon the great wedding feast arrives. The joy is short lived, however. Loyalty and trust had not been among the attributes that he had sought in his partner because he had only been focused on the physical. Now, threatened by arson if she fails to comply, his wife is forced to play the serpent by enticing Samson to divulge the secret of his riddle (as if he hadn't already allowed himself to be enticed!). After seven days of weeping and urging, Samson can take it no more. Each of us is only strong up to a point, and he caves in to this pressure as he will again with Delilah. He may have been physically strong when the spirit of the Lord came upon him, but his emotional strength was no match.

Even while the emotional histrionics and deception are taking place there is a clue from Samson that things aren't going to turn out well. Even before he is deceived he shows a lack of trust when he lets her know that since he hasn't even told his father and mother there is no reason why he should tell her (14:16)! He should tell her, of course, because she is his wife – that is why he is meant to be marrying her: because he loves her, trusts her, and wants to share everything with her. Except that we know otherwise: we know that he is not marrying her for those reasons, he is marrying her because he *saw* her and he *wanted* her, and he thinks this is enough. Samson ought to privilege his wife over his mother and father in the information he is willing to share, but instead he ranks her lower than them, though she is going to be his wife. This isn't the 'leaving and cleaving' that we read about in Genesis 2.

Even from the outset, then, this is not a relationship built on trust, from either partner's perspective. Samson could not bring himself to tell her the riddle's secret until her emotional blackmailing wore him down; she could not bring herself to tell him how the Philistines had threatened her and thus to seek for his protection. There is again a strikingly contemporary note here because there is a very real challenge to people in trying to build their marriages on trust today. It is hard to trust when you know that so many other people's marriages are failing all around you – what basis do you have to trust, or to believe that your marriage will be any different? This can be a very real fear, potentially preventing a person giving themselves completely and without qualification to another in marriage as they should. Instead there can be a tendency to live, whether consciously or unconsciously, with a constant glancing over one's shoulder, an implicit unease. This can lead to a utilitarian approach to marriage which focuses on taking rather than giving, serving ourselves while we can because we are not quite sure we can trust someone else enough to invest ourselves fully in them. A good starting point here is to make sure that, unlike Samson, we are looking for the right sort of person in the first place, someone whose promises will matter to them; from that point on we must trust, commit, and give our all.

Of fire and fox

You can't be a husband just when you feel like it, when the mood takes you and you happen to want to be one. Yet finding his early experience of marriage disappointing, this is exactly what Samson attempts to do. Having given the changes of raiment to the riddle-'solvers', he then disappears ("in hot anger he went back to his father's house", Judges 14:19, ESV), feeling that his wife's behaviour justifies his abandonment of her. Eventually, however, he cools down from the rage in which he had stormed off, returning with a peace offering for his wife. By this time, though, it is too late; his choice to be a husband now that it suits him once again has been rudely interrupted by his wife having been given to someone else – no less a person than his best man!

> "After some days, at the time of wheat harvest, Samson went to visit his wife with a young goat. And he said, 'I will go in to my wife in the chamber.' But her father would not allow him to go in."   (15:1, ESV)

When he had left in his fury he had been thinking only of himself, telling himself that her behaviour had merited his reaction. Now that he is over his anger he realises either that he is lonely or that there might be some advantages to being married after all; thus he returns with his make-up wares. But when he can't have his wife he takes vengeance on the Philistines using a group of foxes to set light to their fields. But he fails to put in place any protection for his family when the Philistines retaliate (why so? perhaps again because he is not thinking about things from the perspective of responsibility for others, only his own selfish desire for recrimination). The fire Samson makes unleashes more fire as the Philistines burn the family and their property to the ground. Samson is hurt again as his wife burns in the flames, the violence escalating further until Samson finally has the last word, for the moment at least.

What do we see in these scenes? We see a man unable to control his emotions very effectively, one who is not able to think through the consequences of his actions and how both he himself and those he loves are hurt when he pursues a path of self-seeking and escalation. We see a man who clears off in the heat of the moment and then wishes he hadn't and ends up paying the price. We see a man who clearly cares something for his wife (or he wouldn't have returned with the kid), but is easily distracted into personal vengeance when his own honour is under threat. In short, we see a man who's got it all wrong when it comes to marriage. No wonder it doesn't work out; the whole thing literally goes up in flames.

Consumer

Author Tim Keller has described the dominant way people treat marriage in Western culture today as being a 'consumer' approach, a description which fits Samson's marriage very well. As a consumer I can go into a store and if I like the look of something or if I think it will meet some needs I have then I may choose to buy it (let's imagine it's by means of monthly instalments), considering that the price I have to pay is worth it for the benefit I shall receive. A consumer approach to marriage is the same: we see someone we like, we evaluate the benefits we hope to gain by being married to that person and compare them against the price we shall have to pay on an ongoing basis (the giving up of other options, the sacrificing of a big part of one's freedom, the sharing of financial resources, and so on).

This all sounds fine on the surface (if rather self-centred) until we think what happens down the road. Suppose, on the same analogy, that we decide we are no longer getting the utility we desired from our consumer product any more – it is no longer meeting our needs. Suppose, alternatively, that we see a different product that we like better. Or suppose, again, that we no longer feel we want to keep paying the monthly instalments for the product – the sacrifices or investment we have to make in order to have it no longer merit or match the benefits we are getting. What happens then?

The answer is that everything breaks down. It won't give us the kind of marriage where we can look forward to growing old together because we can trust that we shall each be there for the other's needs whatever the circumstance. Instead it creates an environment where we are constantly looking over our shoulder because we can't really trust our partner to be there for us if things get difficult or they get a more appealing offer somewhere else. Imagine a couple in which one partner falls sick and the other says, 'I never signed up to push you around in a wheelchair now that you are sick; that price is too high and one that I'm not prepared to pay'. It contrasts nicely with an anecdote about a man whose wife was very sick with Alzheimer's and didn't even recognise her husband any more. His friends told him he should put her in a home because her care was too much for him – 'She's not the woman you married any more' they told him. The man's reply was telling: 'She may not be the woman I married, but I'm still the man she married, and that man would look after her and cherish her for as long as he was physically capable of doing so.' You would never get that in a consumer marriage.

A broken model

The prevailing consumer approach we've been exploring goes a long way to explaining why so many marriages fail today. If we only invest and make sacrifices while we judge we are getting out corresponding value then the marriage is constantly at risk. If we consider it an option that we might meet a better version of our partner at some point down the road for whom we might exchange our current mate, then the same will apply. If we regard our marriage partner like a consumer product that we only 'pay for' (that is to say, make sacrifices for or 'stick with' in the context of marriage) as long as they are meeting our needs and we are getting out what we expect, then we shall never be safe and neither will they. A consumer approach to marriage is essentially a selfish approach. We can put this selfishness bluntly (need for sex, need for security, need for entertaining companionship, need for affirmation, need for someone to raise the children we'd like to have) or we can dress it up in more acceptable terms about finding self-actualisation and fulfilment – but it is all essentially the same. Many self-help books on marriage are built on the same premise – if you behave in these ways (i.e., pay this price) and communicate better, you will *get* more (as a consumer) from your marriage. It is usually true in one sense – you will get more – but this is still not a good reason for making *self* and making *consumption* the basis of marriage, as Samson seemed to do.

Samson's marriage was a consumer marriage – he saw, wanted and took, but he did not love enough truly to share himself with his wife since trust and true sharing were never high on his agenda either in what he was looking for or in what he was prepared to give. When he was wronged he opted out and went off in anger, only later to realise it may not have been entirely his wife's fault. He hadn't got out of marriage what he'd expected, so he ran away. Later, when he thought about her and realised that he did actually want her after all, he goes back but is only able to swallow his pride for a moment before descending into a cycle of revenge with the Philistines in which his wife and her family are first marginalised and then destroyed. It's always all about Samson and his needs; it's never really about his wife or what Samson can *give* to please her.

Is there an alternative to this unattractive and ill-fated model? Yes, there most assuredly is. It is laid out in the sacrificial example of Christ and in mutual submission. It is seen when we realise that the Biblical model for marriage is not the consumer model, it is the *covenantal model*. It is not about what I can get and what I'm prepared to pay for it – that model *can't* work because it can never deal well with the weakness and change that is inherent in all of us; instead the Bible model works on the basis of a promise – a covenant made between two people in the presence of God which applies come what may. Whatever other reasons there might be, whatever else we might get or not get, and whatever we might have to pay or not pay, this is our commitment before God and this is our bond. It is because of this promise, this marriage covenant, and the marriage of Christ and his ecclesia to which it points forward, that we may trust – that we *must* trust – so that we may look our partner in the eye and say, 'Until death do us part or until the Lord returns'.

Postscript: maleness reconfigured and redeemed

Topics: Bad role models; The Bible's vision for maleness; Marrying one of God's daughters.

WE started our sequence of negative male models for marriage with a particularly harrowing example – it's extreme, but it highlights the issues at stake and shows the contrast between ego-driven self-absorption and the kind of model for maleness that the Bible holds up through the example of Christ. Later in the section our studies of Haman and Lamech showed how childish and self-centred we can be (and how *pathetic* it is to witness!), while the case of Samson and his Philistine wife showed what happens when there is no real trust between partners and we are only invested and present in a marriage when we can get out of it what we want.

In contrast to these examples and in contrast to modern society's uncertainty about maleness and the proper role for a husband within a marriage, the Bible contains an inspiring vision. Males can and do bring something to the table and God has asked of them a crucial role within marriage and family life, as well as in the congregation of believers. Though God has equipped us with the physical, psychological and emotional tools we need to execute these responsibilities, they don't necessarily come naturally to us. We have to work at them and show dedication and discipline, just as with any activity that is worthwhile and has lasting value.

Over the course of human history men have a lot to answer for in terms of their behaviour towards women. The Bible's model of male headship provides no licence for lording it over another and wielding power in that sense. Instead, leadership should be about seeking the salvation of one's wife and family, leading in love, in worship, in forgiveness, in prayer, in the scriptures, in provision, in direction-setting, and in example. Society has no need of any more men who are overbearing or boorish; what it needs is more men who have been moved by Christ.

It is an act of immense daring and faith for a woman to enter into Christian marriage with the intention of following the Biblical pattern of treating her husband as the head. She needs to be confident that her husband sees Christ's pattern of leadership and aims to follow it in his own life. We've examined Paul's fourfold injunction that the husband is to concentrate on loving his wife – 'love her, love her, love her, love her' he says in Ephesians 5, more insistently than he says anything else – and if she knows that this is really what he will try to do with all his heart then it will be a wonderful reassurance to her.

For his part he should think of the tremendous privilege into which he is entering when he embarks on marriage. It is no longer as customary as it once was for young men to ask their girlfriend's father if they can have her hand in marriage, but that practice yields an interesting thought from a spiritual perspective. We are all sons and daughters of God as believers, and if that is the case then what we are effectively doing in marriage is not only marrying the daughter of Mr Jones or Mr Smith but in addition marrying *God's* daughter! This is a striking and transformational concept. How would husbands treat their wives differently if they really kept the consciousness of that thought at the forefront of their minds: that they are in a sense married to one of the daughters of God.

Part 4
The wife

Introduction: Biblical norms, cultural norms

Topics: Positives from female emancipation; Bible responsibilities – Old Testament and New Testament consistency; Deborah and Jael; Respect and influence; Neither male nor female – common responsibilities.

The main purpose of this part of the book is to examine a set of scriptural role models for wives both positive and negative rather than to rehearse what has been covered in other chapters about the wife's role in the family and in relation to her husband. Nevertheless, since the material on that topic is spread across a number of different places in the book it seemed sensible to draw together a brief summary in this chapter in order to make this part of the book a bit more complete in its own right.

IF a man's role in society has shrunk or become ambiguous in the modern world, a woman's has significantly expanded. There are many wonderful benefits to this – the possibilities of education, more diverse career options when women choose to work commercially, help with childcare, not to mention equality of other kinds which does not stand in contravention with scripture and which significantly improves the lives of women versus what they might have expected one hundred or even fifty years ago. There are certainly significant positives which have come from the feminist movement and the general direction male-female relations have taken in recent times, for which we should be grateful. Meanwhile the corollary of men helping out more around the home and perhaps taking more of an active role in childcare is beneficial to all – gone are the pipe and slippers of yore and any male expectation of being waited upon at every turn – and this is no bad thing.

There is further still to go. While women have been 'liberated' in many respects in the West, the increasing sexualisation of women in society seems to have gone in the opposite direction. Furthermore, there are still far too many instances of the abuse of women by men even in what are supposedly the most sophisticated and enlightened of societies. The full extent of these problems will sadly not ultimately be resolved until the return of Christ.

Yet while we may observe the positive and negative dynamics in society and perhaps offer comment on them, the real question is, 'What does the Bible say?' The Bible is at once fully up to speed if not ahead of some of these trends. It preaches the equality of women both in Genesis (chapter 2 of this book) and in the New Testament ("Neither male nor female … all one in Christ Jesus") – teaching which put it far ahead of its time and rendered it significantly 'liberal' compared with the prevailing views during many parts of human history, for all it might seem conservative today. Men and women stand side by side before God in Bible teaching, in equal need and with equal opportunity of salvation before Him. There is nothing, therefore, in the Bible that stands against a woman participating in the same educational opportunities as men (for instance), or as having other 'rights' in line with those of a man from a societal perspective.

Yet we have also seen that the Bible does prescribe a specific role for the female in family life and in the formal worship of God (see chapters 2, 4 and 5 for more details). Genesis sees man as the head of the family, the one who receives the commandments of God and who is responsible for seeing them put into action in his household. His wife is to be the helper at his side in the carrying out of this task, and together they receive the blessing of God in order to do so. Together they are to be fruitful, not only by bearing children if God so blesses them, but also by doing good works and exercising wise dominion over the assets God has put under their charge. The woman's role is thus characterised in Genesis 2 in terms of 'helping'.

When we get to the Fall and the punishments of Genesis 3 two aspects come out. One is the crystallising of Adam's headship role in the statement of his 'rulership' or responsibility – we've considered extensively what this means in chapters 2 and 4, and it may also be an aspect of the 'desire' or 'turning' that she has towards him (Genesis 3:16). The second aspect that arises from Genesis 3 in terms of the woman's specific areas of responsibility is the matter of childbirth and her responsibilities towards children and family. We argued that God has made man and woman differently – in terms of the physiology of their bodies and brains and also in terms of their psychology and emotional responsiveness; given God's supremacy as a designer it would make complete sense to assume that He has prepared us specifically and precisely for the roles He has asked us to carry out within marriage. It is telling how scientific discoveries about the differences between men and women in these regards as recently as the last few decades have supported what the Bible has always claimed – that men and women are indeed different and that it makes perfect sense for them to have different areas of responsibility in God's sight.

A consistent message
When we come to the New Testament we find there is a perfect match with this picture from Genesis. The New Testament teaches that women should 'submit' to (i.e., allow and help to nurture) the spiritual headship of the male within marriage (and within congregational worship), and we considered extensively what this meant in chapter 5. This has nothing to do with chauvinism or patriarchy and everything to do with a simple trust that the One who made us knows best. It is about encouraging husbands to step up to be all they have the potential to be as spiritual men – to take responsibility for the spiritual

course of their families as Adam failed to do – and it is about a wife showing her appreciation of Christ by treating her husband, not as a man with all the annoyances and shortcomings that he possesses, but as if he were Christ himself. This is a great way to esteem and honour one's husband and to elicit from him the kind of Christlike love to which the scriptures call him to aspire.

A wife thus 'submits' to her husband by allowing him to be the spiritual head and helping him in that task – his position of responsibility in that respect is in a very significant sense within her gift. She has a calling to show him respect, a respect occasioned not so much by his worth as by her appreciation of Christ. Very little of this sits well in a modern cultural context, but modern culture has significantly failed in its own recipe for marriage as demonstrated by the fifty per cent divorce rate. Once the true model of Biblical headship is appreciated then submission to it is no longer a scary thing; it comes down to whether we are able to trust God to know what is best for us in what He has said about marriage.

Not surprisingly the New Testament also focuses on the woman's responsibilities towards children and family, exactly in line with Genesis.[1] Again, God has given women the emotional, psychological and physical characteristics required for this task and we must be careful not to look down on this role just because society is inclined to do so. It is in many ways the most important role that there is (in the case of His very own Son God entrusted this role to a woman) – what could be more important than giving birth to and being given primary responsibility for the growth and nurture of the next generation of God's potential servants? If it is true that God is seeking godly children as a central part of His grand purpose (and it *is* true – the Bible tells us so very clearly as we discuss in Part 6), then it is also true that He has put women in the position of having the greatest influence of all over those children as they develop and grow. This is not to be sniffed at or sneered at or regarded as somehow a lesser role as

---

1   See chapter 33 on the Titus and Timothy passages.

though a woman who accepts this call is somehow making less of herself than she ought. On the contrary, she is fulfilling the very commandment of God Himself, the highest honour that one could have! We shall go into this more in chapter 33 and examine how it is entirely consistent with the passages in the Pastoral epistles about a wife's responsibilities.

What this means (coming back to our opening discussion of female 'emancipation') is that whether or not a wife decides to work commercially is thus to some extent a non-question – a side show. It is not the central issue. The central issue is that she fulfil the scriptural command towards her household and towards her children if she has them – since this is a Biblical mandate whereas whether to work or not to work commercially is not. Whether or not she works, this responsibility towards children and family remains because it is divinely ordained. What a wife then has to decide is whether commercial work would help or hinder her in carrying out those responsibilities that God has asked her to take care of. *That* is the real question, and it is one on which we may very well have our opinions (which it is fair enough to express as long as we don't impose them on others), but one which she and her husband must prayerfully consider, discuss, and answer for themselves.

The 'how?' of it
What picture emerges when we look beyond Genesis and Ephesians 5 to other models for womanhood from a scriptural perspective? We see the immense power of influence that women wield towards their husbands and families, an influence which can be used for good (Esther) or evil (Jezebel); we see the emotional perceptiveness and intuition of women used to good effect (Esther again), and more ambiguously (Job's wife). Elsewhere there are plenty of other examples of female qualities at work for both good and bad (Abigail for good in her tact at dealing with both Nabal and David, Rebekah for bad in her manipulation of her family). The examples of Sarah and Ruth illustrate further positive aspects of womanhood, while several

passages in Proverbs refer to the detrimental impact of a wife who nags ("like a continual dripping" – either a broken tap or water-torture depending how you think of it!) rather than finding a more positive way to communicate (Proverbs 21:9,19; 25:24; 27:15). The examples of Ruth and the Virtuous Woman both illustrate that being a female is no passive role; it is instead a calling of massive responsibility, one which requires intellect, resolve, energy and fortitude. We'll be picking up some of these examples in the next few chapters.

Two further examples of female proactivity, not covered elsewhere in this book, would be Jael and Deborah from the book of Judges. In Deborah's case there seems to be an implicit criticism of the men in Israelite society for not being suitable or not having the courage to spot the need and take on the leadership role she is obliged to assume ("there was no one ... until I arose ...", Judges 5:7). She is the wife of Lapidoth, but nothing else is known about him, and the scriptures hold forth her example of bravery, leadership and decisiveness as a model – a role that she seems able to accomplish without neutering her husband or usurping his role in their private household. She is described consecutively as: a prophetess (her role as a spokesman of God), the wife of Lapidoth (her role in her family with respect to her husband), and the one who judged Israel and carried out the exploits of Judges 4 & 5 – see 4:4, this passage encapsulating her various roles. Rather like Zipporah's stepping into the breach when Moses had not acted as he should (chapter 23), Deborah is obliged to take ever-increasing involvement in the crisis to the point of going into battle herself with Barak the son of Abinoam. This interaction is an interesting one – although it is not husband-and-wife it is a male-female pair and one in which the woman has to cajole the man first to be involved at all, and then has to make a further concession by agreeing to go into battle at his side so that he has the courage to go at all, instructing him what to do and where to go at every step of the way. From a human perspective this going into battle like a military captain puts her at considerable risk, a world away from male chivalry and the willingness of men to put their own lives on the line to save their women. But for all it shows up the males, it is an inspiring illustration of the capacity of women: of this particular woman's mettle, her willingness to step into the breach and do what needed to be done, and her ability to go 'above-and-beyond' to save her people.

Deborah's self-description as a 'mother in Israel' is also highly appropriate. Being a mother is not necessarily just about showing vision, courage and tireless energy towards one's own immediate family but can in fact be a much more encompassing role that benefits a wider set of God's people. It is a paradoxical role because a woman can be such a 'mother' no matter her age or the age of her own children – in fact, she can take on this role even if she has no children or even a husband of her own! Furthermore, if we take Deborah's 'mothering' as a case in point, it had in this particular case nothing to do with babies or childcare or any of the various other aspects that men might traditionally associate with what it means to be a mother. It was rather a role of insight – of spotting a need and being willing to act – a role of oversight, care and protection, a role which required an understanding of God's plan and purpose, and a role which demonstrated immense character and fortitude.

Jael's example is slightly different but not unrelated. She is the wife of Heber the Kenite who appears to have somehow misaligned himself with Sisera the enemy. But he seems to have gone AWOL as the narrative unfolds and is simply not present in the scene (one might ask, where are men when you need them most?! – actually in this case because he had an alliance with Jabin, it was perhaps for the best and part of God's grand design that he wasn't there). The ambiguity of his absence only serves to heighten Jael's actions. She knows where *her* allegiance lies, and it is one hundred per cent in the right place with God and Israel even when her husband might be leaning in the wrong direction. Making use of her female and motherly airs she encourages the fleeing Sisera into the house and puts him to sleep – only to impale his skull to the floor with a mallet and an enormous tent peg! The echoes here of Genesis 3 and the bruising of enemies heads are not difficult to spot – her action standing both as a type of the Lord Jesus and as a fitting monument to the clear-sightedness, strength and courage of all women through the ages of human history who have acted bravely and decisively to fulfil God's commandments on their family or people's behalf.

The neck and the head

Turning to the wider question of male-female interaction, it has been said that if the husband is the head then the wife is like the neck – and it's the neck that turns the head! There is a lot of truth in this – a man wants to please his wife as far as possible (it is part of *his* responsibility to do so, as long as this doesn't involve contravening his other responsibilities to seek her salvation and lead the family in the right spiritual path), so his wife needs to think carefully about what it is that she wants and the direction in which she will seek to influence her other half. Another witticism, attempting to capture the same idea, says that while the man may wear the trousers, it's the wife who usually chooses them. The point of these little sayings for believers ought not be that she has ways and means of circumventing his objectives and getting what she wants anyway despite him – rather that she has huge scope to help him and the family as a whole in the right direction by the way in which she exercises her influence.

As to respect (a key feature of the specific requirements laid at the woman's door), we've already had cause to discuss how this validation is something which is very important to a man and his sense of self (chapter 5). It can be a challenge for her to show it, especially when his behaviour doesn't always merit it, but this is what she has been asked to do – and for the sake of Christ rather than her husband. Selwyn Hughes put it like this in addressing his female readers: "God has given you the power to turn your man into the man both you and God want him to be – that power is the power of respect." He then went on to quote someone who was once an unbeliever but converted to Christianity, initially because of the impact of his wife's spiritual behaviour: "When my wife began to show me respect, although I didn't realise what was happening, it created for me a bigger mould into which I wanted to pour myself. I wanted so much to be the man she saw me to be. And it was this that led eventually to my desire to receive Christ." It's a nice illustration of the power of some of the divine principles for marriage in action.

The same aim

In conclusion, there can be a danger in discussing the specific callings of male and female of focusing too much on what distinguishes them and too little on what is the same. There are two reasons why we might do this: first, when the scriptures talk about wives and husbands they naturally concentrate on what is different in their roles rather than what is the same (the latter would be redundant to the discussion after all), and second, because the topic sits awkwardly with the current cultural view in Western society there can seem to be a need to elucidate or even defend the scriptural position (whereas in reality it needs no defence since it is divine).

It's worth remembering, though, that these specific gendered areas of responsibility are but one aspect of our total calling and that most aspects of what a man or a woman is called to do, think and be are identical. These shared responsibilities arise from our common status as human beings, our common need as sinners, our common salvation in the Lord Jesus Christ, and our common calling to follow in his steps. Our mission to love the Lord our God, to love our neighbour, to cultivate the mind of Christ and to obey God's commandments is identical whatever our gender, race, age or background – and these things unite us all. It is impossible to put a number on it, but if we were to approximate what proportion of our spiritual responsibilities and activities as a married believer relate to our gender (i.e., our calling as a man versus our calling as a woman, for instance) perhaps it might be as little as ten per cent or less (this is just a guess!) of our total mandate to be a spiritual person in God's sight. We can get a sense of this by asking what proportion of the commands and advice of Jesus and the apostles in the New Testament relates to us equally versus what is specific to the role of the man or woman. The answer is a very high proportion indeed. The vast majority of New Testament teaching applies to us equally whatever our gender and we should not lose sight of this when we think of the specific commands to the husband and the wife, important though they are. It's useful to keep in mind a sense of proportion about the balance of New Testament teaching – there is indeed clear guidance on male and female roles within the family and for worship which should be appreciated as a recipe from God and which should be put into practice – but we should ensure that we set this against the context of a much larger set of commands, responsibilities and aims that affect us all equally whoever we are. Being a man or a woman is *mostly* about being a human being in relation to God rather than being a gender; what unites us in our calling to become like our Lord is far greater than what distinguishes our particular role as husband or wife. With this context in mind, therefore, we can turn to some of the further inspiring examples of spiritual women the Bible presents.

Esther and Ahasuerus

Topics: Inner versus outer – becoming the right (kind of) person; The wise use of influence, Broaching difficult conversations and situations; Preparation and prayer.

It was the spa treatment to end them all, shaming into insignificance modern-day exotica like ayurvedic exfoliating body scrubs, Balinese deep tissue massages, or Hungarian thermal mud. No, Ahasuerus took this matter seriously, stipulating that the girls in his harem underwent a preparation process lasting a mind-bending twelve months: six months purification with oil of myrrh and six months with sweet odours, not to mention "other things for the purifying of the women" (perhaps the writer was somewhat baffled him or herself by the various concoctions and techniques that were employed!). Only at the end of this were the girls finally ready to appear before their king.

AHASUERUS was either a patient man or had a lot of girls in the queue – how else to explain the twelve month waiting period? But when the king's chamberlain saw Esther, the rules appear to have been bent ("Hegai speedily gave her her things for purification, with such things as belonged to her", Esther 2:9), suggesting either that she didn't have to go through such a long purification process as the others, or that she somehow jumped the queue into the twelve month purification pipe.

The reason for this? No doubt her beauty and figure were stunning, but surrounded by the finest that Persia could offer, would this *alone* have been enough to so distinguish her? It might, but then again perhaps there was something else about her which was distinctive, her way of speaking or her intellect, maybe, perhaps an uncommon spirituality or grace in her manner, a demeanour that bespoke a concern for others – a rare find in that environment of coquetry and preening self-promotion.

Accessorize

There is another detail in the passage concerning Esther's distinctiveness that is most intriguing. It was apparently the practice for each woman to select an accessory of some kind to accompany her on her night with the king, a prop to get his attention in the bizarre world he inhabited where beautiful girls were ten a penny. Unthinkably, however, Esther turns down this opportunity, contenting herself either to go unaccompanied or to take whatever Hegai the king's chamberlain deems appropriate for her:

> "Thus came every maiden unto the king; whatsoever she desired was given her to go with her out of the house of the women unto the king's house ... Now when the turn of Esther, the daughter of Abihail the uncle of Mordecai, who had taken her for his daughter, was come to go in unto the king, she required nothing but what Hegai the king's chamberlain, the keeper of the women, appointed. And Esther obtained favour in the sight of all them that looked upon her ... And the king loved Esther above all the women, and she obtained grace and favour in his sight more than all the virgins; so that he set the royal crown upon her head, and made her queen instead of Vashti."   (Esther 2:13,15,17)

Anyone who has experience of getting dressed up for a Very Important Occasion will know how agonising it can be, especially for a woman. Deciding what to wear, which colours are best, how to do one's hair ... the list could go on to levels of detail well beyond this author's competence. Imagine yourself in Esther's shoes – how you might have fretted over the selection of your accessory, the one 'extra' you were allowed to take with you to distinguish yourself above all the others who had preceded you.

But Esther is not going to over-think this. In fact, she is not going to think about it at all for she knows that it's all in God's hands anyway. She doesn't spend time deliberating over what accessory to pick; if Hegai wants to choose something for her, fine, she will take it and bow to his superior knowledge of the king – but if not she will go as she is.

Now this might be simply a lesson about not over-thinking one's appearance too much, but we might be able to extrapolate a bit more broadly than that. Could this be about the value of being the *right person* – that it's who you are, you yourself without embellishments and trappings, which is important. This is not just about female accessorising – there are accessories of all types which people bolt on, airs they assume, possessions they feel they need to surround themselves with, tones of voice they adopt, status they must demonstrate in order to impress others or feel good about themselves. Esther was simply herself, and it was enough because she was the *right sort* of person, the sort of person she should have been in both the sight of God and man.

We have to be a little bit careful with this conclusion of course; it wouldn't be right to argue that we can just 'be who we are' without thought for the impression we make, or without taking care of ourselves physically or spiritually. The 'natural man' is not good enough as he or she is, so it's no good to think we can do the spiritual equivalent of someone who rolls out of bed and shows up any which way. That's not what Esther did. Rather, it's a calling to focus on making sure the essential person underneath is what it should be and letting that person speak – rather than our trappings or some projected 'image'; secondary and external matters can then take care of themselves. Esther was the queen of choice, accessories or no, because of who she was as a whole person; she didn't need stage props or 'illusion' of any kind.

Getting what you want

The other aspect of Esther to consider is the way in which she influenced the king to overturn the edict of Haman, a masterstroke of persuasive communication and intervention. The example is a little complicated because in a sense Esther was a kind of double agent, married to Ahasuerus but working with Mordecai to achieve purposes contrary to what the king had originally agreed. The scriptures record that Esther did the commandment of Mordecai as if he was her father, even after she had married the king, to some extent a contravention of Adam's description of what it means to be married in Genesis 2. Nevertheless, we can still learn lessons about persuasion from her behaviour, without entangling ourselves too much in the complexity of her divided allegiance.

In an important sense the subhead "Getting what you want" is a misleading one – Esther didn't *want* to manipulate the king into changing his mind and her life would have been far easier if she had kept quiet, at least as long as no one discovered she was a Jewess. In a very real sense, then, she was going against her instincts of self-preservation in speaking to the king. The reason why she took these steps was in order to achieve what *God* wanted and her people needed – the deliverance of the Jews. This is an important distinction. If she uses wiles and cunning to achieve her designs, she does so for no selfish purpose; she does it to see the will of God fulfilled. Any female who uses her powers of persuasion to influence a male (this is a God-given ability, after all, and can be used for good or ill) might measure her goals and objectives against those of Esther. It's a far cry from using one's influence for self-seeking than it is to achieve spiritual goals in the family, or to seek gently to reorient one's husband if he seems to be heading in the wrong spiritual direction as Ahasuerus certainly was here.

The end and the means

Esther's strategy is deliberate and carefully considered, her goal so critical that she gives it intensive forethought and preparation, fasting night and day for three days and requesting that others do the same in her support (4:16). The risk of rejection is real for she hasn't been called before the king for thirty days, a concerning fact given the ample supply of concubines and other interests that he will have, not to mention the Persian kingly prerogative of executing anyone who ventured into his presence unbidden. Not knowing how he will react Esther will try to bridge the gap that seems to have opened up between her and her husband in their relationship, her fate hanging in the balance as she does so.

There are modern analogues of this uncertainty, particularly if a couple has become somehow disconnected from each other's wavelength for a period or if there has been an awkward issue or disagreement that has not been addressed. Trying to bring about positive change in these circumstances can be daunting and therefore needs both preparation and bravery – you just don't know how it will be received by your partner, and there is always a risk that it may make things worse rather than better. Esther's example suggests that if the goal is good and right then there may need to be this element of risk-taking and forethought. No wonder there is a need for prayer, fasting, and dedication, a need to share her concerns and anxieties with others, carefully thinking through her strategy rather than simply running into the king's presence and blurting out what she wants.

But once she is in his presence, she knows exactly what to do! Why? Because of female intuition and charm, because she knows her husband and the things he will respond to, and because she has thought it through beforehand. The crucial step in the case of her particular husband, she knows, is not to come to the point too quickly, but rather to develop his curiosity slowly. This she does by inviting Haman and Ahasuerus to a banquet which they greatly enjoy, but where there is by design notably little furthering of Esther's real goal – she is too smart to reveal her secret too easily! The king is intrigued at the first request, but after the second, he's positively *desperate* to know what it is that Esther wants! She is patient: she waits for the right time to say it. She does not use histrionics; she doesn't say, for example, 'How could you possibly let this happen to me and my people? What kind of a king are you?' Nor does she load guilt onto Ahasuerus ('I can't believe you let this happen!' 'I suppose you do everything that Haman tells you! Isn't it time you thought for yourself a little bit?'). She shows him respect even though he may not necessarily deserve it.

How to speak

The phrasing of her requests, when they finally come, is notable for its deferential tone:

"My wish and my request is: If I have found favour in the sight of the king, and if it please the king to grant my wish and fulfil my request, let the king and Haman come to the feast that I will prepare for them, and tomorrow I will do as the king has said."   (5:7,8, ESV)

"If it please the king, and if I have found favour in his sight, and if the thing seems right before the king, and I am pleasing in his eyes, let an order be written to revoke the letters devised by Haman the Agagite …"   (8:5, ESV)

The lesson here is not so much that wives should speak to their husbands quite like this, nor husbands to their wives – there is a royal setting to the scene here which perhaps requires a certain etiquette and the use of obsequious language. But there is still a lesson. Esther was Ahaseurus' wife, and she might have reasoned that this was enough to license her to talk in a certain way, not to show the respect that others had to show her husband. She didn't need, perhaps, to say 'if' quite so many times, to put him first and herself second so clearly ("if I have found favour … if it please the king … if it please the king … if I have found favour … (if) I am pleasing in his eyes … *then* let an order be written …"), but she does so as a mark of respect to the authority of her husband.

Communication skills are an essential art in marriage, one of its challenging aspects being the danger that our familiarity with our partner can breed contempt in the way we speak. If we catch ourselves talking to our partner in a way which is harsher, less compassionate or less respectful of the other's view than the way in which we would speak to someone we didn't know so well, or similarly, if it is different from the way in which we would expect *others* to talk to our partner, then a small dose of Esther's approach, even greatly diluted, could make a good corrective. If we love, cherish and respect our partner, then we ought to talk to them in a way which shows it.

Not just for wives

Just as Esther saves her husband from himself, cunningly intervening to prevent him from making a bad decision, so too there may be times when modern-day disciples, whether wives or husbands, may be presented with the opportunity to do the same. Prayer, preparation and planning will be important ingredients, not to mention a healthy dose of courage.

There are two steps to the process. One is to have the right goal, the right spiritual objectives for which you are striving – all the persuasive powers in the world are pointless if you are not going to direct them to achieve something spiritually worthwhile. But once those objectives are in place, there is also a need to think about *how* we achieve them: what is the right way to ask, to suggest, or to motivate? How are we most likely to be effective in bringing about the change that we believe is needed? Both aspects, the goal itself and the method of achieving it, need careful and prayerful thought.

The good news is that at heart the two partners within a marriage *want* to please each other, want to meet each other's needs and desires, and want to give the other what will make them happy. Sometimes this can get obscured or temporarily buried under a heap of 'baggage' as we work counter-productively for a time, but at heart this positive self-giving desire is usually present underneath if only it can be unearthed or reinvigorated.

As soon as Esther successfully opened communication channels with her husband and went about getting her message across in the right way there was nothing Ahasuerus wanted to do more than fulfil her request. May it be the same when we share our spiritual aims with our partners in a similarly thoughtful and well-prepared way.

Ahab and Jezebel

Topics: A remarkable woman with talents grossly misapplied; A wife's influence on her husband; Strong partnerships; A wife's support and perception; Lessons from Jezebel's diligence and proactive character?

Is there anything good that can be said about Jezebel? No doubt not very much – she is the epitome of evil, an example of female marital dominance out of control and bent to all the wrong ends. And yet as a personality type she remains an interesting study, one from whom lessons can be drawn; if only her drive and determination could have been focused on diametrically opposing goals the outcome could have been so very different.

BUT first, what of Ahab her husband? In comparison with her he is almost a non-person, so etched is her character into every narrative in which she appears. Though a much weaker-willed personality, he too is an evil man, one prone to sulks and despondency (could it be that her dominating ways exaggerate this tendency within him?). The Kings' record draws the following conclusion:

> "But there was none like unto Ahab, which did sell himself to work wickedness in the sight of the LORD, whom Jezebel his wife stirred up." (1 Kings 21:25)

This puts the matter beyond doubt: Ahab was strikingly evil of himself (and quite capable of being that way in his own right), but she influenced and incited him, exacerbating the problem in a material way. He sold his soul, as it were, for the sake of evil, and she was right behind him urging him to do it. She is a 'helper' sure enough, and a helper 'meet' for him given their combined enthusiasm for sin. She was helping him all the way to his grave.

A sticky end

As for *her* grave, she never got one:

> "And the carcase of Jezebel shall be as dung upon the face of the field in the portion of Jezreel; so that they shall not say, This is Jezebel." (2 Kings 9:37)

As the dogs dismembered her body, all that remained was the palms of her hands. How, then, and in what way was she so evil? 2 Kings tells of the servants of the Lord whom she had killed (9:7), of the considerable support she gave to the prophets of Baal, of her expertise in witchcraft and whoredom (verse 22), and of the fear she inculcated even in Elijah – but it is the comments of Revelation which perhaps provide the greatest insight:

> "Notwithstanding I have a few things against thee, because thou sufferest that woman Jezebel, which calleth herself a prophetess, to teach and to seduce my servants to commit fornication, and to eat things sacrificed unto idols." (Revelation 2:20)

She is an enabler, a motivator, and an inciter of others to do evil. She knows how to appeal to the basest instincts of others to educate and encourage them in the ways of evil (note the prostitution language with the term 'seduces'). Not content to do wickedly herself, she leads whole hosts of others into sin through the strength of her personality and her understanding of what will compel them to follow in her path.

Epitome of evil

As the epitome of all things evil it seems unlikely there would be much to learn from Jezebel, and yet there is. There are some wonderfully strong aspects of her personality from which lessons may be drawn as long as we keep in mind the massive proviso that these attributes need to be applied in completely the opposite direction from the one she chose.

Let's think about it. She is a great provider and protector who regularly hosts and provides for 450 prophets of Baal and 400 prophets of the groves who eat at her table. She is a tremendous mother-figure, a patron of worship, supporting the institutions in which she believes in practical, hands-on ways. Of course she is supporting utterly the *wrong* worship, but the energy she commits to her cause is nevertheless notable and may well shame the efforts we may expend on something much more worthwhile. She doesn't just *talk* about support – she is right there giving it, enabling and providing like a (false) mother-in-Israel.

There is a phenomenal industry to her actions. She is a doer, a go-getter, a person who makes things happen. She could martial prophets, nobles, and elders as well as servants; she had confidence and self-assurance ("I will give thee the field of Naboth ..."), and she was supremely industrious and committed within her own frame of reference – to Baal and not to God.

This level of industry and commitment seems almost unparalleled in terms of what is said of other women elsewhere in the scriptures except in the case of the Virtuous Woman. With respect to these aspects of drive, influence and provision Jezebel and the Virtuous Woman seem well-matched – other than the all-critical distinction of the goals to which they were dedicated. Would Jezebel have made excuses for herself or weakly complained that there was nothing she could do about a particular situation? It's hard to imagine a more unlikely scenario as her response to Elijah's triumph on Mount Carmel illustrates. Indeed, when all the chips were down and she was surrounded by Jehu's men before her death, she *still* puts a brave face on things:

> "And when Jehu was come to Jezreel, Jezebel heard of it; and she painted her face, and tired her head, and looked out at a window."   (2 Kings 9:30)

She is still proactive and prepared to give it a go, even in this remarkably bleak position! Perhaps, then, in her energy and outlook she can serve as an example, if only those attributes – the very ones shown by the Virtuous Woman also – can be harnessed not to a harmful cause like Baal worship but to a good and spiritual one. If only Jezebel had been pointed in the right direction, what she might have been able to accomplish!

Why so sad?

The most interesting scene involving Jezebel, at least as far as relationships are concerned, is the one in which Ahab sulks about Naboth's vineyard:

"But Jezebel his wife came to him, and said unto him, Why is thy spirit so sad, that thou eatest no bread? ... And Jezebel his wife said unto him, Dost thou now govern the kingdom of Israel? arise, and eat bread, and let thine heart be merry: I will give thee the vineyard of Naboth the Jezreelite."

(1 Kings 21:5,7)

She is perceptive of her husband's feelings, noticing when he is sad and off colour, and immediately doing something about it to make him feel better. Despite the external toughness males may like to project, there are times when they are perplexed and down, and it would not be uncommon for them to find difficulty in expressing this. A perceptive wife like Jezebel is able to read the situation and work out what can be done about it. While wives perhaps ought not to indulge their husbands' sulks too much (especially if they are a frequent occurrence), her proactive approach here is noteworthy – helping her husband to do something he didn't have the courage or gumption to do himself, even if the action she chooses to take is utterly evil. As soon as she commands her men they jump to attention to execute her plan (verse 11), and her influence both over her husband and her wider entourage is again noteworthy.

The incident raises a number of questions which can't be answered definitively – there isn't enough data in the text – but which are nevertheless interesting to reflect upon. Her emotional intuition about her husband seems admirable and part of what being a true partner to one's spouse ought to be about; so does the idea of working as a team, each partner bringing something to the relationship that the other partner may not (it's much clearer to see what Jezebel brings to the relationship than Ahab in this particular instance, but there was presumably something that appealed to her about him, even if it was only the power he wielded). It's quite possible to live in one's own world in a marriage and *not* notice what our partner is thinking and feeling, but Jezebel certainly does not make this mistake.

On the other hand there is the question of who 'wears the trousers' in the relationship, and here the answer would seem very much to be Jezebel, something which sits ill with the scriptural model of male headship. Here the example of the Virtuous Woman is instructive. If Jezebel crosses the line into dominating her husband in an unscriptural way (and it's not completely clear whether she should be seen as this kind of 'battle-axe' wife or not), then the woman of Proverbs 31 shows that a woman can bring energy, industry, commitment and the powers of influence, resourcefulness and productivity into a marriage which are thoroughly right without undermining a husband's headship and without needing to get his blessing at every step because she knows her activities are consistent with the goals of the household: the Virtuous Woman does all these things wonderfully well and still allows her husband the space to take on his Biblically mandated role. If wives can harness some of Jezebel's get up and go (exhausting though it may be to consider it!) and apply it in the same direction as the Virtuous Woman does, then the result will be something quite remarkably good, just as Jezebel was quite remarkable for her sin.

Job and his wife

Topics: Female insight and intuition; The importance of listening even in an argument; Benefitting from one's partner's observations; Bad advice.

"Curse God and die!" is perhaps the most spectacularly memorable piece of bad advice ever given to a husband by his wife. Yet the observation of Job's wife which immediately preceded this outburst contained within it the kernel of a truth which Job might well have usefully taken to heart. It is no simple task carefully to sort through the words spoken by partners in their emotionally-charged disagreements to discern the wheat from the chaff, especially when we ourselves are involved. Often our statements and motives can be highly complex to unravel, containing paradoxes of good advice and bad, insightful perceptions and crass misevaluations. The famous words of Job's wife form a fascinating case study.

THE background to the incident is well known: one by one the externals of Job's life (property, possessions, family) are stripped away, and now he faces another harrowing bout of suffering as his own body is attacked and his health obliterated. It is in that context that his wife offers her evaluation of the situation:

"Then said his wife unto him, Dost thou still retain thine integrity? Curse God and die! But he said unto her, Thou speakest as one of the foolish women speaketh. What? Shall we receive good at the hand of God, and shall we not receive evil? In all this did not Job sin with his lips."   (Job 2:9,10)

The exchange is a heated one; tempers are frayed and there is no beating about the bush in what either party says (note her use of the word "still" which suggests exasperation with Job perhaps arising out of previous circumstances and conversations, not to mention Job's likening her suggestion to that of a fool). This is what difficult circumstances do: they put relationships under pressure, they reveal what is underneath. Furthermore, they can cause us to go overboard in what we say, bringing to light attitudes and resentments that may, in kinder circumstance, have remained hidden. It is familiar territory to consider Job's sufferings as a crucible for *him* (that's surely one of the main purposes of the book within the larger framework of scripture); but they were a crucible for his wife too, and for their relationship. If we care about each other at all as partners (and perhaps even if we don't), when we suffer, we suffer *together*, at least in some measure.

Identifying the issue

First Job's wife says to him, "Dost thou still retain thine integrity?" Her use of an aggressive questioning style here highlights her frustration, but with whom and about what exactly? Is she exasperated with Job, and if so, is it for being or trying to be too righteous ('Why can't you just be more like everyone else?') or is it rather for making such a big deal of his righteousness?

These two, though similar, are not quite the same thing. The first is a criticism for the preoccupation with being righteous (the focus is on the *righteousness* – why does Job have to put so much effort into doing good things – are good things sufficiently worthwhile as to put so much effort into doing them?); the second is a criticism of *Job* for valuing his own righteousness so much. In the language that she herself uses, the first focuses on the *integrity* and whether it is worthwhile ('what's the point in integrity for anyone; it's just not that valuable'); the second focuses on *Job* ('Why do you care so much about *your* integrity? This isn't about *you*; just give it up, and stop being obsessed with your own righteousness so much').

There is also a third possibility – that she is exasperated with *God*. How could God allow this to happen to them, and if this is the kind of God He is, then Job may as well curse Him and be done with it (so she would be reasoning). If this is the correct interpretation then we're witnessing an interesting and not uncommon phenomenon – a person is angry about one thing (in this case, God), but they take it out on someone or something else (in this case, Job, because he is immediately available to her to attack, whereas God is not). This can often happen in strife between marriage partners – the quarrel is ostensibly about one thing, but somehow we manage to make it about something else. The best course of action here is simply to be ruthless with ourselves in trying to be fair: we need to identify objectively what the real issue is and address that. If there is something in a set of circumstances which cannot be changed, there is no point in blaming something or someone else for it, least of all our partner.

Retaining your integrity
It's particularly worthwhile, I think, to focus on the idea that she might be frustrated with Job's insistence in holding on to his integrity. This idea ("Dost thou still *retain* thine integrity?") has such important echoes with the rest of the book that it is highly suggestive in terms of the book's overall message – perhaps giving us a quite specific reason why the comment is recorded.

At the very end of his speeches and immediately prior to the intervention of Elihu, Job says:
"Let me be weighed in an even balance, that God may know mine integrity."   (Job 31:6)

This is very interesting. Job *has* become focused on – perhaps even obsessive about – his own righteousness or integrity; he feels it's the only thing he has left to hang on to, but in doing so he has started to put his own righteousness in first place and thus in some way to marginalise the righteousness of God. This is not what he sets out to do, but it is where he has ended up. His sufferings have shown that he has too high a view of his own righteousness, and in the course of his trials he has allowed this sense of his integrity to dominate and compromise his sense of the righteousness of God. He concludes his speeches with a long passage proclaiming his own righteousness, and the verse quoted above ("[let] God know mine integrity") is characteristic of his closing monologue.

Needless to say, this is all wrong and the very opposite of the sort of argument that Paul lays out in Romans 1-3 about man's sinfulness and *God's* righteousness. Although it is true that Job has not sinned in all the ways that he lists, his righteousness is *still* irrelevant as a basis of commending him to God, and he therefore needs to let go of it and trust in God with both hands, as it were, and with full concentration. That this is indeed an issue that Job's sufferings have brought to light[1] is supported by passages like the following:

"I will never admit you are in the right; till I die, I will not deny my integrity."   (Job 27:5, NIV)

"... till I die I will not remove mine integrity from me." (KJV)

"My righteousness I hold fast and will not let it go."   (27:6)

"I will maintain my righteousness and never let go of it; my conscience will not reproach me as long as I live."   (NIV)

The truly fascinating point about this is that the very point that Job needs to let go of his righteousness is identified right back in chapter 3 by his wife when she asks him why he insists on holding on to his integrity! Whether she intends it that way or not, she is, either deliberately or ironically (given the overall foolishness of her suggestion that he curse and die), correct in that part of her analysis! Job needs to cease and desist in retaining his own integrity as if it were sufficient to commend him to God or to require that God should give an account of

---

1   Though crucially it is not a *sufficient* explanation of them. There are many potential reasons – and no reason (that we can understand) – for Job's suffering.

Himself to Job. This is wonderfully ironic, and a delightful extra dimension to the riches of the book.

Right analysis, wrong conclusion

There are two practical points to draw out from this as far as relationships are concerned. The first is that Job's wife, in picking out such a key issue of the book in her comment, is shown at one level to be highly intuitive, perceptive and smart, as women often are. When men stop and think about it, they realise that this is a very special skill that women often have: how quickly they understand the dynamics at play in relationships, for example, or take stock of an interpersonal problem. Ironically, Job's wife 'gets it' in chapter 3 – Job has to let go of his sense of righteousness – but it takes a further thirty-six chapters and the intervention of the Almighty Himself to get *him* to appreciate it! God Himself has to intervene to put Job's integrity in a proper context before Job finally sees the point and repents in dust and ashes.

This is female intuition, then, at its best for a brief moment – only for it then to all come crashing down in what she says next! If it is right for Job to let go of his integrity, his sense of *self*, then it is certainly, absolutely and categorically wrong for him to curse God and die, as he well knows. Right premise, wrong conclusion! What she *ought* to have said is that he should cling instead to *God's righteousness*, the knowledge that God always does what is best, even when we don't understand what He is doing or why He is doing it.

Her proposed course of action *was* foolish (as Job points out); she was indeed talking as one of the "foolish women" talk when she angrily advised him to be done with God rather than offering him her love and support; it was awful advice. And yet her words contained within them the kernel of a perspective, intentional or otherwise, that *was* correct. I wonder if Job would have looked back later and wondered if he should have considered a bit further the first half of what she had said.

This highlights another point. When under pressure or in an argument we are often listening for what to reject, a trigger to discard the other person's idea so that we can continue guilt-free on the course we're already on – winning the argument or proving that we are right. This is sometimes called 'ego-speak': being so busy thinking what we're going to say next and how we're going to prove ourselves to be right that we are not listening to what the other person is saying. We often *refuse* to hear the correct parts of what our partner may be observing because we take objection to some other part of it, such as the implication that there may be aspects in which *we* need to change. Even if we end up disagreeing with the overall conclusion our partner might suggest (as Job correctly does here), this example suggests that we should always listen carefully to see if there is something in what our partner is saying from which we can learn. We are trying to become like Christ, after all, and our partner's observations, even when they are not kindly expressed or when they do not include the full picture, can often show us where we are falling short.

Moses and Zipporah

Topics: Wives can save their husband's lives; Taking action if one's husband doesn't; Spiritual responsibilities of men and women.

God's model for marriage is that the man take on the responsibility of spiritual headship – but what happens if the man has no interest in this requirement or fails to rise to the challenge? Certainly his wife should help him and encourage him to take on the role God has asked, but she cannot *make* him do it; ultimately it is a matter for his own free will for which he must answer to God. What, then, in this situation? Should she sit back and see spiritual goals and priorities not actioned in her family because of her husband's unwillingness or lack of spiritual perception? The account of Moses and Zipporah in which she dramatically saves Moses' life by taking the initiative in a moment of his spiritual and practical failure provides an interesting precedent.

EXODUS 4:24-26 is one of the most cryptic passages of scripture containing both intricate word plays and a number of unanswered questions. Nevertheless, the basic thrust of the action seems clear. Moses is en route from Midian back to Egypt to take up God's commission to liberate the Israelites from the hand of Pharaoh. One would have thought, therefore, that as God's chosen deliverer, he would have his own house in order before he set off.

But it is not so. Midway into the journey Moses and his family stop at an inn, presumably to rest for the night. While they are there Moses gets the shock of his life as God's angel arrives on the scene on a mission to kill him (that's right – to kill Moses, the very one God has just called to serve as His agent of deliverance!):[1]

"And it came to pass by the way in the inn, that the LORD met him, and sought to kill him. Then Zipporah took a sharp stone, and cut off the foreskin of her son, and cast it at his feet, and said, Surely a bloody husband art thou to me. So he let him go: then she said, A bloody husband thou art, because of the circumcision."   (Exodus 4:24-26)

The issue is Moses' failure to have circumcised his son and it is this which precipitates the angel's hostility. Quite simply, he should have known better. Why he hadn't done it we don't know – maybe he was squeamish, maybe he didn't think the matter was such a big deal, maybe he excused himself because he had been living amidst Midianite rather than Jewish culture for a good while, maybe he simply forgot. It doesn't matter; whatever the reason, he didn't do it, and it wasn't good enough.

But why should God's angel take issue with Moses at this particular moment rather than some other? Why on the journey at the inn rather than, for instance, back at home when the original sin of omission had taken place? The answer probably lies in the fact that Moses is now about to go back to Egypt to be the leader of his people, God's representative and chosen deliverer. To whom much is given much is required: it would be quite hypocritical for Moses to attempt to bring the people out of Egypt and demand spiritual reform from them when he

---

1   Alternative interpretations are possible, for example that it is Moses' son Gershom that the angel attempts to kill – for more details see my article in *The Christadelphian*, January 1999, pages 14-18; see also *The Exodus* (Norwich: Testimony, 2009), pages 70-72,78,79. In the main text I have presented what I believe is the most likely interpretation rather than continuously caveating with alternatives the points being made. Even if some details of the passage are interpreted differently the point about Zipporah's action would remain unchanged, and this is the part which is relevant to the discussion of relationships.

had not fulfilled this basic part of God's covenant to Abraham in his own household. The angel functions as a kind of border-patrol: now that Moses is going back to his people to take up his responsibilities as deliverer the angel blocks the way, seeking to kill him rather than allow him passage while his son remains uncircumcised.

While Moses seems to be quite nonplussed by the whole incident (his very silence through these cryptic verses suggesting as much), Zipporah knows exactly what to do when danger strikes. Her husband's life is threatened (and perhaps her son's as well), and she apparently knows what God's command concerning circumcision required. On seeing the safety of her family in peril in this way she therefore immediately takes action. If Moses has not been prepared to circumcise his son as he should and is now endangered because of it, then she will do it for him. She immediately grabs a flint and performs the circumcision, the danger instantly averted.

Of course she is not pleased by this sequence of events. The KJV's 'casting' of the foreskin at Moses' feet may be too strongly worded, but irrespective of that her twice recorded, "A bloody husband art thou to me!" in two adjacent verses makes her anger pretty clear. She should never have had to be doing this job; it was Moses' responsibility to circumcise his son as it was Abraham's for Isaac – but she is forced to step in to save her family because Moses had neglected his responsibility. It causes friction and anger but it brings salvation to the family and assures its ongoing integrity.

We don't know what Zipporah thought about circumcision or what her spiritual persuasions were. Her father seems to be a spiritual man (though there are ambiguities around precisely which god he worshipped), but we have little on which to judge Zipporah other than this incident. She certainly knew what the problem was and what she had to do to avert the danger when disaster was about to strike, but whether she personally disapproved of circumcision and this was the cause of her anger, or whether she did approve but resented the fact that she had to carry it out, we cannot say.

For our purposes here, however, it is beside the point. The lesson seems to be that if a husband cannot be persuaded or influenced to do what is right and see to it that spiritual actions are carried out in his family, then the wife ought not to sit back and allow them to go undone (on the basis, for instance, that she is usurping his authority). This might suggest, for example, that if Bible readings are not being done or spiritual things not being discussed, if a husband refuses or cannot be motivated to do them, then the wife ought to do so for the salvation of the family. It is not the ideal, but it is better than the alternative and what we are dealing with in this kind of example is a question of competing principles. It is right to obey the laws of the land until the point when they start conflicting with the laws of God, at which point it must be they that take priority ("we ought to obey God rather than men", Acts 5:29); similarly the suggestion from this incident is that although it falls to the man to be the spiritual head of the family, if he has no interest in such matters then the wife should do what she can rather than allowing his indifference to lead to the family's spiritual demise.

Othniel and Achsah

Topics: Wanting the best for one's marriage and family; Spiritual ambition.

Like the Moses and Zipporah incident of the previous chapter the account of Othniel and Achsah is brief and rather cryptic, yet it provides an interesting illustration of a wife's ambition for her household.

THE intriguing incident is recounted twice: once in Joshua 15 and then again in Judges 1 during the annals of the conquest of the land. Here is the Joshua version:

"And Caleb said, He that smiteth Kirjathsepher, and taketh it, to him will I give Achsah my daughter to wife. And Othniel the son of Kenaz, the brother of Caleb, took it: and he gave him Achsah his daughter to wife. And it came to pass, as she came unto him, that she moved him to ask of her father a field: and she lighted off her ass; and Caleb said unto her, What wouldest thou? who answered, Give me a blessing; for thou hast given me a south land; give me also springs of water. And he gave her the upper springs, and the nether springs."

(Joshua 15:16-19)

'Winning' a bride by virtue of a military conquest for her father is not usually the way it would be done today, but no matter; the important thing for our present purposes is Achsah's request on learning that she is to be married to Othniel and what this reveals about her family ambitions.

Knowing that Othniel is particularly in favour with her father at the moment she 'moves' or persuades him to ask for a possession of land – an inheritance – to go along with their marriage. Perhaps the mention of this request at the point of marriage suggests that it was not the normal practice for an inheritance to be passed on precisely at this juncture, or perhaps Achsah is identifying a specific parcel of land that she would like to be her dowry (rather than whatever her father might happen to choose). This would be an interesting option because it would suggest that Achsah didn't want her father to give merely money to Othniel as a dowry, but that what she really cared about was the land – the Land of Promise. If this is right then it would be her desire to maintain a stake of inheritance in the promises which is paramount.

Whether or not this is a discussion about a dowry (the text simply does not say), the key fact seems to be that Achsah persuades Othniel to ask her father for this field. Having accomplished the military victory he just has and become the (likely) favoured son-in-law it makes sense in Achsah's mind that Othniel should be the one to ask. In the society of those times matters such as property transactions were probably the usual preserve of males, so she encourages her husband to pursue her request on her behalf.

The text does not reveal whether or not Othniel's request is in fact made. It could be that it is, but that Achsah is not satisfied with the field she receives; it could be that the request is refused or even that it is not made. All we know is that the next thing which happens is that Achsah is getting off her donkey to speak to her father. This implies that she has been travelling (after all she lives with her husband now, not her father, which is why she needed the donkey), so she has gone to visit her father to speak to him about this matter. The dismounting from the donkey seems a surprising detail to mention but perhaps it serves to indicate Achsah's respect and propriety in addressing her father, even though she may be making a somewhat unusual – even audacious – request.[1]

For his part, Caleb seems surprised to see his daughter and knows immediately that there is something significant on her mind. The point seems to be that she is not content with merely receiving a parcel of land from her father; she wants now to improve the prospects of the land that she has been given. Stepping in now to communicate with her father herself she points out that the land in question is of poor quality ('south land', 'desert land' or 'Negev land' – probably an analogy of quality rather than a statement of location) – and that she needs to have springs of water also in order for the land to be maximally fertile. Only then will it be possible for Othniel and her to make of their inheritance all it can be.

Now what is going on here? Is this a materialistic or spoiled daughter not content with what she is given and always asking for more from a father who can't bring himself to turn her down? More likely, I think, is that her efforts show her ambition not only for a family and a future which can be successful from a practical perspective but from a spiritual one as well. The things she asks for are:

1. a possession or inheritance;
2. a blessing;
3. springs of water;
4. fruitfulness (implicitly this is what springs of water will enable in a desert land).

---

1   The reference to a woman dismounting from a donkey to ask for life-giving water sets up a contrast between the beginning and the ending of the book. At the end a dead woman (the slaughtered concubine) is put up onto a donkey to be carried home and there dismembered. A further contrast comes in Caleb "giving her *according to (her) heart* the upper springs and the lower springs". The italicised words are in the original but not in the KJV translation; they form both a pun on Caleb's name ('according to heart' in Hebrew is 'c leb' – the very consonants of his name) and an allusion to the concubine incident in which the Levite went to speak to his concubine's heart, but ended up making only his own and his father-in-law's heart glad in their self-indulgent male-bonding – see chapter 14 for more details. Everything that goes right in male-female relations with Achsah, Othniel and Caleb goes wrong between the Levite and the concubine at the end of the book.

The interesting point is that these have spiritual analogues –
fruitfulness, blessing, water, possession are all concepts that
resonate in terms of eternal things as well as the purely physical.

The suggestion then is that her twofold request, first
through her husband and then in person to her father, illustrates
her ambition for her family, first from a natural and then from
a spiritual perspective. If she is going to be married and have a
family then she wants it to be the best that it can be in terms
of ownership of a stake in the Promised Land and in terms of
its potential for fertility and fruitfulness. Her request shows
her ambition for a big possession, for good territory, for a good
base on which their marriage and their future can be built. She
colludes with her husband in order to accomplish this aim but
she is also prepared to get personally involved to achieve her
goal, negotiating with and influencing the men in her life (her
husband and her father) to enable her to achieve the best for
her future family. It appears that neither Othniel nor Caleb
have themselves really thought through the implications of
inheritance and what sort of land will be needed to bring forth
the best for the family – but she has, and when she 'moves' them
and makes her request in that direction her father seems to have
no hesitation in seeing that she is right and granting her request.

Commentator Daniel Block puts it like this:

"She recognises that the desert (Negev) land she and her
husband have received offers little promise. Accordingly she
concretizes her need for a blessing with a request for a field
with springs of water, without which she will be unable to grow
the garden she needs to feed her family. Although she remains
graceful and respectful, she will not be simply a passive object
of men's deals. Instead she seizes the opportunity to achieve
something neither her father nor husband contemplated.
But she does so without overstepping the bounds of female
propriety."[2]

---

2   Daniel Block, *Judges* (*New American Bible Commentary*; Nashville: Broadman and
     Holman, 1999), page 96.

The scene is perhaps reminiscent of several others in the scriptures which have to do with spiritual ambition. One of these is Solomon's request for wisdom at the beginning of his reign. He does not say, as wicked Ahaz later did, "I will not ask, neither will I tempt the LORD". No, he asks for wisdom. Perhaps an even closer analogy is the prayer of Jabez that God would 'enlarge his coasts':

"And Jabez called on the God of Israel, saying, Oh that thou wouldest bless me indeed, and enlarge my coast, and that thine hand might be with me, and that thou wouldest keep *me* from evil, that it may not grieve me! And God granted him that which he requested." (1 Chronicles 4:10)

For her part Achsah asks for both a possession and for springs of water to give that possession fruitfulness and productivity. She wants her land to be fruitful just like her marriage, and she wants to claim a big stake for herself as a 'mother in Israel' in the Promised Land. It is much more than her leaning on her father to buy her a big house or give her a bigger piece of the family estate. Her ambition, resolve and action within the sphere of her influence also recalls the Virtuous Woman who at every turn sought to maximise the good of her household.

The Virtuous Woman and her husband

Topics: Energy and industry; Internal responsibilities – internal and external activities; What the woman does for her husband and family; A husband's appreciation and response.

The famous chapter on the Virtuous Woman (Proverbs 31) can be read in various ways: as an ode to a real woman, as advice on choosing a wife from a mother to her son, as an idealisation of all the virtues of womanhood, or, perhaps most fruitfully, as a portrait of the bride of Christ or Wisdom personified. Here the focus is a practical one reflecting on the woman's role in relation to her husband and family.

FIRST, a brief portrait of the Virtuous Woman in her own right. What are some of the attributes she possesses and the skills she brings to bear? Consider, for example, the following:

"She rises while it is yet night and provides food for her household and portions for her maidens ... She is not afraid of snow for her household, for all her household are clothed in scarlet." (verses 15,21, ESV)

This brings out the sheer level of industry she is able to sustain, her bravery and courage. She is a wonderful provider, embracing all her household (including the maidens, who are presumably meant to provide for and serve *her* – yet she includes and takes care of them!).

Or again:

"Strength and dignity are her clothing, and she laughs at the time to come. She opens her mouth with wisdom, and the teaching of kindness is on her tongue."   (verses 25,26, ESV)

This is an interesting choice of clothes ("strength and dignity"), but a fine one to aspire to. The object of her laughter is also surprising, but it bespeaks someone with nothing to fear because she is well-founded, well-prepared, and courageous. The only way you can be that way with any reasonable basis is because you trust in the Lord – and this, as we discover later in the poem, is precisely what she does.

There are lots of ways one might complete a sentence that begins 'she opens her mouth ...' (for instance: '... and puts her foot in it', '... and then wishes she hadn't', '... and it's all downhill from there'), but it is none of these options as far as this woman is concerned. The virtuous woman opens her mouth "with wisdom", the chief virtue of Solomon's book, "and the teaching of kindness is on her tongue". This woman is not just a pretty face nor 'merely' a hard worker and a devoted provider. She has intellectual and spiritual capabilities aplenty ("wisdom ... teaching") and she knows how to share them ("she opens her mouth ... teaching ... is on her tongue"). She does not specialise in knowledge without kindness (as a crusty intellectual might) or kindness without knowledge (as a do-gooder devoid of the right framework of understanding). Instead the one attribute tempers the other and coalesces in the perfect blend: mercy and truth have kissed one another once again, if in different words.

Implicit trust

Now to the heart of our topic: to examine how the virtuous woman behaves in relation to her husband and family specifically. This is brought out in three passages which we shall look at in turn.

"The heart of her husband trusts in her, and he will have no lack of gain. She does him good, and not harm, all the days of her life."   (verses 11,12, ESV)

It might be thought obvious that a wife would do her husband good not harm, but this is not necessarily always the case; she might *generally* do him good, she might even mostly *intend* to do him good – but there might be times when it doesn't quite work out that way: times when she fails to respect him or his views, times when she makes him feel small or inadequate, times when she minimises what is important to him, or when she doesn't really think about what is best, whether for him as an individual or for them as a couple.

Instead there is a consistency and longevity – a reliability – to her support, such that his heart can "safely trust in her". She is a refuge for him, faithful to the last, just as her Heavenly Father is faithful. She is also a source of productivity ("he will have no lack of gain"), whether through her support and enabling of his endeavours or through the industrious pursuits of her own, amply spoken of elsewhere in the chapter.

She also gives him space to interface with the world outside the family, enabling him in this particular case to take a leadership role in his community:

"Her husband is known in the gates when he sits among the elders of the land."   (verse 23, ESV)

She supports and enables this function and helps to sustain his reputation and role outside the household, not demanding that he always be at home concerning himself exclusively with family matters. This can be a hard balance to strike, because there is another extreme in which the husband is never at home and offers no support to the family – this is clearly not good either. Both partners have a responsibility to sacrifice in these areas, and of course to discuss them openly together in order to agree an appropriate strategy.

He praises her

The final passage is a longer one, one which contains further admirable attributes of the woman herself, but which also flips things around for an important discussion of how the husband ought to respond to his wife. It is this reciprocal aspect that we now want to focus on.

"She looks well to the ways of her household and does not eat the bread of idleness. Her children rise up and call her blessed; her husband also, and he praises her: 'Many women have done excellently, but you surpass them all.' Charm is deceitful, and beauty is vain, but a woman who fears the LORD is to be praised. Give her of the fruit of her hands, and let her works praise her in the gates."   (verses 27-31, ESV)

In response to her abundant care and marvellous foresight the family are quick to notice and to show appreciation. Even the children do this (not always the case, by any means – maybe the father needs to teach them by example how to do so!).

All this raises some important questions. Is the husband able to praise his wife for the work she does? Even if she is not perfect and her self-sacrifice does not quite seem to match every detail of Proverbs 31, there is surely a huge amount that she does which is worthy of note and appreciation. But *does* he note it? And if he notices, does he *bother* to say anything or do anything to express it? The words of the husband here are poignant: "Many women have done excellently ...", and it is worth stopping for a moment just to consider the excellence of the ways of women from a man's perspective: their more natural empathy and appreciation of the feelings of others; their patience, gentleness, attentiveness and kindness when compared to many men; their ability to carry out acts of provision and care day after day without showing frustration or complaint; the amazing instincts of motherhood; their seeing into the heart of matters and intuitive sense of what relationship dynamics are 'about' – all these and many others, without even mentioning the physical aspects of grace, poise and beauty which so captivate men.

There can be for many women – especially mothers – an unrelenting and monotonous list of tasks to be accomplished, the burdens of children which she often largely bears, key aspects of running the home and the sheer hard work that it all implies. There are the different roles she is called upon to fulfil, often in the compass of a single day (wife, educator, confidante / shoulder to cry on, mother, woman, cook – and all in the context of her first role as a disciple of Christ). There is plenty of scope, then, for any man who is even modestly observant to exclaim with Solomon, "Many women have done excellently ...!"

In the special case of his own particular 'Virtuous Woman' the poet goes beyond this and exclaims "... but you surpass them all!" Now these words might be considered to be true because this particular woman is an idealisation and amalgamation of the various virtues of womanhood or because she stands as a symbol of wisdom or the bride of Christ. But there is also a sense that any husband who is at all appreciative of the virtues of his wife can join in with these words of praise: that *for him* her virtues surpass those of all other, that he is so grateful that she is *his* wife and that he has truly found "a good thing" from the Lord – the best thing for him, according to God's gracious provision.

He is not frightened to say so, because he is aware of the abundant blessings that have come to him because of her partnership. He is only too happy to appreciate and celebrate the unique virtues and performance of his wife; so glad, in fact, that he exuberantly tells anyone who will listen, whether in the gates of the city where her example shines forth just as much as his words of counsel as a community elder, or whether it is in the gates of his own home where he sets an example to the rest of the family by showing just how much he values the goodness of his wife.

The key question for husbands, then, is implicitly posed by the end of the poem. A woman who fears the Lord is to be praised, for this – the fearing of the Lord – is the most important characteristic of all. But *is* she?

Part 5
Intimacy

Introduction: sex and its symbolism

Topics: Sex is a gift from God not a taboo; The marriage context; Symbolism
– why it's a big deal; How the culture got it wrong; Pornography; The different
needs of men and women; Difficulties within marriage; Giving versus getting.

SEX is one of the most remarkable human experiences and
one of God's greatest gifts; at the same time it has been
severely misunderstood, abused by society and can be the
source of considerable awkwardness and even dysfunction in
a relationship. In this section the aim is to try to set a proper
context for sex from a scriptural perspective – its purpose, its
wonder, its appropriate setting, its boundaries – then to explore
a set of scriptural examples. The first of these, from Song of
Songs, explores the positive aspects, the remaining examples
some of the 'problem' areas (sex before marriage, the breakdown
of good sexual relations in a marriage, and affairs).

Although sex has a specific context – that is, within a
marriage rather than before or outside it – within that context
it is thoroughly good. Let's start with this positive side. It is so
good, in fact, that the physical, psychological and emotional
union that it creates and celebrates between a man and his wife
is a scriptural metaphor for the ultimate union of Christ and
the worldwide congregation of believers in the kingdom of God.
Sex is fundamentally about expressing and feeling unity with
one's partner – it is about *oneness* just like marriage as a whole,
and in many ways it is the ultimate expression of that oneness.
It is the way one says, 'I love you and am one with you' with

one's whole body and mind. Once we appreciate this we can see why it's such a big deal from a spiritual perspective as well as a physical and emotional one – God is one, we are meant to be one in marriage, and in a wider sense we are meant to be one as a group of believers united to our Lord and to our God. The 'high' that intimacy creates – perhaps unparalleled in any other human experience – is thus in a sense a glimpse at the nature of God and at what God wants for His people (such that we might exclaim 'so *this* is why oneness is such a big deal: because it is how God is, because it is so much better than division, because it is so *right* – in the sense of how things ought to be between a man and his wife – and because it feels so good').

There was a time when society as a whole and some parts of the religious world in particular were prudish about sex. I once heard of a book written at the end of the nineteenth century which provided advice for pastors' wives. It exhorted them to make sure they made it apparent to their husbands during sex that it was an uncomfortable and unpleasant experience for them – this way their husbands would be less likely to seek it often and so would be less contaminated and distracted. Few will be tempted to think like this today, but if that tendency does exist then a good remedy will be a re-reading and reflection upon the Song of Songs (the next chapter), or a passage such as Proverbs 5:

"Drink waters out of thine own cistern, and running waters out of thine own well. Let thy fountains be dispersed abroad, and rivers of waters in the streets. Let them be only thine own, and not strangers' with thee. Let thy fountain be blessed: and rejoice with the wife of thy youth. Let her be as the loving hind and pleasant roe; let her breasts satisfy thee at all times; and be thou ravished always with her love."

(Proverbs 5:15-19)

There is no embarrassment or prudishness here; sex is compared to a delightful and refreshing fountain of water (think how this becomes a spiritual metaphor in the New Testament), a source of satisfaction and renewal for a couple. Little further comment should be needed therefore by way of saying that intimacy within marriage is not something to be embarrassed about, shied away from, or felt inappropriate, dirty, sinful, or in some way less than thoroughly right and good.

Similarly there is no scriptural evidence that sex is purely for procreation – the burden of evidence from several passages like Proverbs 5 and the following New Testament verses pointing strongly in the other direction:

"Marriage is honourable in all, and the bed undefiled ..."

(Hebrews 13:4)

"The wife hath not power of her own body, but the husband: and likewise also the husband hath not power of his own body, but the wife. Defraud ye not one the other, except it be with consent for a time, that ye may give yourselves to fasting and prayer; and come together again, that Satan tempt you not for your incontinency."   (1 Corinthians 7:4,5)

When we ask *why* it is such a wonderful and powerful thing there are a number of interesting points to be made. The first is because God made it so – it is a wedding gift from Him, if you like, a crowning celebration of the institution of marriage that He created for us and wants us to enjoy. Second, one of the reasons for its power is that it brings together both the physical, emotional and psychological realms and ties them all together, binding a couple as one in these different ways. In that sense it *creates* unity: walls, partitions and barriers are broken down and a couple are truly rendered one. Third, it embraces and involves so many of the human senses: touch, taste, smell, sight, hearing can all be involved in the act so that it is quite literally a whole body experience in which two separate bodies are fully intertwined. Fourth, it is a spiritual parable – it has symbolic power – as we have already seen; it is so much more than a mere physical act or a bodily function. I find the following quotes from the writer Mike Mason helpful in capturing some of this:

"Exposure of the body in a personal encounter is like the telling of one's deepest secret: afterwards there is no going back, no pretending that the secret is still one's own or that the other does not know. It is, in effect, the very last step in human relations, and therefore never to be taken lightly. It is not a step which establishes deep intimacy, but one which presupposes it ... To be naked with another person is a sort of picture or symbolic demonstration of perfect honesty, perfect trust, perfect giving and commitment, and if the heart is not naked along with the body, then the whole action becomes a lie and a mockery. It becomes an involvement in an absurd and tragic contradiction: the giving of the body but the withholding of the self."   (Mike Mason)

This captures both something of the significance and beauty of sex within marriage, and it also shows why sex outside marriage isn't right, a topic we'll return to in chapter 28. Once we see what sex represents, its significance in building intimacy and unity, it becomes self-evident why promiscuity and sex outside marriage are wrong.

A different view

It goes without saying that society has taken a very different view from what has been set out above and unfortunately we need to face the challenge that this alternative and false world-view presents if only so that we can be alert to its potential influence upon us and be sure to stand up for what is right in God's sight. To some extent there is an inconsistent polarisation in contemporary thinking. In one sense sex is considered the 'great god', the most important thing in the world, the purpose of life, the only thing that matters; it is obsessed over and its significance exaggerated beyond all proportion; we live in a world which worships sex and seems to think of little else. In another sense, though, it has been dramatically cheapened and reduced to a mere bodily function like going to the bathroom or brushing one's teeth – as if it can be divorced from any emotional significance or any real meaning beyond a physical high that lasts for a few moments but is nevertheless to be pursued as if it were life's ultimate goal. From this false perspective intimacy is just a set of physical stimulae and responses that the body is capable of, to be indulged and exploited at every available opportunity –

'good sex' is simply about knowing enough about this physiology and practising certain physical techniques; there is no emotional or spiritual context, and, bizarrely, scarcely an interpersonal or relational one.

Once we step back and see these two attitudes for what they are their shortcomings can be readily seen, but that doesn't mean their bludgeoning impact felt every day through the media and prevailing cultural attitudes doesn't have any impact upon disciples. The effect, then, is simultaneously to make sex into the be all and end all of life (it clearly isn't, even though it is important), and at the same time to cheapen or 'commoditise' it (why would we want to do that with one of God's most precious gifts?).

All of this might be easy enough to deal with and properly contextualise if we were dealing with an abstract concept to which we could keep some personal distance. But of course we're not dealing with something abstract, we're dealing with one of the most powerful forces known to human beings which society is telling us either to worship or indulge at every available opportunity. Purely of itself – without any external stimulation or cultural messaging – the sex drive in human beings is very strong, and society knows exactly how to manipulate it. In the light of this it can be very difficult to keep a balanced perspective towards sex and its place in life, and to help our children and young people do the same.

Cultural consequences
What problems or consequences can the culture's approach to sex have on believers? Most seriously it can raise the level of temptation, availability and perceived 'normality' of sex before or outside marriage (we'll tackle both of these in later chapters and explore why they are serious matters in God's sight). It can make young people feel alienated and out of touch with their peers in society – old-fashioned, prudish, repressed, and perhaps as though they are denying themselves one of the best things life has to offer for no apparent reason; they therefore need to be

provided with good reasons and solid foundations for holding on to the Biblical standard. Similarly for those within marriage who may not be particularly happy with the physical side or even some other aspect of their relationship, society's approach can make the feeling of dissatisfaction more urgent and the temptation to seek fulfilment elsewhere more strong. Indeed, all the talk and portrayal of people's sex lives in society (where once it would have been taboo) can tend to foster feelings of discontent and a curiosity about what else might be available, if not a level of performance anxiety about whether or not one's own life and habit is up to muster.

For men in particular the ever-more explicit sexualisation of women in society and the mass availability of pornography can present a particularly acute challenge. When women are portrayed in advertising and media as sex objects whose main purpose is the satisfaction of male 'needs', it subtly influences and impacts attitudes and behaviours; our vision becomes distorted and our self-centredness increased (as if this wasn't already hard enough to keep in check); in short it becomes harder to have the right attitude towards women and to keep in proper perspective what is truly important in life. As for pornography, if a person once allows themselves to look it can quickly become a deteriorating spiral of increasingly debased forms of voyeurism where the word 'addiction' is not too strong. Is it really a big deal? Yes it is, precisely because it is addictive, because it impacts the way men look at and think about women, because it exploits women, because it is a world of debauched fantasy which tends to worse and worse perversions, because it can lead to dissatisfaction and dysfunction in real-life relations, and because God has made it clear that sexual promiscuity and taking pleasure in the promiscuity of others is wrong. Society may claim it's 'normal' but that is no justification; if one finds oneself caught in its web the best thing is to try to stop as urgently as possible. It will not be easy – rules for oneself, creating new patterns of behaviour and password protection can all help; some have found it helpful to confide in someone to

whom one is obliged to 'report in' occasionally in order to have
an ongoing level of accountability and progress. If we have found
our way into this situation it will not be easy to extract ourselves
whatever method we try, but God has called us to try to put in
our utmost effort to strive against sin.

It is important, of course, to know what the scriptures say
in terms of the boundaries for sex (it's not as though God has not
spoken His mind on this issue), but it is also very useful to have
a sense of *why* He has said it. It is not that He wants to 'spoil our
fun' as it were, it is that the gift God has given us is extremely
valuable and precious and He wants us to handle it with care and
treat it with the appropriate respect. In order to understand why
God has set a context for sex which is different from the tearing
down of barriers and taboos that the culture has undertaken we
have to understand what sex means and we have to trust God to
know what is best for us.

Sex doesn't just mean a couple 'doing what comes
naturally' or 'having a good time' in any way they please, causing
long-term damage to relationships and abusing God's gift for
short-term thrills. It certainly can mean 'having a good time'
within the context of the lives of a married couple, but it means
so much more than merely that. What we need is a 'theology' of
intimacy, so to speak, an appreciation of its massive significance
as the crowning glory of a relationship, the summing up of all
the unity that a couple shares and a celebration of the unity of
God Himself. Once we start to see in God's gift a reflection of
His character and a symbol of the unity a couple shares in the
Lord then our perception of sex can be transformed. This brings
us back to where we began this chapter – it's not (merely) about
a physical act; it *is* that, but it is so much more as well, and on all
kinds of levels.

Difficulties

Even if we manage to get the context right in the aspects we've
considered above by 'possessing our vessels' and keeping our
behaviour and thoughts within the boundaries God has set,

it doesn't mean that all will necessarily be plain sailing. For many couples there are times when the physical side of their relationship is deeply fulfilling, but there can be other times of immense difficulty and awkwardness of a kind that would have seemed inconceivable at the start.

Why is this and how can it be? A key reason is that sex is such an intimate and personal thing that deeply affects one's inner self. To reject one's partner in this area of life or to be dissatisfied with their 'performance' in some way feels to them like a rejection of *them* – all of them, their whole person. It may not be intended in this way, but this is what it feels like, and to some extent the feeling is unavoidable. One writer put it like this: "To touch my body is to touch me. To withdraw from my body is to distance yourself from me emotionally." Because sex is so intimate, to reject someone or to have a problem with someone in this area of life feels to them a hundred times more personal than to reject a concept or an idea that they might hold. This means we need to tread carefully, sensitively and lovingly when we attempt to broach any issues with our partner in this area of life and we really need to try to understand why they may feel as they do. Sex is about a shared vulnerability which enables two partners to become closer to one another than any other activity would allow – but the very vulnerability that it involves is a reminder of what is at stake. If we love our partner as we should then the way we approach any discussions of this area of married life is a great opportunity to demonstrate it.

What's important

It's been said that when the physical relationship between a couple is good it constitutes about ten per cent of what is important in a relationship. However, when there are problems in this area it can quickly become ninety per cent of what is wrong (or at least, what is perceived as wrong!). When things are going well sexually a couple tend to feel relaxed in the relationship, accepted, appreciated and involved. By contrast, if there is a problem it can become a gigantic focus, possibly being perceived as the greatest factor of disappointment. The physical side is in many ways a mirror (and sometimes a mirror with magnifying powers) of the overall health of the relationship. It celebrates what is happening (or isn't happening as the case may be) in the rest of the couple's life.

If this is right – that physical relations more frequently reflect the quality of the couple's whole relationship rather than the rest of the relationship being driven by the quality of the physical – then it would suggest that in times of difficulty, while it's certainly wise to try to communicate and be open about the physical aspects (to make one's feelings and requests understood and appreciated), it can often be better not to put *too* much focus on the physical and instead concentrate more energy on improving the overall health of the relationship, the sense of closeness and unity that pervades the whole range of the couple's interactions. Then in time, with the overall relationship in a better place, there will be ample opportunity to work on the physical (and it may automatically improve in any case). Men, in particular, can fixate on the quantity of physical intimacy they may be receiving, but to make an issue of this (as if the fixing of it is the *first* thing to work on) is often a mistake and can actually cause relations to deteriorate further.

Different needs
It's helpful to understand a bit about the different 'wiring' of males and females with respect to their sexual feelings. To a certain extent there is a physical aspect to the sex drive for a man which he feels needs to be fulfilled almost irrespective of the emotional connection he may or may not feel with his partner at any particular point in time. While intimacy will definitely be more rewarding for him as well if he is at one emotionally with his wife, this may not be a prerequisite for him. While there can certainly be this physical aspect of sex drive for a woman also (probably more contingent on her monthly cycle), in general (and of course all of this is to deal in generalisations) a woman needs to feel more emotional connectedness and oneness with

her husband in order to feel like sleeping with him in the first place. It's been said that men tend to see sex as an end in itself whereas women tend to focus on romance as a route to it – and romance requires that emotional connection we've been talking about. She needs to feel loved emotionally in order to feel like loving physically.

Once we start to to take this on board it helps to explain why focus on the overall health of the relationship – the emotional union and oneness of the man and wife – will create a much better foundation for addressing any physical issues that may have arisen (by contrast, emotional issues and discontinuities will be unlikely to be fixed purely by continued focus on the physical). Marriage counsellors sometimes say that where lack of sex has become a really serious issue in a relationship it can be best for the partners to agree simply to put this side of the relationship on a complete hold for a period of time so that there is no sense of expectation or disappointment from either party; instead, the couple should both concentrate on improving the relationship in all its many other aspects. When this has improved it will be easier to improve the physical.

Giving and getting

Before moving to some scriptural examples there are a few final practical points and guiding principles to consider.

After marriage there can be a tendency for some husbands significantly to reduce any displays of physical affection or only to be affectionate or physically close to their wives when hoping for sex. Needless to say, this is a very poor state of affairs which sends bad messages and is to be avoided at all costs. A wife needs to experience the tenderness and care of her husband throughout the relationship; starved of this she may feel reluctant to be intimate. This can deteriorate into a vicious cycle in which he then shows even less affection because he feels he isn't getting enough sex. If this situation arises it somehow has to be broken through. The husband certainly has a basis for explaining to his wife how he feels and how he would like to be close to her, but his best approach would be to take the initiative by showing her the (non-sexual) affection and appreciation that would make her feel more loved (this comes back to his responsibilities to lead in love which are part of his calling to spiritual headship). If she feels loved she is much more likely to want to be intimate with him, and if he feels respected and loved in the ways he appreciates he is likely to feel much more like the man he would like to be.

In short, effort and attention to this vital area of a marriage is necessary from both partners. While there can be times of difficulty, if both partners are making an effort to act in the spirit of Christ towards their partner within marriage there is huge scope for healing and the rebuilding of closeness when difficulties have arisen. Think for a moment about the huge effort put into conducting affairs by those who make that error; if only they were to put a fraction of that effort into improving their own relationships one wonders how much genuine improvement there could have been and how many more happier marriages.

In the majority of cases most couples *want* to be intimate in principle but for some reason or other some disruption or obstacle has intervened which is making it difficult and which means they are struggling to get in touch with those feelings. It's been insightfully put this way: "many couples who fervently desire a long hug have to make do with a new kitchen or another holiday in the Bahamas." The answer is not to add more external 'stuff' to the relationship – whether it's a holiday in the Bahamas, a new kitchen, or some other distraction. The answer instead is to work at improving the relationship from the inside – honestly and kindly to share feelings and goals which can gradually improve this important area when difficulties have arisen.

A very helpful notion is to think about sex as a way of giving rather than getting. If we can think about it less in terms of our needs and wants (that is, the selfish perspective) and more in terms of what our partner might appreciate (which can sometimes include not being intimate when we might like to be) it can be transformational. Intimacy is a form of giving ourselves away and to do so in a way that our partner will appreciate is in a sense to give our all to them. One writer put it like this: 'the total abandonment of it all (i.e., physical intimacy) is the nearest thing this side of heaven (we would revise this to 'the kingdom' of course) to the spiritual ecstasy and intimacy we will one day have with God.' This is quite a revealing and potentially transforming perspective.

Once we start to see sex as a giving to our partner rather than a taking by ourselves then it automatically rules out demeaning types of sex or practices with which one partner would feel uncomfortable. If sex is a celebration of a couple's unity then it stands to reason that both partners have to feel comfortable and want to express to one another the things that intimacy symbolises. As the Lee's put it in their book, it is committed, self-sacrificing love that will produce the best sex.

An interesting perspective which grows out of this focus on giving is to think of intimacy as an act of communication between a couple. What is it that we want to say to our partner? There is the potential of course to communicate some very bad messages of demand and control on the one hand or of coldness and lack of interest on the other. But there is also the potential to communicate a message of care, need, warmth, love, consideration, interdependence and unity – with one's mind, one's words, and one's body.

Solomon and the Shulamite

Topics: A celebration of love and unity; Mutuality in a relationship; Infatuation and the growth of love; Communication and the joy of sharing; Appreciating each other.

For all its meaning at the allegorical level concerning God and Israel and Christ and the church, on a literal plane the Song of Songs celebrates the wonder of the God-given pleasures of love in courtship and beyond. Love is a God-provided capacity and as one of the strongest forces known to human beings it should be no surprise to find a whole book devoted to this amazing aspect of human experience. Over time, more songs and poems have been written about love than any other topic, but this one stands above the rest – a divinely inspired celebration of love and all that it points forward to in the relationship of Christ and the church.

E SSENTIAL though it is to a broader perspective on the Song, our focus here will not be on the allegorical but on the plain-meaning initial application to the love of a man and a woman. To get a few introductory matters out of the way upfront, we shall be taking the view (without space to defend it, unfortunately) that the book has two main characters (the shepherd-boy and the Shulamite) not three.[1] It is not primarily a 'history' of a

---

1   Some have proposed a love-triangle between these two and Solomon, but this appears to require quite a lot of 'reading in' of a plot line into the text.

particular relationship Solomon had with a specific woman (though no doubt his many relationships deeply influenced his thoughts and feelings about love), but rather an idealisation of what love between a man and a woman can be. Why do we say an idealisation? Even in the throes of passion and infatuation the love between two sinners (as we all are) has its boundaries and limitations, for no couple is perfect in every detail and no experience unalloyed by shortcomings; there is none of that on show in the Song however as the book celebrates the wonder of all that is good and positive about love. The book doesn't have a 'plot' in the normal sense of a piece of narrative literature. Instead it is a series of vignettes, a collection of poems all closely related to one another which depict different aspects of the lovers' feelings and their relationship to one another. The poems are designed to celebrate the love of the couple and their yearnings for each other; it misses the point to look for chronological order or narrative movement.

There is organisation in the work, however. The poems are arranged around a single central section in which he calls her his bride and in which the most obvious references to the sexual consummation of their relationship occur. The term 'bride' occurs nowhere else in the Song – only in this central section (4:8-12; 5:1). Whether they actually are literally married at this point or are simply imagining it in this passage isn't entirely clear and is to some extent by the by; there is a blurring of fact and fantasy as the lovers speak about their relationship and their feelings for each other. But it is significant that the most explicit references to sexual union occur in that central poem where the term 'bride' is repeatedly used. There also seems to be some level of thematic movement in the poems regarding the references to King Solomon, but we shall get to this a little later on.

Two sides of the same coin
Who are the two lovers? He has no name, though he appears to be a shepherd; she is called simply the 'Shulamite' and appears to be a country girl, used to being out in the sun (hence the

references to her being 'dark'). The fascinating thing about this nomenclature is that 'Shulamite' looks very much like a feminine form of the term Solomon! Since this is his song ("the Song of Songs which is Solomon's") then the woman belongs to him, as it were – she is his corresponding partner, his other-half, his mate. The two were meant to be together; they are two sides of the same coin. Solomon and the Shulamite (the connection is more apparent if we put in the Hebrew form of Solomon – *Shelomo* and *Shulamiit* – note the similarity of the main consonants) together form a complete whole so that he might well say to her: "this is now bone of my bone and flesh of my flesh". She is *ishah* (woman) to his *ish* (man).

This isn't to say, however, that the young man in the story really is Solomon the king of Israel; he is instead an imaginary character, a literary projection, the Solomon of the story rather than the Solomon of real life. Real Solomon wasn't a shepherd in the literal way his father had once been, and the love he had with his many wives certainly wasn't perfect as is the love described here. This is an imaginary, idealised, simpler and purer Solomon, the Solomon he might have liked to have been: not a king with all the pomp and ceremony that entailed, but a humble and carefree shepherd. We almost sully the poetry by conceiving of it too literally; Solomon is projecting what the ideal love between a boy and a girl might be like – a relationship to which ours only approximate even though we can relate to what he envisions. Into that world Solomon re-imagines himself, transformed and simplified: he becomes an idealised version of every man, and thus the Song is both his and ours.

Playing on this connection – this 'it is and it isn't' aspect of Solomon – the lovers use the language of kingship to describe one another. This does not mean that he is *really* a king (in the story) – he is a nameless shepherd boy, and she no queen. But they exalt the significance and beauty of their love by speaking of it in regal terms; he is *her* king, as it were, and she a queen to him, even if everyone else looks at her and sees only a country girl. This is the transforming power of love in action and a wonderful example of how we should conceive of our own partners in our hearts! He describes her as a mare amongst Pharaoh's horses (1:9-11), and she calls him 'my king' (verses 12-14). The kingly fantasy continues in 3:6,7, and he later describes her as having "sat him in the most lavish of chariots" (6:12) – again this is fantasy not reality. We are dealing in the language and imagery of amazing poetry.

But while they have described each other in regal terms in order to praise each other and celebrate the significance of their love, there is a lovely passage in 8:11,12 in which the real Solomon is imagined to pass by in his royal procession and pomp. "Keep your chariots, your vineyards and your wealth" she says to the 'real' king in this imagined scene; happiness doesn't consist in those things of worldly riches and pomp, and if the real Solomon were to ask for her hand with all his wealth and power in tow she would spurn him for her shepherd. To be truly happy she needs only her humble shepherd and their love, perhaps an interesting sidelight into Solomon's own thoughts about wealth and fame, something akin to what is recorded in Ecclesiastes. For all his astronomical wealth and might and the many women with whom he became acquainted, a simple and singular love with one to whom he could truly have been united in both body and spirit would have been far more satisfying. It is this latter kind of love that the Song celebrates.

Mutuality
What is beautiful about the two lead characters being masculine and feminine forms of each other (*Shelomo* and *Shulamiit*) is that this is exactly how a relationship is supposed to be – the two halves coming together to form a unity in which each is an essential part. Life can scarcely be conceived of without the other once this has happened, so fundamental is the love which binds them.

A further dimension of this mutuality and belonging comes through in the way the couple dialogue with each other, alternating and reciprocating their speech in praising the other.

Here is an abbreviated example from the first chapter, taken from Ariana and Chana Bloch's translation:[2]

Him to her: 1:9-11

> "My love I dreamed of you
> as a mare, my very own,
> among Pharaoh's chariots …"

Her to him: 1:12-14

> "My king lay down beside me
> and my fragrance
> wakened the night …
> My love is a cluster of myrrh …
> in the vineyards of Ein Gedi."

Him to her: 1:15

> "And you, my beloved,
> how beautiful you are!
> Your eyes are doves."

Her to him: 1:16,17

> "You are beautiful, my king,
> and gentle. Wherever we lie
> our bed is green."

The beauty of it is the way they are lost in the delight of the other – a fine aspiration for married life and one's attitude to one's partner. Humans have a great propensity to be lost in *themselves*, but there is nothing of this here; if the lovers speak of themselves at all they do so only to see themselves as respondents to the other. They find joy in their reciprocation, their extolling of the other's virtues; their love has transformed them through the loss of selfish concerns and in the winning of their partner. The greater whole of their joint relationship is so much more fulfilling than the more self-focused freedom they once knew.

Another example of intertwined speech like this comes in 2:1 (her), 2:2 (him), 2:3 (her). Similarly, both partners devote

---

2   *The Song of Songs – A New Translation* (Berkeley: University of California Press, 1995).

extended poetry to the praise of the other: he of her in 4:1-15; 6:4-9; 7:1-10, and she of him in 5:10-16. This type of poetry (technically called a *wasf*) is a celebration of the other's body as item by item the other's various features are singled out for special praise ("your neck is like ...; your head is like ..."): the pair seem to have noticed every detail and there is not a blemish in sight – such is the elevating power of love!

Infatuation?

One can dismiss all this heady language as a description of '(naive) young love'; we may even have come to look back at that intense early stage of infatuation in courtship and marriage as having all been rather silly (now that one is so much older and wiser, of course!). Yet there is nothing wrong with the kind of fascination and mutual obsession the lovers have as long as the two partners are a good match (as they certainly are in the Song); it is like a God-given glue that can bind a couple together and help them on their way to their new shared life. Recalling one's own experiences of those early months or even years of being deeply in love can be a good way to identify and become comfortable with the language of the Song.

But if this is our entry pass into its world, we must conceive the Song of Songs as more than a great poem about what it feels like to fall deeply in love with someone when dating is going well and you are thinking about getting married. While the infatuation stage may be time bound (the experts say those dizzying feelings typically last between six to eighteen months), as it morphs and develops into a deeper bond there is no reason why the mutuality and reciprocity so defining of the Song's language needs to wear off even if it comes to be expressed in different ways. Physical passion may moderate to a more long-term sustainable level, perhaps, but there is more to a relationship than purely that aspect, and a couple can learn oneness and mutuality on all kinds of levels of which the physical is just one.

What we have in the Song is an idealisation of a human relationship, but it is an idealisation to be striven for in one's own life because in its turn it speaks of a spiritual relationship between God and Israel or Christ and his bride. Now the fact that this idealisation is expressed in physical terms (her neck, her breasts, his head, etc.) doesn't mean that it is *only* about the physical and that we have exhausted the poem when we recall how intensely we once felt about our wife or our husband in a physical sense when in the throes of infatuation. The physical pull the lovers attest stands for *everything* that draws a couple together – the physical, the emotional, the historical, the psychological, and the spiritual.

The praise, then, that he gives her and she gives him, their mutual longing and concern for each other, need not be something confined to 'Phase 1' of a relationship. The couple in the Song love to praise each other – as couples who start dating often do. But why should that behaviour stop? Should it be the case that a young man who once couldn't take his eyes (and perhaps his hands) off his now-wife or think or talk about anything else can now scarcely look up from what he is doing and grunt in response when she speaks to him? Should a woman who once obsessed and fantasised about being married to her man now think more about taking care of her appearance for her colleagues when she goes out to work than she does for him, or roll her eyes when he speaks about something he is interested in?

The couple in the Song *bother* to speak about each other, to compliment each other, to pick out details they find attractive in each other. They look forward eagerly – even desperately – to any time spent together and to their next meeting. They want to be everything they can for each other for they are the male and female forms of the same unity, two sides of the same coin, he the Adam to her Eve, the Christ to her bride. They belong together, she bone of his bones and flesh of his flesh; but the only way they can be like this – and continue to be like this as their lives go on – is if they make the effort to be so.

Perhaps the most powerful expression of mutuality in the Song is the following:

"My beloved is mine and I am his."   (2:16; 6:3)

This is the language of possession, but it doesn't convey any of the negative overtones of possessiveness or of treating the other as an object. It is the mutual belonging of a yin and yang, a mutual possession which meets a mutual need. We must trust ourselves to need like this, and we must endeavour reliably and consistently to be what is needed for our partner.

The unique one

It's a good idea, then, to hold up the couple in the Song not merely as an example of what we might once have felt when we were in the flush of young love, but also as a model for what we might still hope to achieve in our relationships throughout their entirety – that a man might be the sort of lover and friend that is described here, and that his wife would be the same for him. It's a goal that should be reached for in all aspects of the relationship.

Even the very terminology the lovers use to speak of one another is revealing. He is her king, her lover, her friend – at different moments, from different perspectives, and sometimes all at once. For her part she is his beloved, his sister, his spouse – nomenclature which speaks of their physical and emotional connection, the elemental knowledge and experience they share (like brother and sister), and their mutual interdependence as man and wife. These terms and others like them (it makes a great study to look out for them in the Song) speak of the different aspects of a relationship and the different things that one's partner can be in one's life – the different needs they can fill and the multifaceted nature of human relationships.

Another wonderful feature is the way in which the partners pick out each other's uniqueness as their perfect match. "What is your beloved more than another (i.e., any other) beloved?" the daughters of Jerusalem ask her. She doesn't hesitate when asked this question; she answers immediately and knows exactly what to say because she has taken the time to appreciate him and the way in which the two of them fit together so well. He similarly extols her virtues and her singularity in his sight in a way which is both affirming and captivating.

It is by making an effort in these areas as the lovers in the Song so ably do – by mutual praise and appreciation, by words and acts of consideration, by savouring the things that make our partner special and right for us, by valuing all the different aspects of life in which they enrich our lives – that we shall lift our marriages above the humdrum and mundane and transform them to something closer to their true potential. This, after all, is how we shall keep our marriages young. The Song is full of lush, verdant imagery, the language of nature and the language of spring. It is full of life, of greenery, of animals and plants – all of which speak of the fertility of the couple's love. Spiritual relationships are to be productive things, not stale and staid. It is sometimes said that you are as young as you feel and the same thought can pertain in the domain of relationships also. To keep a relationship young and fruitful is hard work, but it is time and effort well spent and so much better than a relationship in which the partners take each other for granted or do their best to pretend the other isn't there. We got married in all probability because we were in love; we owe it to both our partner, to ourselves, and to our Lord to stay that way. The Song is a wonderful evocation of just what that oneness can mean.

Shechem and Dinah

Topics: What the Bible says about sex outside marriage; The Law of Moses and its principles; Sinning 'against the body'; Symbols do matter.

Shechem and Dinah's pre-marital relationship provides a good starting point to examine the Biblical and conceptual foundations for regarding intimacy as something only to be enjoyed by a couple within marriage. In this chapter we'll be focusing particularly on the question of why pre-marital and extra-marital sex is a serious matter in God's sight.

WHILE we don't have as many details as we may like, the evidence seems to suggest that the relationship of Shechem and Dinah was built on genuine attraction and affection, not merely the desire to be self-indulgent and promiscuous. In the modern day too this is where the temptation most likely lies for the believer – it is relatively easy to demonstrate that promiscuous behaviour is offensive to God; the harder test comes when deeper emotional ties begin to be formed and a couple may start to say to themselves: 'but we are so in love; it's only natural and right to express our feelings for each other in the most intimate way – we can't help ourselves.' This is a highly dangerous argument, one which is sometimes even coupled with the claim that 'it isn't hurting anyone; it's an expression of our *love* – how can that be sinful?'

Let's examine the case of Shechem and Dinah:

"And when Shechem the son of Hamor the Hivite, prince of the country, saw (Dinah), he took her, and lay with her, and defiled her. And his soul clave unto Dinah the daughter of Jacob, and he loved the damsel, and spake kindly unto the damsel. And Shechem spake unto his father Hamor, saying, Get me this damsel to wife ... And the sons of Jacob came out of the field when they heard it: and the men were grieved, and they were very wroth, because he had wrought folly in Israel in lying with Jacob's daughter; which thing ought not to be done. And Hamor communed with them, saying, The soul of my son Shechem longeth for your daughter: I pray you give her him to wife."   (Genesis 34:2-4,7,8)

Expressions like "his soul clave" (cf. Genesis 1), "he loved the damsel", "he spoke kindly (i.e., to her heart)", "the soul of Shechem longs for (her)", coupled with his desire to marry her speak to the strength of feeling Shechem had; to his own standards we might well conclude that Shechem was honourable – he was trying to do the right thing as he saw it. For most unbelievers in the present age (and, unfortunately, for some believers too) this would constitute justification enough for a couple to sleep together. Some would even claim that a couple intending marriage or even a serious relationship should do so in order to check that they are 'sexually compatible'.

The account is clear, however: what Shechem did was 'defiling' of Dinah; he took something (her virginity) that was not his to take because they were not married. The strength of his feelings or their attraction therefore has nothing to do with it; what they did was wrong (and the blame, notably, is put at the man's door in the passage). It is a thing which "ought not to be done in Israel", a "folly", a cause of righteous anger irrespective of one's view about the course of action Jacob's sons subsequently followed.

It is instructive to compare this condemnation against what is said in the Law of Moses: there is a clear relationship even though the Law had not been given in the days of Jacob.

Leviticus 18 provides very clear guidance on various sexual relationships that are categorically 'out of bounds', Exodus 22:16,17 speaks of a couple having to marry if they sleep together before marriage (or the male providing financial compensation if the father refuses), while Deuteronomy 22:13-29 provides the most comprehensive guidance on relationships outside marriage. To explore the latter passage for a moment, various different types of extra-marital relationships are defined and corresponding penalties assigned:

- A woman who marries and is found not to be a virgin is to be stoned (verse 21).
- A man who falsely accuses his wife of not being a virgin is to be 'chastised', must pay a fine, and may not divorce the woman (verses 18,19).
- A couple committing adultery is to be stoned (verses 22-24).
- Those who sleep together when the girl is betrothed to someone else are to receive severe penalty including stoning (verses 23-27).
- A man who lies with a virgin must marry her and pay a fine (verses 28,29).

While it is true that believers are no longer under the Law with respect to carrying out these punishments, the passage is nevertheless extremely important because it clearly shows the seriousness with which God views the matter of sexual purity, there being no reason to think that this has changed. There are some particularly interesting phrases that are used: a man's sleeping with a woman in the country when there is no one to hear her is compared to murder – this is the extent of its seriousness. Similarly, those committing adultery are to be stoned – if this were a small matter in God's sight, there is no way we could conceive of this as being the punishment. For a couple consensually to have sex before marriage is to result in marriage and a fine (in other words, sexual intimacy unmistakeably belongs with marriage). If a man sleeps with a woman before marriage like this then he must marry her because he has taken something that properly belongs only in marriage; if the girl's father does not want this (a circumstance conceived of in the Exodus passage – perhaps because he thinks the man is not worthy or is otherwise unsuitable for his daughter or because he does not want to commit some of his inheritance to such a man) then the offender must make financial restitution for what he has wrongly taken. There is no way that one could look at these passages and conclude that from a divine perspective 'sex outside marriage is no big deal' or that it is somehow okay because it (allegedly) 'doesn't hurt anyone'.

Does it apply any more?

The push-back to all this could be that the Law of Moses is no longer relevant. This would be a huge mistake (it is still highly relevant even though it is not to be applied by the letter any more) – there are key passages in the New Testament that show the essential approach hasn't changed: sexual sin (which means sex outside marriage) is still sin, as the following passages make very clear:

- 1 Thessalonians 4:1-8
- 1 Corinthians 6:12-20
- Ephesians 5:3-12

These passages clearly outlaw sexual promiscuity in general but they also hint at why it matters from God's perspective. Our bodies are meant to be a temple for God; they are not intended for exploitation or self-indulgence. If we are to share them with another (other than God) then it is to be in a deep and permanent marriage commitment. To have sex with someone is not merely a physical act but is also to be 'joined' to them in a significant way, to be one with them in a way which involves the emotional, psychological and spiritual, not merely the physical (compare the quotes from Mike Mason in chapter 26). One writer put it like this: "The joining of a man and a woman sexually will always be more than a temporary physical bond. Whether we intend it or not, it affects us at a deep emotional, psychological and spiritual level … God's law prohibiting adultery is not to spoil our fun but to protect family life and to keep us from hurting each other, and ourselves." The same sentiments can be applied with respect to sleeping together before marriage.

In short the pattern is that we should be using our bodies to glorify God, not to indulge ourselves. If we have to ask during dating 'is this too far?' then it probably is. The fact that our body is a temple ought to dictate the sort of activities we are engaged in.[1]

Sinning against yourself

In Corinthians Paul talks about how inappropriate it would be to be "joined" to someone we should not be joined with or with whom we are not one in marriage. The language here clearly goes back to Genesis 1 in which 'cleaving' to one's wife is linked to becoming one flesh. Paul also talks about sexual sin as sinning "against" one's body, whereas other types of sin can be considered as more 'external to' or "without" the body. What does he mean by this?

I think it all comes back to the symbology of the body and the concept of oneness. The body isn't just a 'thing' to be treated however we choose. It represents *us*, our all, our whole person emotionally as well as physically. Because sex is an emotional and psychological act as well as a physical act, to engage in it is to engage our entire person – our very selves. Once we see it this way then sex isn't something external, something that we can 'just do' and it have no impact upon us. It is an act involving our very being, our innermost self as well as the external. In this sense, to sin here is to betray ourselves as well as our God, it is to sin "against" our body, as Paul puts it, the very temple God has given us to fill with His glory.

Furthermore, sex and marriage are fundamentally about *unity*, a concept which is so central because it is integral to the very first definition of who God is ("Hear O Israel, the LORD our God is ... *one*"). If, as we have seen elsewhere, God wants us to

---

1   For more on this topic see chapter 12.

enact His very own nature within our marriages, how can we take the fundamental symbol of it – our physical union and all that it means emotionally and spiritually – and mix and match with multiple partners or sleep with people outside of marriage? It is a betrayal of a fundamental symbol of God's identity. God wants us to be one with our marriage partner forever because *He* is one forever – from everlasting to everlasting. Our unity with our marriage partner speaks of our appreciation of *His* nature (compare the Malachi verse about marriage: "And did not He make one?", Malachi 2:15). There is one Lord, one faith, one baptism – and so the list goes on; the idea of there being only one sexual partner (and then only within the covenant of marriage) fits right in with this. Sex is fundamentally an act of oneness, and there can't be true oneness in God's sight outside the covenant of marriage.

Symbols do matter
In order to understand God's requirements around our sexual behaviour, therefore, we have to understand the symbology behind the body and behind the concept of oneness. Sexual purity – seeking for holiness in our behaviour (a term repeatedly used in the New Testament passages listed above) arises out of the oneness of God. We must never, ever say, 'But it's just a symbol – a symbol can't be so important, can it?' On the contrary, it's important *precisely because* it's a symbol – a symbol of who God is and of what He wants for all of us! Our keeping to His commandments shows our valuing of these symbols. Symbols are extremely important – think of baptism as a symbolic death, or the symbols of bread and wine. Keeping oneself for the person one is going to commit oneself to for the whole of one's life is an act of tremendous meaning, both to our partner, and to the Lord God. Of course it isn't easy – but it is worth it.

A couple of 'what if's' can arise from this discussion. We are human, of course, and periodically serious mistakes are made. While the consequences of this have to be lived with (and there is indeed an impact which we should not be so naive as to deny),

God is able to forgive even serious sins. It should be remembered though that if we have failed or not previously appreciated the real significance of our actions, we show God that we care on a going-forward basis by reforming our behaviour and not doing the same thing again. This will be particularly difficult if lines have already been frequently crossed, but it is the least we can do, surely, to show God that we care about the commandments and the symbols that He has given us and put within our power to demonstrate.

Finally, it is sometimes asked if a couple who have already committed themselves to marriage by getting engaged can go ahead and sleep together. The answer to this is 'No'. Engagement is not the same as marriage, and enough engagements are called off to know that, no matter how sure we think we are, it can and does happen. God has made it clear enough that sex is for within marriage and that outside that we should "possess our vessels". Doing so shows our commitment to and appreciation of the good commandments that God has given us and the wonderful symbology which physical intimacy acts out.

David and Bathsheba

Topics: Avoiding temptation; How affairs can happen; Risk factors to avoid; Painful consequences.

Tragic but true, affairs happen: King David was not the first and nor will he be the last. Sadly they happen too amongst believers from time to time. But why and how do they happen, and is there anything that can be done to be alert to protect oneself and one's relationship and to minimise risk? Perhaps the narrative of David and Bathsheba can provide some clues to help in answering these questions, a starting point from which they can be usefully discussed.

IT all began with a king not going with his men to war, choosing instead to remain behind at the palace. As the well known saying goes, the devil makes work for idle hands to do, David's leisure giving him space for distraction, unprofitable activities and worse. He has time on his hands and opportunity. The next detail in the narrative is that he is looking out of the window and sees a woman. He can't help this, but he can help what he does next:

> "And David sent and enquired after the woman. And one said, Is not this Bathsheba, the daughter of Eliam, the wife of Uriah the Hittite?" (2 Samuel 11:3)

At this stage it seems not so bad – he's only enquiring, after all, much like a man might see a magazine with a stunning woman on it who he doesn't recognise and takes a look to see who it is, perhaps glancing at the following pages to see if there are any more pictures temporarily to stimulate his senses.

But it is the beginning of the descent. Don't ask, David – don't pursue the thought! Look the other way, close the curtains. Get out of the situation. Do what Joseph did when Potiphar's wife takes hold of his garment.

But he doesn't. And why not? Because he *enjoys* looking; he's intrigued, he wants to know more about this possibility even before his action is fully hatched, getting closer to this new source of fascination if he possibly can, wondering about what might be. And soon it is too late.[1]

Temptation

It's unlikely that most of us would face temptation in quite the same way as David does here. Even if we did see a Bathsheba nude or scantily clad, it is unlikely that she would respond to our summons as she did to a king. There can occasionally be circumstances, however, where temptation is overtly sexual and 'in our face' in this sort of way: Joseph's example with Potiphar's wife is a classic case, his response in leaving his garment in her hand and fleeing a fine lesson in how seriously we should treat such temptation, no measure too drastic for getting ourselves out of there as quickly as possible (interestingly the Genesis text states no less than four times that this is what he did – an astonishing emphasis!). Once one's mind has dawdled and flirted

---

1   We might also ask what Bathsheba is doing bathing in this manner in at least semi-public view (or perhaps David's palace occupied an elevated position in the city so that only he could see?). Since we don't know anything about the position of the buildings and washing facilities in the vicinity such lines of reasoning are speculative and it might be best to take a 'presumed innocent until proven guilty' approach as far as Bathsheba is concerned (in either case David's actions are not justified and it is clearly David whose sin is focused on in both the narrative and in the Psalms). It remains a valid point that it is helpful if women are aware of the way in which provocative appearance may incite lust in men and take appropriate steps not to play on this.

with the possibility of sin, it may already be too late, such can be the weak will of man. It is better to be honest with ourselves at the first sign of danger and take evasive action.

There are certain types of places where such stark temptation is more likely to occur (clubs and the like) and there are certain states (alcohol or drugs the obvious enemy) where we shall be all the more susceptible. Sexual sin is serious and temptation strong, particularly in the modern cultural environment, so the smart thing to do is minimise every possible risk factor, not assume we are strong enough to handle it. Joseph shows us the way to go.

More often though, the temptation for an extra-marital affair or a pre-marital liaison does not begin with nudity, nor does it start in the bedroom. It begins more subtly, often perfectly innocently, but ends up where it should not. If this is so, is there anything we can do to spot danger signs and know when to take action to curtail the risk of falling into temptation?

How do affairs start?

Initial physical attraction can be a trigger, but such attraction grows more often from a seed of a thought in the mind which is allowed to germinate and receive mental nurture rather than by some overwhelming and irrepressible force that sweeps over us seemingly beyond our control. The apparently innocuous initial thought develops into something dangerous when we allow our minds to play with possibilities, indulging in speculation, allowing ourselves to be captivated and intrigued by the other person's every detail and gesture.

Flirtatious behaviour can trigger or exacerbate these feelings of possibility. Flirting may well be fun, but it is a dangerous game for married people to engage in, one whose consequences can be relationship shipwreck, permanently harming the lives not just of the couple themselves, but also children, parents, friends, and brothers and sisters. We can soon find our minds entrapped into fascination with someone, mesmerised, seemingly, beyond our control, unable any longer, we may feel, to get the off-limits person out of our thoughts, our desires so much harder to control than we had thought. To be blasé about these things, to think that it's no big deal and that we are strong, is to court disaster.

But sometimes – perhaps often – it is not the physical side at all where problems begin. The writer Voddie Baucham has an interesting discussion about the nature of intimacy (he's using the term not as a euphemism for sex but instead in the non-sexual sense of close knowledge of someone, things shared between two people which are not shared with others, confidences divulged and exchanged, a personal detail, experience or reminiscence revealed and entrusted to another). It involves vulnerability, trusting someone enough to take the risk of being emotionally exposed and finding this act of daring met by understanding on the other side, an exchange which is shared but goes no further.

The point is that once you have been intimate with someone of the opposite sex at this level (again, we're talking about shared thoughts and confidences not anything sexual at this point) it creates a bond, an intimacy, which is real and which can soon be extended into other arenas. A man chats to a colleague at the water cooler, they exchange pleasantries, and over the coming weeks and months they keep bumping into each other periodically. It begins completely harmlessly – perhaps they have some shared meetings and find they have some interests or experiences in common. They seem to be on the same wavelength, they chat some more, gradually sharing more of themselves, not with any intent (though each has noticed the other is not unattractive), but simply because they enjoy talking and they seem to understand one another. She listens to him, and he to her, in a way that perhaps their partners at home no longer seem to do, she appears to admire what he's doing at work, and she is so well turned out (compared to his wife's casual clothes when he gets home) and so considerate.

And now it is starting to happen. He finds himself recounting some detail from his past and then observing 'Funny, I've never told anyone that before', and she shares something about her marriage which is not going so well, and how she wishes circumstances were different. This is intimacy. You can guess where it is headed unless one of them takes action quickly by denying themselves the pleasant feelings the new relationship is giving them. But why should they do that? Why should they desist? It feels so good to be understood and to share, and there isn't any physical aspect to their relationship – they haven't done anything wrong, have they?

Of course they can indeed reason like that, but if they do they are naive and foolish. This sharing of oneself, this developing intimacy, is something which is highly dangerous to share with anyone of the opposite sex who is not your partner, because very soon there may be a touch, and then another, and ultimately desire for intimacy of the other sort (which you can be sure, by this stage, at least one of them has already thought about).

Does it mean we shouldn't talk to people of the opposite sex if we are married? Of course not. But we should be aware of the dangers, of the strength of desire that can grow from a small seed, and of the weakness of the mind. We should be wise enough to spot when a friendship is crossing through the boundary of friendship and into intimacy, when too much confidence is shared and when danger therefore looms. Adultery usually doesn't begin in the bedroom; it begins in intimacy of conversation, in too much of oneself being shared and too great a closeness being allowed to develop into a oneness of mind. Very soon you have persuaded yourself that you have found it at last: your soulmate, the one who understands you better than you understand yourself (and so much better than your partner, it goes without saying). How could you have been living unfulfilled for so long, only to find at last this near-perfect person with the same needs as you, free of all the failings of your partner and the encumbrance of the mundanities of daily life? Of course this reasoning is foolish and unrealistic, but it doesn't necessarily stop us thinking that way if we have allowed ourselves to get into this position of intimacy in the first place.

Risk factors

Doctors speak of risk factors which make heart disease, cancer or diabetes more likely – it doesn't mean that if you tick the boxes on the risk factors you are assured to get one of those conditions, but it makes you much more vulnerable. It can be helpful to think in a similar way about risk factors related to affairs and adultery.

The obvious one is the physical – if a couple do not have a good physical relationship where they feel both loved, cared for and safe, then they will be much more vulnerable to the temptation of this being provided elsewhere. The Apostle Paul knew what he was talking about when he commanded couples not to "defraud" one another (strong language this! 1 Corinthians 7:4,5) with respect to sexual relations, but to ensure that if there was a period of abstinence (only justified on grounds of spiritual dedication – rarely the reason for sexual abstention in marriages today), that the couple join together again. A mutual understanding of each other's needs will work better than belligerent insistence here.

It is not just about sex, however. Other physical manifestations of intimacy – holding hands, a hug, whatever it may be – are important in reassuring each other that we are loved and cherished. If this has disappeared from a marriage then either partner (yes, it is important to men as well as women) will be more readily open to accept or seek this warmth elsewhere. It sends a terrible message if the only time we touch, hold or are otherwise tender to our partner is when we want sex; our relationship is in a much better place if signs of warmth and closeness of all types – physical, verbal and practical – are often present, with both partners bearing the responsibility of ensuring that they are.

But being intimate is about more even than this, more than merely the physical. If a couple rarely talks to each other, if that sharing and confiding aspect of close, attentive conversation has disappeared from a relationship, then something very precious has been lost and no amount of effort should be considered too large to recover it. We are no more two, but one flesh as married partners – yet how can we be one if we only mumble or mutter at each other about what's for dinner or whether or not the dog has had his walk, refusing or unable to share our inner selves in openness and in confidence, that connection broken down? In this state both our and our partner's risk factors for discontent and therefore the susceptibility to temptation will be running very high; we would be wise to try to take preventative action before the danger signs grow larger. We have a responsibility not only to keep ourselves pure but also to help our partner to do the same.

Consequences

The consequences of an affair can be devastating, as David and many others have discovered to their cost. By God's grace David was forgiven and was able to put his life back together again in a measure, even continuing his relationship with Bathsheba as his new wife. The point is that things were never really the same again – they can never be once an affair has taken place. The sin was forgiven by God, but the consequences were not taken away. Similarly at the human level the most deeply wronged partner may find it within themselves to forgive, but they may not feel they can continue to share a roof with that person, particularly in a case where the unfaithfulness is persistent, compulsive or unrepentant. Even if they can, the level of trust that once existed between the couple has in all likelihood suffered permanent damage; the relationship is unlikely to be the same again for either of them, even if the one is able to forgive and muddle through.

There were certainly ramifications of the sin in later life as far as David was concerned. Some of the later problems in his family life feel as though they are in some measure orchestrated by God; others seem to reflect David's lack of confidence in dealing appropriately with issues in his family because he was too conscious of his own failings, his reluctance to take a stand (for instance in dealing with Amnon and then Absalom) reflecting a sense that he was in no position to judge. While we can have sympathy for this if it is indeed how he felt, we cannot allow sins of the past to paralyse us from future action. If one has done wrong oneself it ought not to lead either to the extreme of harshness and intolerance with others (perhaps a reflection of the fact we are still angry with ourselves), or to a lack of ability to take any stand at all lest we be hypocrites. We can still recognise and stand against sin while being all too painfully aware that it has claimed us as its victim also. We can and must stand up for the standards God has set while at the same time recognising both how weak flesh is and our universal need to seek always the forgiveness of our Lord.

Human lives are messy; many things happen which are far below the ideals that God has set. It is worth reflecting, however, that where the love and forgiveness of God is felt and put into practice there is always hope. If both partners are willing to try again to love one another and put godly principles into action in their lives and into their relationship there is always the prospect of rebuilding what has been broken. Our God is a God who can bring good even out of the evil of human sin where He is sought for and given opportunity to work. We can see this too in David's example. There was some good that God was able to bring out of a sin even as grievous as this: "And David comforted Bathsheba his wife … and she bare a son, and he called his name Solomon: and the LORD loved him", not to mention the composition of Psalms like 38 and 51 which have been an inspiration and source of hope for believers struggling through their own weaknesses and imperfections ever since.

David and Michal (2)

Topics: Arguments; Unreasonable accusations; Responses count; Withholding intimacy as a 'punishment'; Sex and power; Caring for each other.

We first looked at David and Michal back in chapter 9. The 'fairy tale' nature of their pairing which looked so good on paper unfortunately did not last. The incident of David's dancing mightily before the Lord as Michal despises him from her window marks the effective 'break-up' of their relationship as unified husband and wife and probably shows that they were never truly on the same page spiritually speaking. In this chapter we shall examine the row they had about David's dancing before thinking about its longer-term fallout. The broken emotional and spiritual unity between the couple led to the breakdown of their physical unity as well.

L ET'S watch, first of all, as Michal confronts David about his behaviour:

"Then David returned to bless his household. And Michal the daughter of Saul came out to meet David, and said, How glorious was the king of Israel to day, who uncovered himself to day in the eyes of the handmaids of his servants, as one of the vain fellows shamelessly uncovereth himself! And David said unto Michal, It was before the LORD, which chose me before thy father, and before all his house, to appoint me ruler over the people of the LORD, over Israel: therefore will I play before the LORD ... Therefore Michal the daughter of Saul had no child unto the day of her death."   (2 Samuel 6:20-23)

There is a big contrast between Michal and David at the start of this passage. David comes home from having worshipped God in wonderful spirits; he has shared his overflowing joy by a generous gift and blessing to all his subjects, and now he returns home with the intention to bless his household also. Twice in his speech to Michal he mentions that his dancing was "before the LORD"; it was a matter between him and God first and foremost, and anyone else who happened to be there to witness what went on was merely incidental to the scene. Michal, by contrast, comes out to David with some of the most memorable sarcasm to be found in the scriptures; she doesn't mention the Lord at all. David is clearly in the right in what he has been focused on and is now returning to do; she, by contrast, doesn't relate to his passionate relationship with God or respect him enough to allow him to have it in peace. Flushed with anger, nor does she have any appreciation for his desire now to come home to bless his family. Before he has chance to explain his actions or convey any of the positive spirit he is bringing home she is on to him with her aggressive and insulting attack.

Responses count

But what of David's response? Up to this point David is clearly in the right and she in the wrong. But Michal's anger and biting sarcasm seems to have riled David and provoked him into saying more than he needs to say in standing his ground. Everything he says is true, but while he should certainly vigorously defend his fervour towards God, does he really need to put her down by emphasising that God has chosen him before her father and before all the people? It's true of course, but does he need to say it? Anyone who has had an argument with their partner will know that sometimes there are things which, while they might be true, are not conducive, let us say, to swifter reconciliation.

Sometimes there are things which are better left unsaid, whether or not they are technically correct.

It's an interesting situation in which a person who seems to be in the right in an argument puts themselves in the wrong by the way they respond (as far as we can judge – clearly this is to make an interpretation which could be mistaken). To refuse his duties as husband for all time from this point forward because she has insulted him is to escalate the matter very significantly. It shames her and destroys the oneness that is meant to exist between them as a married couple. It is true that she has already harmed that oneness by her attitude and her attack on him, but he escalates it and renders it permanent by transferring their emotional and spiritual lack of unity into the physical domain as well.

In David and Michal's case, then, there was no reconciliation. The statement that Michal had no child to the day of her death seems to imply David refused to sleep with her from this point on as a punishment for what she did. While we cannot be certain what to make of this, it is doubtful that it counts amongst the list of David's positives: he insists that Michal return to him as his wife by leaving her interim husband (2 Samuel 3:14-16), but in light of this dancing incident he now refuses his marital obligation towards her (we might wonder whether he would have abstained so readily had he not had numerous other wives). The fact that David's spiritual action (dancing) has been met with an unspiritual response (confrontational sarcasm) would not seem to justify a retaliatory course of action for which Michal has no recourse. David seems to have allowed the disagreement to reduce his own behaviour from a spiritual high to a humiliating power play; it is perfectly true that 'she started it', but in any given situation, no matter the origin, we must try to do what is right. What we see here is that both parties have backed themselves into corners from which it will be hard if not impossible to retreat. The marriage spirals inevitably downwards.

Issues with intimacy

Scripture brings all kinds of uncomfortable issues to the fore and invites readers to reflect on them, even if they would rather not do so. Here is an example of the withholding of intimacy as punishment or retaliation, the use of sex as a means of exerting power or control – one of the most precious God-given bonds being used as a weapon for one to harm the other. It is a very, very dangerous path to go down because it only escalates and exacerbates, never solves. It brings pain, disharmony, resentment and frustration, causing a marriage further harm and putting it in danger of starting to crumble under its own weight.

While David's is an example of a man withholding intimacy from his wife, the more common case might be the inverse, a natural enough consequence of the different way men and women are wired with respect to their physical needs considered in chapter 26. While this withholding can be deliberate, it can also be completely unintentional, though still a consequence of something underlying which is wrong in the relationship. It is an example of the way sexual relations in marriage are often a mirror or even an amplifier of the general health of the relationship: if things are going well, intimacy will tend to be present and rewarding; if they are not, there may well be disappointment and long absence which can develop into a vicious circle.

What can be done if this is the case? Paul spoke very clearly about the responsibility of both partners to one another with regard to physical oneness, so there is no doubt that it is a very important matter (we shall look at this in a moment). Yet while both partners should be prayerfully aware of and discuss these verses, it is no help for the brother to stab his finger at them and demand intimacy from his wife (or vice versa). Both partners need to understand each other's wishes, submitting to one another in their common needs but also in their differences. A woman needs to understand the reality and regularity of man's physical desire (the 'burning' as Paul puts it); a man has to understand that his wife needs to be loved and to *feel* loved and close in order to want to be intimate with him. Insisting on one's 'rights' when one has made little effort to be worthy of them is hardly the way for a husband to proceed – in fact, it may well bespeak the kind of attitude which has provoked the other partner to try to 'reclaim' control by withholding sex (whether consciously or otherwise) in the first place.

Sex and power

Sometimes sex can be about power or the lack of it. A man can feel that he has certain physical needs and that, if he is married, he has an entitlement or 'right' to see those addressed. Sometimes he can press this 'need' too strongly with insufficient concern for his wife and her needs, and it becomes a power play. For her part, she may feel she is being overpowered by his needs, or that she needs to reclaim power – perhaps by withholding sex – because she feels her emotional needs in the relationship are not being met.

It goes without saying that this is not how it should be. The Apostle Paul talks about this very matter in 1 Corinthians 7, interestingly choosing to use the language of power in his discussion. His dramatic and redefining move is to assign the power to the opposite partner in this matter:

"The wife hath not power of her own body, but the husband: and likewise also the husband hath not power of his own body, but the wife."   (1 Corinthians 7:4)

Three points are of interest here. First, Paul subverts 'male dominance' (the usually stronger male need) that can sometimes seem to drive this issue because he assigns power to the wife, saying that she has 'rights' over him! It's not about what he does or doesn't feel like doing, then, but what she feels like doing with him. This would have brought Paul into very harsh conflict with the cultural norms of the day in which the husband would normally have been thought to have control over his wife (one can almost imagine the males in Paul's audience, too steeped in the prevailing culture, shaking their heads in disbelief.

But of course Paul doesn't merely assign power to the woman; he also assigns the same responsibility to the husband over the wife's body. In doing so, some might have considered him to have ducked out of the issue – by saying the reciprocal thing about male and female bodies and the other partner's power it might be thought that the two things have cancelled one another out and he has ended up saying nothing. But that simply isn't the case at all. What he has done is to exalt and foreground the idea of mutuality and reciprocity: to say, in effect, 'it's not about *you* and *your* needs; it's about *them* and *theirs* (that is to say, the partner's)'. If two partners in a relationship can only learn to think graciously this way instead of being frustrated when sex isn't happening on the one hand (on his part, perhaps), avoiding it or going through with it reluctantly or with a bad spirit (sometimes, perhaps, on hers), then the relationship would see a wonderful improvement in many aspects, not just in the bedroom.

The third point is that the mutuality that Paul advises here is the very thing we saw so beautifully acted out in the Song of Songs in chapter 27. It's clear that the couple of the Song would not have had the kind of issues we are discussing here. How do we know? Because they are the perfect illustration of reciprocity, he hers and she his! Paul would never have needed to tell the shepherd and the Shulamite that they each had 'power' over the other's body, because that's exactly how it was for them – they each wanted to give the other that power and along with it their everything.

Difficulties with intimacy may well be a feature of a marriage at some point or other, but they are often the symptom or corollary of some other issue, difficulty or misunderstanding within a marriage which also (or probably first) needs to be prayerfully discussed and resolved. There are occasions when professional advice and counselling can prove helpful, but it can also be comforting to know that many couples have experienced challenges at some point in their discipleship, and that many have been able prayerfully to work through them – sometimes the shared resolution even leading to a greater closeness and depth of feeling than existed before. As with all things in marriage, the principles of self-sacrifice and of considering the other and their needs are very important. This is something that should apply in *both* directions; it is not just about the man's needs, or just about how the woman feels – it is about both of these things and more: it is about *mutual* submission. The fine spiritual standards of unity and love to which we all aspire as disciples can be a tremendous source of help and encouragement as we work through our human foibles and strive to appreciate as best we can in our fallen state the wonderful gift that God has given us.

Part 6
Children and family

31 |

God's work in the family

Topics: The family in God's purpose; The consequences of parenting across the generations; The father as a model of God the supreme Father; The key influence of the mother; Expecting respect from our children; Spiritual education; Brainwashing and indoctrination; Secular education.

The topic of bringing up children could well be a book in its own right so our purpose here must be modest: to examine the lives of a handful of Biblical couples from whom we can take some guiding principles in terms of the purpose and place of children within the family and the critical role parents have in a child's care, upbringing and education. In this first chapter we'll selectively introduce some of these themes.[1]

THE first point to note is that God's mode of working has always involved the family. He began with Adam and Eve, blessing them and telling them to be fruitful and multiply. When He called Abraham He was not calling merely Abraham but also Sarah and, in time, Isaac, and through him Jacob – and ultimately the entire children of Israel. Indeed, their very name as a people – the *children* of Israel – uses family terminology. Believers today are similarly labelled sons and daughters (of God) – He is our Father and we are brothers and sisters of one another and of

---

1 For further treatments of this topic see Don and Ellen Styles, *Family Life in the Lord* and *Preparing a 'godly seed': Scriptural and Practical Advice on Family Life Today* (ed. John Nicholls and Mark Vincent; *The Testimony* Special Issue, June / July 2006); also available online.

Christ as our elder brother. The concept of family is fundamental to the whole of God's working.

While modern societal trends cut against the grain of all this with the increasing number of broken homes, multiple sets of parents and half-siblings and the growing atomisation of the family, God's family pattern remains the model for believers. If you were brought up as a believer just think about the importance of family and parental influence in your own life. In my case (and just to stick to my father's side of the family by way of illustration), when my unbelieving grandparents on my father's side attended a preaching campaign in Leamington Spa back in the 1930s they were not only making a decision that influenced their own lives; instead, through their actions and the way they passed on their beliefs to their children God has called not only them, but also their seven children and beyond them grandchildren which thankfully included me and my two brothers, and through them another six children (so far!). This serves to emphasise that the way my grandparents responded has turned out to be key not only for them but for others of their descendants also; its impact of their decision and the way they chose to pass on the pattern of belief within their family has by God's grace been far-reaching. How they brought their children up has implicitly ended up being felt down the generations, not only by their own immediate children but by later generations they have never even met.

This is quite powerful as a way of reminding oneself of the serious responsibility of parenting. There are times after a hard day's work and the various rigours and stresses of life that one would really rather have the night off and have the children be entertained and occupied by others – but while the occasional break can be refreshing and invigorating – particularly if mum and dad get to spend some quality time together – repeatedly to opt out or outsource to electronic devices and the media is to pass up on an immense opportunity and responsibility that God has given. It is very easy nowadays to subcontract childcare to the media, to technology and to entertainment devices of one sort or another – but these things will not teach our children what God is like and what life is really for, or give them love, instruction and encouragement; that is *our* job. Similarly, the more we outsource – whether to TV, the internet, clubs, friends' homes, day care, nannies or after-school activities – the more we may have to compensate to ensure a good spiritual diet and atmosphere is maintained. It's not that any of those things are intrinsically wrong, but we need to think in a non-naive way about their place and consequences.

Father and mother

How will a child learn what God is like? It will be through what his parents tell him about God and what they show him through their own personal example. If one of the primary metaphors for God is as a Father, then we can rephrase the question: 'How will a child know what a father is like?' Now the answer is obvious, it will be through what he sees and knows of his own father. Once we have said this it is immediately obvious just how important the example of the child's father truly is – his father gets the honour of being the child's first 'model' for what God is like. If his own father is short-tempered, unreasonable, inattentive or apt to strike then this is in first place what the child may start to think of God. By contrast, if his own father is to be admired – if he is wise, patient, kind, supportive, strong, fair, forgiving – then the child will have a great starting point for his understanding of God. What an amazing honour it is for a human father to carry this responsibility of being a living, working model for his child of a greater father, a Father in Heaven.

This point is so important that it is worth turning it the other way round also: if God is the ultimate Father, what does this tell us about what a human father should be like in dealing with his children? We have only to think of His overwhelming love and forgiveness, His faithfulness, mercy, truth and justice to begin to appreciate the scale of personal witness and integrity that is called for from a human father. God is not arbitrary or 'moody'; He is consistent and sure and infinitely reliable; He is never too busy to bother with His children – His door is always open; so this is how a human father should be.

Elsewhere we have also considered the father's responsibility in setting the spiritual direction for his family – of saying, as Joshua said, "As for me and my house, we will serve the LORD". God had confidence in Abraham that he would take just this approach, a fact to which He bore witness just prior to the destruction of Sodom:

> "And the LORD said, Shall I hide from Abraham that thing which I do; seeing that Abraham shall surely become a great and mighty nation, and all the nations of the earth shall be blessed in him? For I know him, that he will command his children and his household after him, and they shall keep the way of the LORD, to do justice and judgment; that the LORD may bring upon Abraham that which he hath spoken of him."
>
> (Genesis 18:17-19)

This tribute stands as a great challenge to all fathers who have come since – could God say the same thing about *us*, and is there anything we could change to make the answer to that question more certain in the affirmative? A father dare not think he can subcontract his role to anyone else while he engrosses himself in his career or hobbies; there is a vital responsibility to be discharged.

Turning to the mother, her role in the influencing and raising of children is of course equally central, if not more important. We've already had cause to consider the significance of the woman's role as "mother of all living": the responsibilities of childbirth in Genesis and the way these are picked up in the New Testament. Paul explains that the wife has particular 'inward-facing' responsibilities with respect to the household and her children (chapter 33 and also 4 and 19). Meanwhile the description of the Virtuous Woman makes it plain that these *internal* responsibilities as she "looks to the ways of her household" will involve her in all kinds of *externally-*facing activities. We'll further consider the responsibilities of motherhood in the next chapter.

Proper respect

As father and mother, parents are entitled to the respect of their children. It goes without saying that they need to show themselves worthy of that respect, but it is scripturally right that children should look up to, honour and depend on their parents. This idea is enshrined in the Ten Commandments and rendered emphatic by the association of a special promise as Paul himself points out (Ephesians 6:2):

> "Honour thy father and thy mother: that thy days may be long upon the land which the Lord thy God giveth thee."
>
> (Exodus 20:12; cf. Deuteronomy 5:16)

This responsibility of children to honour their parents is not a small matter as is emphasised not only by this passage but also many other scriptures along the same vein (Leviticus 19:3; Proverbs 1:8,9; Matthew 15:4; Colossians 3:20). Parents must make plain to their children that they expect and require their respect and their obedience, even if this goes against the spirit of the times in which all authority including parental authority is questioned or regarded with suspicion. While we want to be close with our children and to have fun with them, they are not primarily our 'mate' or our 'buddy'; we have been placed in charge and in that sense we are not their equal. Children naturally want to look up to, admire and respect their parents (even though they will test our authority and character from time to time!), so focusing on setting them the best example we can while quietly and calmly showing that we expect their obedience on the occasions when this is needed is the best way to proceed.

One point which is specifically singled out in the New Testament regarding fathers is that they should not "provoke their children to anger" (Ephesians 6:4; Colossians 3:21), a warning serious enough that it behoves all fathers to consider whether there are any ways in which they may unnecessarily or unreasonably be doing this. One sure-fire route is by being domineering, allowing the child no freedom to think for itself and show responsibility. Being a father is not a power play; for most of their formative years we are already bigger and more powerful than they and we do not have to demonstrate the fact constantly; we should earn the respect we would hope to have from our children not force them into kowtowing or obeying a myriad artificial rules we create so that they know who's boss. Another ready route to their anger and possibly their ultimate despising of us is if we are hypocrites. Making them do things we don't do ourselves or expecting them to show attitudes which are contrary to the spirit of our own lives is infuriating for them and over time terribly destructive. Christ never commanded his disciples to do things he would not do or had not already done himself; his model of leadership was not that of a dictator – it was a leading by loving example, his natural authority speaking for itself and only rarely needing to be pressed. As fathers we are in charge of our children and there will be occasions when we need to be firm and to discipline, but most of the time a calm word, reasoned explanation, and most of all leading by example will be what is required to earn their respect and obedience.

An education

Time now to think a little about the content and nature of what we teach and show our children. There are several passages from the Law which are pertinent, and here is one of them:[2]

"Hear, O Israel: The LORD our God is one LORD: and thou shalt love the LORD thy God with all thine heart, and with all thy soul, and with all thy might. And these words, which I command thee this day, shall be in thine heart: and thou shalt teach them diligently unto thy children, and shalt talk of them when thou sittest in thine house, and when thou walkest by the way, and when thou liest down, and when thou risest up. And thou shalt bind them for a sign upon thine hand, and they shall be as frontlets between thine eyes. And thou shalt write them upon the posts of thy house, and on thy gates."

(Deuteronomy 6:4-9)

---

2   Compare also Deuteronomy 11:18-20. This passage, along with 6:4-9 quoted above form a 'frame' around the material in Deuteronomy 6-11.

No sooner has the paradigmatic statement concerning God's nature been made ("Hear O Israel ... The LORD our God, the LORD is one") and its individual implications emphasised ("thou shalt love him with all thine heart ..."), the very next point is that one's children should be taught to do the same. The words of the Law which God is revealing are not just to be 'taught' but 'taught diligently' – they are to be spoken about as a natural and foundational part of daily life: when sitting, when walking, when resting and when getting up. There are no exceptions to this, no 'ifs and buts' – this is simply what one must do. Daily life is to be about God: it is to impact all one's actions and all one's seeing; when we go out we are to remind ourselves that we are His ambassadors and when we return we are to remember that our home is to be a home not just for ourselves but for God as well.

It's quite clear what the scriptures are saying here in terms of our responsibilities to educate our children in spiritual matters; it is to be our first priority – *nothing* comes before it. Two matters arise from this, the first in relation to the question of brainwashing and the second with regard to education and skills of other kinds. Taking the brainwashing matter first of all: it is not a matter of hiding what others and what society in general believes; we would want our children to understand this so that they can interact effectively with others and so the beauty of what we have stands in contrast to the hollowness of the alternatives (for example: mindless matter coming from nowhere and going nowhere, with no meaning to be attached to any of it on one world-view). It is not about brainwashing, it is about telling them the truth and the reasons for it. Let us be very clear: the education systems of our time will not teach our children the truth about God; to the extent that they teach religion at all it is likely to be in a wishy-washy 'some think this, some think that' kind of way which is unlikely to persuade anyone and makes people believe that it is up to them what is true. One of the beauties of what we have is that it is not blind faith such as is necessary for some religions; there is sound evidence for it which we would want to show our children.

Similarly, we should also be clear that there is no 'neutral' position. The culture and its education system have already taken a view; science has already been confused as being corrosive to religion, and the perspectives of materialism and naturalism have taken hold. These views state or imply that there is no logic behind, no evidence for, and no need of the supernatural or anything beyond matter itself; on this view nature is 'the whole show' and there is no need for God. Those who want Him can invent Him if they wish but there could be no real evidence that could support their position (so we are told) – just personal opinion. Of course the point about this is that it is of itself a faith-position – naturalism and materialism are metaphysical positions which are assumed as dogmas and rarely questioned; the atheist world-view is a faith-position because it can never be proven; the question is whether the evidence points towards it or whether it points to the Biblical God.

The culture, then, does more than its fair share of indoctrination; it does not present a 'neutral' position because it has already assumed naturalism, evolution and a disjunction between religion and science. But it is these views of the culture which have led in a very significant degree to the secularism of our time and the moral values it has generated. It is not, then, as if we can send our children merrily to school for them to be innocently and neutrally presented with the evidence on both sides with respect to scientific, metaphysical, cultural or moral matters; no, they will be 'brainwashed' (if we want to use that term) with the approach of the day. It is not a matter of being a conspiracy theorist about this; it's simply a matter of understanding the spirit of the times we are in and the prevailing world-views it upholds – we should expect nothing less than that the culture should do this, and since society at large doesn't believe that God has anything of direct relevance and certain truth to say about these matters then we know our children will get a human view which represents the cultural and educational leaders of the day. In that light we have a massive responsibility to tell them the truth and why we hold it to be the truth so that as they come to be responsible for their own outlook and decisions they can make a fair choice between God and man.

A second topic to discuss is our attitude to other aspects of education. We may observe that Daniel and his three friends went through Nebuchadnezzar's three year 'education' programme for the top echelons of his civil service and the Bible shows us a multitude of examples of men and women of faith engaged in all kinds of careers from the small to the great. There is nothing to be frightened of, then, as long as we put faith in God first and let that be the yardstick against which all else is judged. Knowing about God and having faith in Him should always be the first priority, but as long as obviously inappropriate forms of learning and careers are avoided this doesn't preclude the acquiring of other knowledge and skills – indeed we are expected to work to eat and to use the skills and talents God has given us as we see in the scriptures. Daniel and his three friends retain their distinctiveness as they pass through their worldly education by choosing an aspect of life (in this case their daily diet) where they will make a deliberate distinction in their behaviour and which will be a constant reminder to them that in the most important sense they answer to God rather than to the king of Babylon.

The phrases used of Joseph, David and Jesus as they were growing up are very telling: that they grew in stature and in favour with both God and man (Genesis 39:2,3; 1 Samuel 18:5; Luke 2:40). Though their dedication to God and to spiritual matters was never in doubt, they appear not to have been perceived as 'religious freaks'. The fact that they found favour with men as well as God indicates that they were all-rounders – they worked hard in their daily activities, they were trustworthy, diligent, quick and responsive as well as servants of God. They seem to have been 'well-adjusted' children, teens and young men, as we would say today – not recluses who were 'holier than thou' or stood apart just for the sake of it, but instead people who knew how to engage with and relate to others. They were 'well-adjusted' in the typical sense that phrase is used, but they were 'God-adjusted' as well which is even more important. Paul's "all things to all men" comes to mind here, an approach which allows us to interact, help and witness to others which is a core part of God's plan. There is nothing wrong, then, with acquiring learning and skills – social as well as intellectual. In fact, it is to be encouraged as long as there is the proper context that in everything God and the seeking of His kingdom come first. Education, careers and business may well enable us to live and eat and they may even be enriching and fulfilling – but they will never (or must never) take the place of the meeting of our spiritual needs through fellowship with God. The sooner we help our children understand this the better; there is a danger we become more focused on their academic, sporting or musical success than they, driving them on to greater and greater accomplishment as if this were the thing that mattered most. But it is whether or not they are learning to be in tune with God which is far more important and where we should focus even more of our attention.

Children also need to have fun, of course. One of the pictures of the kingdom is of children playing in the streets of Jerusalem – there is no one wagging the finger at them for not learning their memory verses in this scene. There is a place for both memory verses (for example) *and* playing, whereas to be always in serious mode – always pressing scriptural learning and rote – can drive them away. Children do love facts and obscure details of all kinds so there is plenty for them to get their teeth into as they grow in their experience of the scriptures, but there is also a time for enjoying other things that humans do and that children do particularly well – like creativity, humour, enjoying God's world, going on adventures, playing games and having fun. It's keeping the balance between all these things which is the great art.

POSTSCRIPT

In writing this and the following chapters about children and family I am very conscious of those couples who would like to have children but have not been blessed by God in that direction and instead have a different calling. It can be extremely painful emotionally for couples to face this situation – one only has to think of Hannah, of Sarah, Rebekah, Rachel, Elisabeth or Manoah's wife to be brought face to face with the sorrow to which it can give rise. The scriptural examples just cited end in a happy resolution, however, whereas not all instances do – whether in Biblical or modern times. Hannah's prayer or Isaac's entreating of the Lord for Rebekah show us that we should certainly take this matter to God in fervent prayer, but ultimately He must be trusted to decide what is best and right for us, difficult though this may be. It is a wonderful thing that as a family in Christ there are very real possibilities for working closely with children and young people and experiencing something of the blessings of family, but of course this is not the same experience as having children that are physically one's own. Adoption is one option that can be prayerfully evaluated; another is to regard the absence of children as an opportunity to serve in other ways. Much as Paul says regarding the benefits of the single life it can be the case that marriage without children presents opportunities for service not available to those with children, but clearly this does not make the sadness of not having children for those who would easier to bear. For a very helpful treatment of this topic see Nigel Bernard's article "'And they had no child' – A Scriptural Consideration of Childlessness", Testimony, May 2002 (available online).

Tamar, Er and Onan

Topics: Children as part of God's purpose; "Be fruitful and multiply" – God's desire for spiritual children.

The reason to consider this rather unpleasant account is not because it offers insight on interpersonal relationships as such but because of what it reveals about the importance of fruitfulness and children. This turns out to be one of the key purposes of marriage.

L ET'S first take a look at what the text says:
   "And Judah took a wife for Er his firstborn, whose name was Tamar. And Er, Judah's firstborn, was wicked in the sight of the LORD; and the LORD slew him. And Judah said unto Onan, Go in unto thy brother's wife, and marry her, and raise up seed to thy brother. And Onan knew that the seed should not be his; and it came to pass, when he went in unto his brother's wife, that he spilled it on the ground, lest that he should give seed to his brother. And the thing which he did displeased the LORD: wherefore he slew him also."

(Genesis 38:6-10)

The nature of Er's sin is not stated, nor do we have any details about his marriage to Tamar. We do know about the nature of Onan's sin, however; if we were to read this account for the first time most would be surprised if not shocked to learn that the Lord would take his life for the failure to provide an heir to his brother. Was the crime really so serious?

It was, and in a number of different ways. It was serious in one sense because it took advantage of a person and a situation. Onan was prepared to take the upside of sleeping with his sister-in-law, but he didn't want to pay the price of the consequences (marring his own inheritance in some way, perhaps; having to be in some way responsible as a father-figure to the child; or perhaps he simply resented doing a good turn to his late brother). At that level it's an example of pure selfishness which can plague relationships from time to time: a preference for take rather than give.

The real issue though is about the seed. Onan's was a serious sin because he failed properly to undertake a duty later to be codified in the Law of Moses: that a man should raise up seed to his brother (to carry on the family line, to preserve the inheritance, to allow the woman to bring up a child and descendant). We can dismiss all this as not having that much relevance in today's world: inheritance laws are different now, and it was a cultural 'requirement' in those days to have children and a social stigma if you didn't, particularly for a woman. Those conditions have changed, we might think, so there are few conclusions to draw here.

This might be a bit hasty, however. While it is true that cultural norms have changed massively, is the imperative to have children if God blesses a marriage in that way purely a cultural one? The answer is no; there are physical, psychological and emotional aspects to that desire too, for a woman in particular. The first command that God gave to the man and woman after blessing them in the Genesis 1 creation account is that they should be fruitful and multiply (that is, have children: 1:28). Indeed, it may be that the being fruitful and multiplying actually *is* the blessing which God pronounces upon them.

Could it be that the command of Genesis is purely one of practical expediency – that there was a world to be populated and this was the way God had chosen to do it? Perhaps so at one level, but there is probably a spiritual aspect to it also. A man and his wife may think that it is their choice as to whether they will have children (assuming they are able to do so) – and indeed it is in one sense. But they should also factor in whether there is a spiritual dimension to the question: it ought not to be just about what *you* want or what your wife or your husband wants; we should consider what God might want also.

Seeking a godly seed

Onan's failure to raise up children to his brother might not just be about inheritance. That was clearly one purpose of the Levirate law, but the law also suggests that it is generally part of God's purpose that couples have children. If we can sum up His purpose as manifesting Himself in the earth, it is not a big step to say that one of the key ways He will do this is through the families that He has created – through children being born who are shown and taught by their parents how good, right and fulfilling it is to serve God and give glory to His name.

A key passage here is Malachi 2 in which the prophet takes his listeners to task for their devaluing of marriage and the importance of marital unity. He emphasises that a man and a woman united in marriage are under a covenant and that this covenant is instituted by God:

"… (Your wife is) the wife of thy covenant. And did not he make one? (i.e., a unity out of the individual components of husband and wife) Yet had he the residue of the spirit. And wherefore one? (i.e., Why is unity in marriage so important?) That he might seek a godly seed. Therefore take heed to your spirit, and let none deal treacherously against the wife of his youth."   (Malachi 2:14,15)

This passage is often quoted in connection with discussions about marriage and divorce, but it should also be quoted in discussions about the purpose of marriage and whether or not to have children. Implicit to the reasoning is that one of the prime purposes of marriage and a key driver of a couple's need to be spiritually one in the Lord is because God wants 'a godly seed' –

that is, He wants godly children. God Himself as a father wants to have godly children (that would be us) who themselves bring forth godly children (the "godly seed"). As part of His whole purpose of filling the earth with His glory and seeking a people for His name God wants us to have children who we can bring up hopefully to be more in the image of God than the image of man. That He would seek to involve even our very own children in this is the most fantastic thing.

When God told Adam and Eve to be fruitful and multiply back in Genesis, therefore, it was part of His bigger plan that there would be a spiritual 'filling' of the earth, not just a natural one. It's our responsibility to do our best to be fruitful in all aspects of marriage (there are all kinds of ways in which a couple with children or without can bring forth fruit to God), but for those of us who have children this is essential for us to think about. Of course we cannot guarantee the fruit will be good, just as a farmer cannot guarantee the weather, the quality of the seed or the non-intervention of pests that may harm or destroy his crop for all the care he gives it. Our children will ultimately have to make their own choices about whether to follow God or not, but until that day comes our calling to 'tend the crop' to help the seed develop into fruit as best we can is imperative – giving our all to help our children grow in a spiritually as well as physically healthy way. Malachi's concept of God's desire for a godly seed has the power to transform our thinking about children and family.

NOTE

It is occasionally argued that the Onan incident suggests or offers supporting evidence that couples ought not to use contraception and that sexual intimacy should only take place for the purposes of procreation. The passage has also been used to argue against masturbation. There are two points to note here. First, the passage is simply not about masturbation at all (in fact that is a topic nowhere covered in scripture). Second, Onan's sin is that he failed to raise up seed to his brother, the main and probably only purpose of their union. This has very little to do with whether a married couple may enjoy intimacy outside the purpose of procreation. In Onan's case, procreation was quite clearly the purpose of their union, but one which he shunned. In a marriage procreation is only one of the purposes of intimacy, albeit a centrally important one. Other scriptural passages show other purposes as discussed in chapter 26; when the writer to the Hebrews says that "marriage is honourable in all things and the bed undefiled" he is saying that it is perfectly proper and good for a husband and wife to enjoy intimacy for its own sake: for the unity it creates and celebrates.

Manoah and the woman

Topics: "The woman" and the symbolism of childbirth; "Saved through childbearing"; The special responsibility of motherhood; Preparation for being a mother; "And his mother's name was …"; Smart wife, slow husband.

While the name of Manoah's wife is not known, she leaves an indelible impression upon the narrative of Judges 13, her common sense and good heed to God's angel a notable contrast with the excitable and over-anxious temperament of her husband. She provides a great example from which to consider the responsibilities of motherhood.

THE narrative of Samson's birth opens like this:
"There was a certain man of Zorah, of the tribe of the Danites, whose name was Manoah. And his wife was barren and had no children. And the angel of the LORD appeared to the woman …" (Judges 13:2,3, ESV)

The man is introduced and named, his geographical and tribal background appropriately identified, yet straightaway the narrative focus passes from him and onto the woman to whom he is married. The angel does not appear to Manoah himself but instead to the woman, announcing Samson's birth and providing constraints around her behaviour and that of the child. The boy is to be a Nazirite with no razor coming upon his head, while for her part she is to be careful to drink no alcohol and eat nothing unclean. The child is to be special as a unique gift of God so she must accordingly dedicate herself by ensuring that the angel's prescriptions are carefully followed.

The woman

The way in which the narrative repeatedly refers to Manoah's wife as "the woman" is very distinctive; it refuses to name her or provide other details about her identity:

"The angel of the LORD appeared to *the woman* ..."

"Then *the woman* came and told her husband ..."

"The angel of the LORD came again to *the woman* ..."

"So *the woman* ran quickly ..."

"Are you the man who spoke to *this woman*?"

"Of all that I said to *the woman* let her be careful ..."

She is also referred to as "his wife" on several occasions, but as the foregoing list demonstrates, it is the expression "the woman" which predominates by some margin. Why this particular styling?

The reason is to heighten the typology. She is not just *any* woman, nor is she *some particular* woman who happened to live at that specific point in history and be called Rebecca or Susannah (or whatever it happened to be). She stands instead in representative or parabolic form. One way to think about her is as a woman representing her kind, womanhood in general. It is through *women* that new life is born into the world and with it hope, whereas the man Adam was the bringer of death. She represents all women and thus the wonderful process of childbirth through which new beginnings are made. In this sense, then, what the angel says to this woman can be seen as a microcosm of what could be said to *all* women as they prepare to give birth to a new life.

But she represents more than merely this. She stands too for *the* woman, the typological woman spoken of in Genesis 3. It would be through a woman that ultimately the promised seed (the "seed of the woman") would come, a seed bringing salvation and joy not just for women thus saved in childbearing but for all people on the earth. This woman is a descendent of Eve to whom the promise of the seed of the woman was made, and she is a type of Mary, a type of the one who again represents her class and had the special privilege of bringing forth the promised seed. The woman who is Manoah's wife stands as a representative woman, a woman to whom the promise of a Saviour is given. Like her successor Mary, her son would be a great deliverer, endowed with the Spirit of God, one whose death would bring about an even greater salvation than was possible in the life that preceded it. If Samson is at all a type of Christ in the deliverance he achieves for his people (and the points of connection are too close for it to be otherwise, even if Samson sometimes does the *opposite* of what Christ would do), then the woman must surely be a type of the woman to whom the seed was promised and the one to whom the saviour was born.

Once we have this perspective it makes perfect sense why she is not named but instead insistently called "the woman". As the typical woman, what is said to her is of tremendous importance to all women, her example shining forth to all who follow.

The woman and the man

The woman is quick to take on board the angel's message and its implications for her behaviour. The first thing she does is to go and tell her husband:

> "Then the woman came and told her husband, 'A man of God came to me, and his appearance was like the appearance of the angel of God, very awesome ...'"   (verse 6, ESV)

Manoah, though, wants reassurance. He hasn't seen the angel and therefore he hasn't fully believed. He wants a repeat of the message to give him the opportunity to clear up any details that he hasn't quite grasped; he wants to see the angel himself so that he can know for sure that the woman hadn't simply been hallucinating. He is a man who wants more evidence and more facts and who at this stage doesn't appear to have a particular abundance of faith:

"Then Manoah prayed to the LORD and said, 'O Lord, please let the man of God whom you sent come again to us and teach us what we are to do with the child who will be born.' And God listened to the voice of Manoah, and the angel of God came again to the woman as she sat in the field. But Manoah her husband was not with her. So the woman ran quickly and told her husband, 'Behold, the man who came to me the other day has appeared to me.' And Manoah arose and went after his wife and came to the man and said to him, 'Are you the man who spoke to this woman?' ... And the angel of the LORD said to Manoah, 'Of all that I said to the woman let her be careful ... All that I commanded her let her observe.'"

(verses 8-14, ESV)

While granting Manoah's request, the angel is careful not to appear to him directly but to go instead to the woman once again. Even when Manoah and the angel finally meet, the angel does not deign to tell Manoah the details of his message, he simply says 'Let the woman make sure she does all that I told her': "all that I commanded her let her observe." He doesn't tell Manoah what it actually was that she should do, just that she should do as she had been told!

Why this unwillingness to speak directly to Manoah? It reinforces the earlier point that the scene is about the typology of *the woman*; it is not about man. Jesus was the "seed of the woman", but he was not 'seed of the man' because he was begotten of the Father, the type here reinforced by the angel's determined focus on appearing to the woman and giving detailed instructions only to her.

But a second and related point is that by so deliberately instructing only the woman the text emphasises the responsibilities of a woman over against a man with respect to bringing up her children. The woman in this passage is to dedicate herself because she is going to have a special child – but there is a no less important sense in which *all* spiritual women should dedicate themselves to the hugely important task ahead as they prepare for childbirth. The woman in this passage is

given instructions about how the child is to be raised and what
he should and should not do – but *all* spiritual women should
focus on how their children are to be raised and how they should
behave, what ought to be done and what ought not. The point
here is not that the man should *not* think about these things or
that he has no responsibility in this regard (clearly he does, he
is to set the spiritual direction for the family as a whole, and is
to be deeply involved in instructing and disciplining his children
– he cannot and must not pass the buck to his wife and say 'the
children are your affair'); but there is a very special sense in
which the responsibilities of child-rearing belong especially to
the woman, her role and influence incalculable in this regard.

Woman and mother

This interpretation seems to fit with what we read elsewhere with
respect to rearing children in the Bible. Right back in Genesis 3
it is the woman who is to bring forth children "in sorrow" (this
perhaps refers both to the physical pain of childbirth and the
almost physical level of emotional attachment a mother carries
for her children her life long). The New Testament similarly
emphasises her responsibility to family and children on several
occasions, exhorting her to "bear children, guide the house"
(1 Timothy 5:14), and stating that she should be a "keeper at
home" (Titus 2:5: the word means being a guardian, carer, or
someone on the lookout – someone concerned with dangers and
threats that might overtake her family, one whose concern for the
health, nurture and protection of her household is paramount).

A key aspect of this guiding the house will relate to
childcare if the family is blessed with children. This does not
mean that the husband's role is unimportant or that he has
any excuse whatsoever for shirking his responsibilities, but it
does mean that a particular responsibility (and, let us say it, a
privilege) is laid at the wife's door. Paul uses the Greek word from
whence comes our English 'despot' when he talks about guiding
the house, so the role is an active, industrious one; she is to be a
proactive manager of the sort we meet in Proverbs 31. None of

these passages exclude a woman taking on other responsibilities such as going out to work and having a career, taking part in volunteer work for charities, or doing all kinds of work in the ecclesia. But those roles, whether she takes them or not, do not nullify or otherwise cancel out the Biblical mandate for her role with respect to the children and the household. God designed and made us for the roles He has asked us to fulfil, and a woman has talents and patience in these areas that it is hard for a man even to comprehend, instincts and abilities that are to be utilised and valued not suppressed as if they somehow disadvantage us or make us less. New evidence for this is emerging all the time as we understand more about the communication skills of women (according to one study the average woman speaks around 20,000 words a day versus a man's typical 7,000 – this would seem to provide a great environment for children to learn language skills and grasp both how to understand and be understood), and their superior ability to recognise and interpret facial expressions and emotional states even as babies and toddlers when compared to males of an equivalent age. It will usually fall to the mother to provide the majority of the hands-on care and nurture for the children as they grow, to be the one they turn to for comfort and guidance when the world becomes too much – and she has been specially equipped by God for this important task.

The woman's charge from the angel thus speaks of the huge responsibilities of motherhood brought out elsewhere in the scriptures by that little refrain, "And his mother's name was …", often used to introduce the various kings of Israel and Judah and most likely an influential determinant in their future course. Motherhood is not something that ought to be entered into lightly, as though we shall automatically be able to do well enough or offer our best without thought or preparation. As the angel said to Manoah, "Of all that I commanded the woman, let her be *ware*": the idea of looking out and being on watch here is precisely the same one in the Titus passage when he talks of women being "keepers" at home (it would be overly heavy-handed to translate this term "keepers" as 'look-out guards', but one of the underlying root words here can indeed carry that sense in one of its fields of meaning).

Most people who have been married and brought up children will admit that, aside from their relationship with God, it is the most valuable thing they have ever done. In this light, what could be more appropriate than proper reflection, preparation and diet both before and during the process? The woman of Judges 13 is explicitly commanded to pay attention to her diet, and while the modern world is expert at applying this at the natural level during pregnancy in making sure pregnant mothers have their proper supplies of iron and calcium and the like, the spiritual counterpart is at least equally worthy of thought and attention.

There are things a mother can be for her children that the father will struggle ever to be, no matter how hard he tries. Of course there is a uniqueness in what *he* brings also and the whole task of parenting is a partnership, but there must be many times in a father's life where he looks at his wife's relationship with their children and shakes his head in wonder; it is just something else to his own relationship. This passage from Judges which focuses particularly on this relationship and responsibility of mother-towards-son evokes all this very beautifully.

Spiritually tuned in

In the case of Manoah and his wife there seems also to have been a gap in spiritual aptitude between the pair. Manoah certainly had a belief in God and a keenness to know and to be sure, but he seemed a bit slow to understand what was going on, as illustrated by the comment in 13:16 that "Manoah did not know that he was the angel of the LORD". This becomes even more obvious in a later scene in which Manoah clearly doesn't think things through and has to be calmly put on the right track by his wife:

"The angel of the LORD appeared no more to Manoah and to his wife. Then Manoah knew that he was the angel of the LORD. And Manoah said to his wife, 'We shall surely die, for we have seen God.' But his wife said to him, 'If the LORD had meant to kill us, he would not have accepted a burnt offering and a grain offering at our hands, or shown us all these things, or now announced to us such things as these.' And the woman bore a son and called his name Samson." (verses 21-24, ESV)

It's a nice example of a woman calmly reasoning with her man when he has not quite got things straight. She might have called him an idiot at this point, or belittled him in some other way; in the cold light of day he certainly seems a bit slow when compared with her, failing to realise the angelic nature of their guest until he had already left, whereas the woman seemed to get it all along without once needing to be told. But this was no excuse to ridicule or demean him.

In terms of the Biblical model of the husband as the head and the spiritual leader of the family, things might come together more naturally if the woman is able to find a husband who has an equivalent scriptural understanding, say, or as strong a spiritual drive as her. But there are occasions when this will not be the case – where the woman has a greater aptitude for spiritual matters as here. Manoah's example shows that this need not be an insurmountable issue provided the wife is prepared to help her husband raise his spiritual game without usurping his headship, empowering him to take on his divinely appointed role. It doesn't mean that he has to pretend to understand things that he does not, and he would be unwise to be heavy-handed in trying to assert his authority to somehow 'prove' he is her equal. If she is wise she will leave behind frustration, pride and ridicule, in love trying to help her husband to develop his understanding and appreciation of spiritual things. If he is wise he will value this help, striving to use her abilities to help him grow and fulfil his role, not so that he can over-compensate for his lack either through posturing or pretending to be something he is not.

The calling to be "the woman" as illustrated in this chapter is a great calling. It is not a human calling imposed by patriarchal society; it is a divine calling, the responsibilities it entails being godly responsibilities. To do them with the proper preparation and diet, with the full care and attention that they deserve, is both a great privilege and an honour, even if it may not always feel that way. To be granted more influence than any other human being over the life and character development of a new child during its most formative years – there can be few responsibilities more important than this.

Joseph and Mary (1)

Topics: Parents' anxieties for their children; The fear of 'losing' a child.

This chapter is a short reflection on one particular aspect of parenting – the way in which parents, particularly mothers, carry with them the cares of the children. This plays out in the lives of Joseph and Mary with respect to their musings about Jesus' uniqueness and the nature of God's purpose with him, but their concerns reflect in a heightened degree those all parents share. Similarly their anxiety at having lost Jesus when he was in the temple is mirrored in parental anxiety about the possibility of 'losing' their children in an emotional or spiritual sense.[1]

MATTHEW'S Gospel depicts Joseph as a thoughtful man, carefully pondering the right course of action on learning of Mary's pregnancy. But if Joseph was a thoughtful man, so too was his wife. Luke's account is more focused on Mary, twice noting that:

"Mary kept all these things and pondered them in her heart."
(Luke 2:19)

"His mother kept all these sayings in her heart."   (verse 51)

---

1   For a fuller examination of Joseph and Mary's relationship see chapter 48.

On top of these a further reference, Luke 2:33, captures the wondering of both parents following the words of Simeon. Together these passages evoke a parent's concern for the well-being of the family and in particular the future of their children; all parents wonder about such things and they often worry too.

We cannot control the destiny or choices of our children; that must ultimately be a matter between them and God. But we can and do wonder all the same – we wonder if we have said too little (or too much), whether we have indeed done the best we could, and what will become of them when they go out into the world and leave our more immediate sphere of influence. There is nothing wrong with these ruminations – they show a natural and healthy engagement in the lives of our children and an awareness of our parental responsibilities, though it is important not to go overboard with worry on things of 'tomorrow' which are beyond our control.

A lost child

The scene in which Mary and Joseph unwittingly 'lose' Jesus is particularly poignant, not only for those who, in a moment of panic, temporarily fear their child is missing but also – on a more metaphorical level – for those times when we worry that we are losing our influence over our children, or that they are losing their way and we don't seem to be able to come up with anything to help them find it ("Son, why hast thou thus dealt with us? Behold, thy father and I have sought thee sorrowing", Luke 2:48). There may be times when we feel like saying very similar words to our no-longer-so-little ones.

The anxiety of thinking that we might have lost the one God had entrusted us with – as Mary and Joseph certainly thought for a moment – can bring trauma in its wake and be one of life's most unbearable burdens. But thinking of Mary and Joseph's role in Jesus' upbringing is helpful here. Were they important, and did they bring to bear significant influence in Jesus' early life? Most certainly. But were they *responsible* for Jesus' sinless life – or, had he chosen a different path, the opposite? Of course not. It was Jesus' victory over sin and not theirs, and though Mary was his literal mother and Joseph a stand-in, this can serve as a reminder that in the fuller sense God is the ultimate Father to our children, and our task is to represent Him to them as best we can so that they can be well equipped to determine whether or not they will be obedient children of His. This is ultimately more important than whether they will be obedient children of *ours*. Our relationship with our children is tremendously important but it is neither our nor their most important relationship. Our responsibility is to introduce them to Him as best we can – but then it will ultimately be up to them to make their own choices about their relationship with God. Of course it will hurt us if they don't choose wisely, but it must and will always be their choice rather than our own. Meanwhile, we must speak of Him and illustrate Him in the best possible way we can even as we ponder their ways and their futures in our hearts.

Arrows and olive plants

Topics: Letting God build the house(hold); Children like arrows in a quiver –
the missionary purpose of family; The wife at the heart of the house; Children
like olive plants – assets not liabilities; The wider family.

This chapter is not really a study of a Biblical couple at all, but
the sentiments of Psalm 127 and 128 are so relevant to the
topic of family and children that they cry out for at least a brief
consideration. Both psalms are short so it's worth quoting
them in full before drawing out some observations about their
wonderful vision for family life.

PSALM 127 – A Psalm for Solomon
"Except the LORD build the house, they labour in vain that
build it: except the LORD keep the city, the watchman waketh
but in vain. It is vain for you to rise up early, to sit up late, to
eat the bread of sorrows: for so he giveth his beloved sleep.
Lo, children are an heritage of the LORD: and the fruit of the
womb is his reward. As arrows are in the hand of a mighty
man; so are children of the youth. Happy is the man that hath
his quiver full of them: they shall not be ashamed, but they
shall speak with the enemies in the gate."

The first point is that a household is just like a house – it
does not just happen automatically; it has to be built. While this
sounds like hard work the good news is that God hasn't left us
to our own devices: He wants to be – and is – the great Master

Builder working among us. We need Him to build our homes and to look out for us, because without that all our efforts will be in vain. We need to be receptive to His working and shaping, aware that our family is His project before it is our own. This way we shall be able to relieve ourselves of some of the stresses and anxieties of our labours, resting soundly in the knowledge that He is in control.

With this background the psalm proceeds in verses 3-6 to extol the virtues and blessings of children. They are a heritage (i.e., inheritance) and a reward, a blessing from God rather than something that we have produced of our own cleverness, genetic prowess or virility. The notion of an inheritance makes us think about the future – it sounds almost a platitude to speak of children being our future, but of course they literally are in the way that our hopes and thoughts are bound up with the twists and turns of their unfolding lives and also in the way in which we might hope they will spare a thought for us in our old age. But they can be an inheritance from a deeper spiritual perspective also if they come to share our faith – the joy of worshipping God with one's children and looking forward with them to the hope of living in God's kingdom must be one of the greatest joys there is.

The next simile is a more striking one – children are like arrows in the hand of a mighty man, and the more one has the more blessed and better equipped one is! This is a far cry from Mao's one child policy and even from the general trend of economic and social development amongst nations in which the more affluent a country becomes the more its birth rate tends to fall.

So what does it mean to compare children to arrows in the hands of a mighty man? Arrows are weapons and the metaphor implies that there is a battle to be fought and won, a mission to be accomplished. And indeed there is: from the Old Testament context of the kingdom of God on earth and the military engagement it sometimes implied, it is evident that more children would in time mean bigger resources with which to defend and conquer, and a step closer to the "sand of the seashore" fulfilment of the promises to Abraham. But the more important context to a modern believer is the spiritual warfare that is to be waged ("we fight ... against spiritual wickedness in high places", Ephesians 6:12), and in particular the work of *mission* which is to be accomplished (that is, witnessing and preaching and the endeavour to fill the earth as far as possible with the knowledge of God). Arrows are offensive weapons, and there is a mission to be accomplished – spreading the news of God's plan, defending the territory, being ambassadors for Him. The image of one's offspring speaking with enemies in the gate with which the psalm concludes tellingly implies that the children are either to be conquerors or ambassadors. Once we call to mind God's purpose of filling the earth with His glory, of begetting children 'in His own image' and of 'seeking a godly seed' then the notion ceases to be surprising. It might not be conventional wisdom to think about having children from this perspective, but God's calling has never been about convention.

It's not merely that a couple might be proud of their children, it's that the children will actually take up and participate in the campaign, so to speak. The 'default' expectation the scriptures imply is that they will come to know and love God – not that we can guarantee it, and not that we can allow ourselves to crumple if they choose a different path, but that it is what we should hope for and in a measure expect (we are nurturing and admonishing them in that direction, after all). Viewed from this perspective, then, the more arrows a man has in his quiver, the faster God's presence and work will come to be known in the earth. *This* is what it is about – not that our children should become doctors or C-level executives or some other type of high achiever (fine if they do, fine if they don't), but that they should be ministers for God.

Time now to turn to the second psalm of the pair ... Psalm 128:

"Blessed is every one that feareth the LORD; that walketh in his ways. For thou shalt eat the labour of thine hands: happy shalt thou be, and it shall be well with thee. Thy wife shall be as a fruitful vine by the sides of thine house: thy children like olive plants round about thy table. Behold, that thus shall the man be blessed that feareth the LORD. The LORD shall bless thee out of Zion: and thou shalt see the good of Jerusalem all the days of thy life. Yea, thou shalt see thy children's children, and peace upon Israel."

God's blessing is delivered from Zion (verse 5), the centre of His concern and the location of His earthly throne. It is a blessing which seems to be expressed in concentric circles:

- You yourself will be happy and well (verse 2).
- Your wife will be a fruitful vine in the heart of your house (verse 3).
- Your children will be like olive plants round your table (verse 3).
- You will see your grandchildren (verse 6).
- And peace upon Israel (verse 6).

The psalm begins with the man's responsibilities (fearing the Lord, working to be fed and to feed (Genesis 3:17+) and then proceeds to his wife, then to the children, grandchildren and Israel. As husbands we are first responsible for ourselves in God's presence, and the next most intimate relationship is with our wife. After this come the children, then the wider family (here signalled by grandchildren) and then the community at large.

Given the context of labour and food introduced in verse 2 it is interesting that the blessings of wife and children are described in agricultural or horticultural terms (a wife like a fruitful vine and children like olive plants round one's table). Tending a garden with fruit trees in it was a core element of Adam's initial responsibilities and work. Interesting, then, that a wife and children should be described in the terminology of plants that produce edible food. A man's labours are not just tilling the physical ground to encourage it to bring forth fruit, but also his labours in his family. The blessing of the Lord is correspondingly not just that the earth will bring forth fruit for him (albeit restrainedly after the curse), but also that his family will be fruitful and that his labours in that sphere will not be in vain. With God's blessing a man's family will bring forth fruit to sustain, fulfil and satisfy him, a satisfaction no less nourishing than the one provided by the literal food on his table.

Wife and children

His wife, then, will be a fruitful vine "in the very heart of his house" (this is a better translation than KJV's, "by the sides of your house"). A vine is not only a plant that brings forth fruit; specifically, it brings forth the fruit which produces wine which makes glad the heart of man, an apt metaphor for many of the good things in marriage shared between a husband and wife. This includes the physical aspect but also the practical help as well as the intellectual, emotional and spiritual companionship they will share. The wife is not just 'in' the house, she is at its very heart, core to its proper functioning and survival.[1] To change the metaphor she is a well-spring for the family, nourishing and sustaining both her husband and her children.

The children are depicted as olive plants round about the table which means that they bring something productive and positive to the family, they are not merely a drain on its resources or an encumbrance to what the parents would rather be doing – nor are they merely there to 'have a good time' as they sit privately entertained by some electronic device. Olive plants bring forth olives, a central part of the Mediterranean diet, the source of olive oil used both for food and light as well as the special purpose of anointing. Children can be expected to be productive, bringing enormous riches and blessing that one can only really know by appreciating it first-hand. While they can seem demanding and draining in the early years with their constant need for attention and care, the olive metaphor used here is an apt reminder that in fact they are the most wonderful productive assets.

---

1   Compare this wife "within the heart" of the house to the false woman of Proverbs who is "without" in the streets (Proverbs 7:11, etc.), seeking to lure in a weak-willed passer-by. The husband must make sure he obtains satisfaction from within the house, not outside.

The bigger picture

The second part of the psalm moves on to consider the wider blessings of godliness:

> "The LORD shall bless thee out of Zion: and thou shalt see the good of Jerusalem all the days of thy life. Yea, thou shalt see thy children's children, and peace upon Israel."   (verses 5,6)

This psalm tells us that if we try to get it right ourselves (the individual responsibilities of verses 1,2), this unlocks potential not just for us, nor even just for our immediate family – but for the generations to come (verses 3-6). Here the specific blessing of grandchildren ("thy children's children") is called out, but it potentially goes well beyond that for many further generations.

It is intriguing that the blessing of grandchildren comes 'wrapped' in the blessing on Israel:

- you will see Jerusalem (verse 5);
- you will see your grandchildren (verse 6);
- you will see peace upon Israel (verse 6).

Our eternal future and the eternal future of our children and of our grandchildren is bound up with the hope of Israel. They are a 'natural' blessing from God whether or not they choose to accept the Gospel's call. But if they do accept that call they are guarded and kept by the hope of Israel. If God cares for Israel as the apple of His eye and our children are bound by that hope, then we truly have nothing to fear for their future and every reason to be glad.

Postscript: further thoughts on parenting

Topics: Having a vision for the family; Learning from one's own parents; Avoiding well known pitfalls; It's not just about the children – putting God and the marriage at the heart; Allowing children growing independence; When the children have gone ...

This chapter continues some of the topical thoughts begun in chapter 31, looking at various issues ranging from learning from one's own parents to avoiding some common pitfalls, to making God and the marriage at the heart of the family rather than the children. We also take a brief look at the 'life cycle' of children in the home – their growing independence and the time when they eventually move home and the marriage must continue to grow without them.

THROUGHOUT our experience of parenting it is very helpful to have a vision for our family, a model for what we want it to be like. We often won't achieve it – with all those human beings involved it is bound to have its fair share of messiness so it is no use to be unreasonably idealistic – but the vision of what we are striving to achieve will be a very useful anchor. Our children are not only *our* children but God's as well, the language of stewardship being used on a number of occasions in the New Testament to cause us to think about how we are managing all the assets God has put in our charge. While we might be more inclined to think of children as liabilities than assets for the first twenty or so years of their lives, of course in actual fact they are massive assets, amongst the most precious God has asked us to steward. We have to make big investments (time, money, emotions) in order to do our job in taking care of them, but parents almost universally conclude that it is one of the most worthwhile things they do, off the scale, perhaps, when we compare it to our day jobs for those who are out at work all day. Thinking of our parental role as an act of stewardship and investment for God does form a helpful context for our responsibilities.

The path our parents trod

Our default model of parenting will most likely be what our own parents did. It might therefore be worth asking them what they learned from their experience of having been our parent – what they themselves now think about the way they did it and whether they would have any advice on what to change. We're not obliged to accept their advice or do what they say, but since they are likely to have had more experience than us it might be interesting to ask. Similarly it can be useful consciously to go through the exercise of thinking about our own experience of having been parented ourselves and what we have learned from it about what makes a good parent. Sometimes when I'm dealing with my own children I can catch myself saying exactly what my father and mother would have said to me – sometimes I'll even use precisely the same words. There is nothing deliberate about this and there is nothing wrong with it if what they did made sense and was effective; in fact, it's great to have had the example of how to deal with particular situations. Sometimes, though, we can assume that our approach is better than our partner's simply because it happens to be what our parents did and what we therefore conceive as 'normal', rather than it being an intrinsically better approach. We owe it to our husband or wife to be open to another way and to consider carefully and weigh things up rather than simply to assume.

The central point is that we have undeniably been influenced extensively by our own parents in our parenting actions and assumptions. This can be good and it can be bad, depending on what those actions and assumptions were. It's therefore very useful proactively to think through the strengths and weaknesses of what they did, whether and how we might do some things differently, and what it would be wise to do the same. All children are different, of course, so what worked for us or our naughty sibling (if such they were!) may not necessarily work for our own children.

Pitfalls

There are some very obvious 'big picture' traps to avoid in parenting, well known but perhaps worth reiterating. One is to spoil our children, to try to give them everything we never had: the perfect experience with no lack of anything. This gives them a false sense of their own importance and inclines them to the view that any want or ill feeling can be solved through the acquiring of physical things or experiences. It can also inculcate a view that the world somehow owes them a certain level of lifestyle and perhaps even whatever they demand. The expression 'spoiled brat' is not a pleasant one, but what it describes is far worse.

Another error is to strive to live vicariously through our children – giving them the experiences we've missed and wanting them to succeed where we fell short or did not have opportunity. We are who we are because of what we didn't have as well as what we did – the hardships and the knocks, the things we had to wait for. Our children are not us or projections of us; they may have very different skills, aptitudes and interests so what worked for us may not work for them. Nor can we compensate for our failures by somehow forcing them to succeed and be passionate about a particular thing.

The expectations of those around us can be another factor that can be problematic. Just because society does or believes this or that with respect to bringing up children doesn't mean that it is necessarily right. We can want to keep up with the Joneses or even do better than they in terms of the experiences and activities we provide for our children, running them hither and thither to different clubs, sports and gatherings when sometimes to spend quality time together as a family might be far more rewarding. We have expectations and hopes for our children of all kinds: spiritual, educational, social, experiential; this is entirely to be expected (how could we not have?), but we need to ensure that these are realistic and appropriate and that they are not too culturally defined. If and when our children fail to meet our expectations we can feel disappointed – sometimes even frustrated or angry – and we can be tempted to take this out on them or on ourselves. This is unlikely to be helpful, and before we do decide a course of action in response it is worth stopping and asking ourselves again whether the expectation was realistic, sensible, necessary, helpful, worthwhile or spiritual in the first place. Is this area of failure or disappointment something that really matters? If not, we can let it go; if it is, then depending on the child's age and the matter in question we are often better to think in terms of how we can smartly influence it to the positive rather than how we can control and enforce.

Keeping the balance
It's important to understand that children are not the centre of the family; everything does not revolve around them. Sometimes it can feel that way – when so much attention is needed for babies and toddlers and their pressing needs, when a teenager's moodiness settles darkly on the whole household or when life outside work seems to resemble a taxi service – but it remains the case even in these trying circumstances that the family involves *all* its members with their needs and desires not just a particular child or the children as a group. The family is not there solely for the servicing of the children's needs; that is but one of several central functions.

The family is to be considered as centred on God first and foremost, but if there is a centre at all amongst the family members themselves then it is mum and dad who form it rather than the children. It was the parents who established the family unit in the beginning through marriage before the children came along, and it is they who will be there when the children leave to live their own lives and potentially form families of their own. They are therefore the constant and the bedrock of the family which is why their relationship as husband and wife is so critical. Having children is one of the marriage's purposes – if God has seen fit to bless the couple in that way – but it is not its only purpose; the acting out of the Christ-bride parable and the learning and demonstration of the unity of God is another equally fundamental one as is the wider showing forth of God's glory. Mum and dad are at the heart of the marriage and their feelings and needs are important all the way through. Of course as adults they are able – and must – make sacrifices of their own wants and the immediate fulfilment of their needs for the sake of the more immediate need of feeding the baby (or whatever it is), but that doesn't mean their own needs go away or that the quality of their relationship ceases to be critical.

This can be a particular challenge when children first come along and the changes and challenges seem so huge, particularly to the mother. She may well feel exhausted for large parts of the day; she will be constantly on the alert to her baby's needs; her body and hormones will be going through significant post-natal changes and in some cases she may even suffer from post-natal depression. In that environment a husband needs to be maximally understanding, supportive and patient even if he seems to have temporarily 'lost' his wife, her emotions and energy seemingly sucked into a vortex the baby has created. Physical intimacy can be difficult for a while (which will tend to make him feel rejected), but the sheer potential for physical exhaustion his wife may feel coupled with the emotional energy her baby is now demanding can also make him feel isolated and wonder if things will ever be the same again. While they may never be *quite* the same, there is every possibility for them to return to being very good indeed and in some respects to be significantly better (after all, to produce a new baby together and see it grow into a healthy and increasingly responsible child is one of the greatest accomplishments a couple could wish for). Just as it is helpful for a husband to be understanding and supportive of his wife during this time, it is important too for the wife to be conscious of the feelings of her husband, including the possibility that he may feel somewhat 'disconnected' by what is going on. If she is wise she will find ways of showing him that she still loves him as she ever did and that nothing has changed in terms of their feelings for one another. Both must find ways of ensuring the marriage is not neglected at this time because it is the marriage which forms the core of the family unit. We mustn't lose focus on the marriage just because children have come along.

When children come onto the scene the identity of the couple changes in many respects from being husband and wife to being mum and dad. This is a very significant change – one which can take some getting used to both for the couple themselves in terms of their own self-image, and for the way one partner sees the other. They also need to see though that 'mum' isn't just mum – she also has an identity as wife (confidante, friend, helper, lover) and an individual, just as dad has an identity as husband and both have identities as servants and children of God. It's important that these other identities don't get subsumed into the one aspect of parenthood; instead they must all get proper space, attention and development.

It has been wisely said that the best way for a father to love his children is to love his wife; the benefits of doing so are immense both to his wife and to the children. When children see that mum and dad care for, respect and support one another they have a wonderful foundation from which to grow in their exploration of the world. It is one of the best gifts we can give our children as it centres them and grounds them, reassuring them that whatever else happens – whatever uncertainty there may be with friends or peers at school and whatever they may come across in life that puzzles or even troubles them – back at home mum and dad are there for each other and for them, united in their love as a family and in their love of God.

Converging and diverging paths

When we think of the dynamics of a family through its life cycle an interesting pattern can be seen. As children grow they move from a state of complete dependence and helplessness as babies to increasingly being able to fend for themselves, make decisions, and ultimately take responsibility for their own life choices. This growing autonomy continues until one day they will most likely leave home completely. What we have, then, is a gradual parting of the ways. As the children grow parents have to let go, no longer able to control their children's behaviour directly but still able to influence – educating and showing their children by example how to make good decisions and making sure they understand the implications of the choices they will make.

This 'letting go' can be very difficult. Sometimes it involves watching our children make mistakes – sometimes serious ones – and picking up the pieces afterwards. Because of our love for them we can want to keep them close and perhaps retain some measure of control, whereas ultimately they will have to stand on their own two feet and answer to God for what they do. What we can do is provide them with a toolkit to help them on their journey, tools to help them think and reason, a perspective on life which approximates God's. As we watch them take their first faltering steps into the world outside it can be traumatic for us as well as them.

This process of letting go yields a fascinating insight into what God must go through as our Father in Heaven. He, too, does not control us, though He could. Instead He allows us the freedom to exercise our free will and make our choices. He provides us with all kinds of examples positive and negative, including the most powerful example of all in the life of His only Son; He provides us with the toolkit we shall need to make our decisions (His word, our conscience, the nurture and nature we have received), but He allows us the freedom to choose and chart our course. He tells us about the consequences of our choices and sometimes He watches us make foolish mistakes which He wishes we never would have made; but while He can and does influence us to make good choices, He will not control us.

When we think of a parent's anxieties for their children and the pain they suffer when they have to watch their children make bad choices it gives us a massive insight into God's role as the Heavenly Father of us all. We can note in our anguish over our children's failures something of His pain when His children go astray; this can be a very valuable and a positive motivator in our own service of Him. But the flip-side is also true: we can see in their successes and the joy it brings something of the joy of God when He sees His children living their lives to be pleasing in His sight. The joy of a parent in seeing their child head in a direction which pleases God is surely one of the greatest this life can know, a mirror of the joy in heaven when sinners repent and try to do what pleases God.

Parenting, then, is a huge piece of learning for us as well as our children. We learn more of selflessness than we learned even by getting married; we learn of love and forgiveness, how to care and to nurture, how to sacrifice ourselves for the greater good – a plethora of spiritual qualities in fact. We gain a raised awareness of our own failings, weaknesses and hypocrisy; we learn more of our nature as human beings but we also learn more of the character of God. We shall have made mistakes as parents, but it is reassuring to know that there is forgiveness for our parental sins just as there is for any others.

We've spoken of the growing independence between child and parent, a parting which is right and fitting as the child becomes an adult. This arc, moving from dependence to independence moves in the opposite direction from the one between a man and his wife who are striving to become ever more one, the very opposite of couples who grow apart and find they have nothing in common once the children leave home. Their experiences as a couple – including the experiences of raising children if they have them – are intended to unite them as one through the things they have shared. This movement towards increasing unity highlights again the point that a strong marriage is what should lie at the centre of a family. Strong marriages don't happen by accident; they happen because a man and his wife are committed to each other and to their marriage and because they make the effort to invest in each other and in their unity in God's presence. Raising children and being unified and united before them is one of the great opportunities to practise this principle as well as one of the greatest gifts we can give our families.

Part 7
Difficult times

Introduction: living with differences and imperfections

Topics: External and internal challenges to happy marriage; Accepting differences and making them strengths; What it means to be a sinner married to another sinner; Destructive behaviours – what sin can look like in a marriage; How we argue; The more you win the more you lose.

Marriage isn't easy; it is at once one of the most potentially rewarding and at the same time challenging undertakings on which we can embark. Bold adventurers, then, all of us who have set sail on this course need a healthy dose of realism in terms of our expectations so that we are not quickly frustrated or disillusioned, along with a good helping of courage and fortitude. Having a vision for marriage – a model, pattern or recipe – is an enormous help because it means we know what we are striving for and why we are doing it: Christ has shown us the perfect example of behaviour and we know that the more we can adopt this and bring it into our relationships the more we shall be able to work through our difficulties and overcome.

SOMETIMES difficulties can result from things external to the marriage itself – from work schedules or loss, by illness, by pressures or exhaustion created by children, in-laws, or financial hardship ... the list could be very long. Sometimes it feels as though these things come in waves perhaps too powerful to stand against. What is certain here is that the stronger a marriage is heading into such times of crisis, the more the strength of the relationship will be able to be drawn upon in order to survive.

By contrast if the marriage bond is already thin and fraying such circumstances can be almost too much to bear. What is also certain is that through prayer God can provide the necessary strength to face even the most bleak crisis; even though it may not always feel like it, He has assured us that He will not try us beyond what we are able to bear.

Sometimes the challenge, the gnawing imperfection, is a matter within the marriage itself, something between the couple which divides them or causes friction or isolationism. What then? The Bible is not a book of rose-coloured spectacles in this regard. It presents some great marriages but it presents them realistically including their problems and misunderstandings, not to say their occasional dysfunction. Examples such as Jacob and Leah, Hannah and Elkanah or Isaac and Rebekah encourage us that even if there are some difficulties in our own marriage, great characters of the scriptures had their challenges too and were able to live and in a measure survive and serve God in that imperfect state. In some cases we shall suggest difficulties were worked through and the relationship improved (Jacob and Leah), in other cases God presented a dramatic solution (Nabal and Abigail), but in others the relationship carried on and survived with both strengths and weaknesses (Isaac and Rebekah) and we cannot really say how it changed over time. All these examples are encouraging, however, because they show us that it is still possible to serve God successfully in all these different circumstances. Spiritual growth and survival is possible even when life is not a fairy tale and in many cases things can be improved through the application of forgiveness and investment.

In this chapter we reflect on two key aspects which can make marriage challenging – the differences between our partner and ourselves and the implications of the fact that both partners in a marriage are sinners. Then we shall have four chapters of scriptural examples followed by a concluding chapter which examines more serious marriage difficulties and offers a few simple suggestions.

One brief note before we proceed: this chapter does not deal with extreme marital difficulties such as physical and sexual abuse, addiction and substance abuse or repeated unfaithfulness. In these cases specialist help will most likely be required and the ecclesia may also need to be involved in helping with remedial action. The comments in this chapter about the imperative to continue to stay in and work at improving a marriage should not be taken to apply to a case where you or your children are in a position of physical danger or abuse; similarly there are circumstances when a marriage is so physically, emotionally and spiritually counterproductive that it is better to live apart even though this is contrary to the scriptural ideal. The purpose of this section is to try to say something useful about the 'everyday' difficulties in marriage, and also to offer a few comments regarding those marriages that have grown cold or are in grave difficulty but can still be improved through the application of the spirit of Christ. We live in a consumer society which tends to discard things rather than seeking to mend them; this must never be our approach in marriage.

Dealing with difference

We must recognise difference in a relationship and learn to live with it in an understanding and productive way. Every individual is precisely that: one of a kind with a unique fingerprint, a unique iris print, even a unique voice print (to name just three perhaps relatively superficial physical differences). We are different physiologically, socially, psychologically, genetically, sexually and historically – and perhaps in other ways also; we need to learn to manage these differences and use them as a strength rather than a weakness. It makes the marriage of two absolutely unique individuals for life fascinating and challenging, because they must live in closer union than in any other human relationship despite their differences. Those differences really come to count and can form the basis of what can be one of life's great triumphs, or its tragedies.

No one aspires to a cold and lonely marriage in which two people continue together under the same roof but lead essentially separate lives with no emotional support and connection. Such marriages usually happen because couples have failed to deal with their differences, allowing themselves to be backed into separate emotional and perhaps physical parts of the house rather than resolving their differences and finding a way of living together with the strength that diversity brings. Two different people have, in aggregate, a greater set of skills and capacities than one, even before the productive capacity of their uniqueness to generate *new* capabilities is considered. There is wonderful potential, but it has to be unlocked.

When we first meet someone and start dating we're often attracted by their differences from us in addition to the things we have in common – there can be a natural complementarity which is delightful. But we have to be careful that we don't allow those very differences which once appealed to us to turn into sores if we eventually choose to marry. To use a rather basic example to illustrate the point, a quiet more reflective person might well be attracted to the more buoyant, gregarious and socially active character of their partner. This is great – but the socially active partner may well want to remain socially active after marriage, and if the quiet one is going to resent this, not give their partner space to express this side of their personality, or try to change them, then there are likely going to be tensions. What is going to be required here is both mutual appreciation of the other's personality, and space and sacrifice so that they can both be 'who they are'.

Couples often find that it is the same issues that cause them disagreement and upset which come up over again; most of these issues relate to their differences as people. The fact that sometimes these same issues arise over and over again shows that they've only been partially successful at learning to live with their differences. We must use differences as a strength and not a basis to disagree or go off in a huff.

It can be tempting to look down on the differences of one's partner: somehow, the way *we* are always seems to be better and more logical than the way others see or do things. We can think that the way we approach life is 'common sense' and that everyone would (or ought) to approach it that way – but once we are married we shall soon realise that our 'sense' was not so common after all; it was just *our* sense rather than a common sense. While there are some differences to which value judgments can be applied (it is better to be punctual than to waste other people's time, for example), my way or yours is not necessarily better; as Olive Dawes pointed out in her book *Choosing to Love*, being different is not a weapon to use against one another; instead it can and should be used as a potential asset for a more complete life together.

Differences between the sexes are worth touching on briefly once again. There is increasing evidence that brains themselves are 'gendered' – that men and women tend to have different types of brains just as they have different physical characteristics. We should not expect our husbands necessarily to think through or respond to problems in the same way that we do (there is probably nothing 'wrong' with them if they don't!), and likewise husbands should not expect their wives to be identikit versions of themselves. There is often not just one way to approach a situation, and we should think very carefully before we impose our own way on others or chastise them for handling things differently from the way we do ourselves. We need to look for complementary attributes (for instance: I don't need to be as sensitive and emotionally aware as my wife because she is already providing that function within the family; conversely because of my presence she doesn't need to be as linear and logical as I may be; this is a far better approach than she criticising me for not caring when something upsetting happens, or my attacking her for not evaluating our financial position in the same way as I). We are different; that is that, and we need to live with it because it isn't going to change!

Then we can get into differences of personality or viewpoint: extrovert versus introvert, logical or intuitive, thinker or feeler, structured or flexible. There are no rights and wrongs here, and we mustn't make wrongs out of them where none exist. Habits and behaviours can change, but basic personality is unlikely to.

The difference in our own upbringing and socio-economic background will also have an impact on some of the areas that couples most often disagree about: debates about money, how to bring up the children, and relationships with parents. We need to take time to listen and to try to understand each other, if necessary making clear what assumptions we are working on rather than taking them for granted. It's worth remembering, however, that there are some things we might never understand about our partner nor they about us – it's just the way we are. We shall never see things exactly through their eyes, so it is good to know when simply to accept things and let them be.

Likewise there are some things on which you may never agree. This is fine as long as you or your partner do not insist on picking at them! Instead it's necessary to get emotional closure – to allow yourselves the space to disagree on something but nevertheless to be united in your overall aims as man and wife. You may never quite agree, for instance, on just how firm to be in disciplining the children. It's almost a cliché for the wife to think the husband is being too firm and the husband that the wife is being too soft; this happens again and again in countless marriages and it may never be fully resolved in your marriage. If you *have* to agree on an issue like this there will be constant antagonism. A different perspective on the matter might be that when the father's firmer approach and mother's gentler one are brought together the child gets just about the right mix of nurture and discipline that he or she is meant to get. If mum were to persuade dad or dad mum that only their way would do then that balance might very well tip too far in one direction or the other. This 'problem' between the couple may thus not actually be a problem at all if they can but trust each other to be doing their best in an uncertain situation.

We must try to avoid letting specific areas of disagreement take over the whole relationship so that it degenerates into a vicious circle of mutually frustrating interactions. We must avoid thinking that our relationship would be great if only we could get our partner straightened out and make them more like ourselves. Far better to be friends to one another, focusing on what is good and right in the relationship – what unifies us and draws us together – rather than what divides us. It is a big mistake to let our interactions be primarily problem-driven. Our relationship won't ever be perfect but there is a lot to be said for focusing on what is good within it rather than constantly picking at the weaknesses.

The imperfect marriage

All human marriages are imperfect – necessarily so because they have humans in them. As Fosdick the bygone preacher once put it: "It is not marriages that fail; it is the people that fail. All that marriage does is show people up." In the early infatuation stage of a relationship we can be so obsessed by the other person that we almost idolise them, putting them on a pedestal as if they had no faults. Of course in our rational mind we know that they do have faults, but the reality of what it really means to be a sinner oneself and to live with another sinner in such close proximity can take a while to sink in. There are bound to be mistakes; there are bound to be moments of failure and disillusion and we do well to set realistic expectations. Harry Tennant once quoted someone who said: "You should go into marriage with your eyes wide open (to a person's shortcomings). And then half close them afterwards!" Often it is the other way round, we go in with unrealistic expectations of the perfection of our partner (something that *we* not they have projected!), and then our eyes are opened to all their foibles and shortcomings. Instead, the quote exhorts, we need to do it the other way: understand and consider everything we can about our partner while dating

– their quirks and idiosyncrasies and the implications for daily life – and then, on entering marriage, look through or look over as many of the faults and imperfections as we possibly can. We need to be prepared to overlook and forgive again and again and again, always being mindful of how annoying some of our own peculiarities must be!

We have all married sinners, but the harsh truth is that we are sinners ourselves also. Jesus' parable about the debtor who was forgiven a great debt and then went and threw one of his own petty debtors into prison is powerful here. We can sometimes want to exact from our spouses for their faults, particularly when we feel they manifest themselves as injustices towards us; in these circumstances it is wise to remember that we may well be disappointing our partner's expectations and hopes just as much in other ways.

Let's take a long hard look at ourselves (not our partner!) and think about how sin manifests itself in our behaviour towards our partner. We won't do all of the unworthy things listed below, but we shall likely do some of them from time to time; we need to look these behaviours in the eye, denounce them and try to eradicate them. There is within each of us the bad spirit – the mind of the flesh – that part of us which is irrational and emotionally destructive, immature, selfish, controlling, and power seeking. It is the part which does things like:

- Score-keeping (doing good things for brownie points so that your partner owes you a debt you can cash in later; taking note of their wrongs to demonstrate on another occasion how unworthy they are).
- Fault-finding ('We had a great day out except for when you ...'; this is the attitude that lies behind statements like 'you should have ...', 'you always ...', 'you never ...').
- Seeking to dominate (treating your partner with condescension and intimidation, or bossing them around).
- Taking the moral high ground (sulking or acting like a martyr if you are not recognised as right or if you don't get your way).

- Showing passive aggression (seeking to control or win by insidious and underhand means; opting out, giving the silent treatment).
- Losing one's temper (causing a scene, seeking to take control through power and fear).
- Deflecting (pretending to be angry or upset by one thing when you are really upset about another; having a hidden agenda).
- Withholding sex as a punishment to one's partner when a reasonable attempt at reconciliation or the fulfilling of their obligations has been made.
- Refusing to forgive (making them pay for their wrongs, refusing to trust so as not to be hurt again).
- Giving up (behaving as if failure and misery is inevitable; refusing to try again; refusing to show emotion or commitment).
- Using threats as a lever ('If you do that one more time I'm leaving...'). Escalation.

When do these sorts of behaviours show up? It can be at any time, but there are two particular circumstances to be alert to. One is when we are tired, fed up or irritated by something else (for instance something bad that has happened at work). In these circumstances our partner can be way too handy as an object to bear the brunt of our frustrations: we can use them as an outlet for our bad feelings, taking out on them the irritation or anger that we feel. We can end up talking to them and treating them in ways we would never treat those we know less well, using them as the recipients of our venting. All of this is completely unfair and not conducive to a good relationship.

Another time to be wary is when we argue; it is these times of disagreement which are a true test of the quality of our character and our love. How we handle disagreements is key, with restraint in an argument being part of the cost of true love (while what we say can be forgiven, when it is cruel, cutting, personal or humiliating it is much harder to forget). What we want to avoid is the classic pattern of marriage trench warfare – the blazing row followed by a total lack of communication. In fact, those two extremes bring out two poles of behaviour towards which individuals tend to cluster with respect to disagreements. There is the 'rhino' type who charge in all guns blazing and say whatever comes into their head, whatever the cost. At the other extreme is the 'hedgehog' who would rather not say anything at all when under stress, the conflict avoider who would rather curl up into a ball to avoid the issue, only coming out again to resume normal life when the tension has passed. It is worth understanding where both we and our partner are on this continuum and making allowances for it. The hedgehog needs to understand that their partner cannot just ignore issues and pretend they are not there; they *need* to deal with them in some way, so an opportunity to do so must be found. The rhino needs to understand how much a hedgehog hates conflict and that they don't want to discuss or argue to the death about every issue; the rhino must keep calm and give their partner time and space until they are ready to discuss. Only by understanding and making allowances for one another will progress be possible.

The psychologist John Gottman, considered by some to have done more empirical analysis on couples' interactions than anyone else, has claimed to be able to predict with considerable certainty after just a few minutes observing a couple whether or not their relationship will succeed or will end in divorce. While we might be sceptical about this claim and while we should note that his observations take no account of any religious imperative that might drive a husband and wife to stay together, his observations based on a study of thousands and thousands of real life couples are at least interesting. In his opinion the key predictor of divorce is the way couples argue – not *that* they argue (all couples will, and many may do so frequently and with some passion), but *how* they argue. In particular he identifies four traits which he ominously calls the 'four horsemen'. They are particularly destructive and are strong predictors that a relationship will not fare well, especially when found in combination:

1. *Criticism* – attacking the person or character rather than disagreeing with a particular thought or action; 'you are so ...', 'you're the type of person who ...'
2. *Contempt* – being deliberately nasty and hurtful; name-calling, sarcasm, mockery, sneering, rolling your eyes.
3. *Defensiveness* – refusal to take criticism or recognise fault, deflecting or denying the issue, making excuses rather than accepting responsibility; 'yes, but ...', 'it's not my fault ...' 'I wouldn't have done it if you hadn't ...'
4. *Stonewalling* – withdrawing from the discussion by walking away abruptly and existing in another room, opting out, disconnecting, refusing to discuss, aloofness or smugness, the silent treatment.

Needless to say, none of these constitute Christlike behaviour and given their destructive impact on a relationship it makes good sense to be on the look out for them in one's own behaviour and to refuse to give them the time of day.

A final point about disagreements is that *we don't have to win*. There is nothing to prove; what we should be seeking for is not some hollow victory but a solution through which we can both live together in unity as husband and wife before God; oneness, once again, is key. We need to realise that usually the harder we fight to win the bigger we lose in terms of the toll it will take on the relationship. It doesn't feel good to be humiliated and ground into submission – in fact it feels absolutely horrible so why would we want to attempt to do this to our partner? Do we think that it won't have an impact, that we can go through life attempting to prove over and over again that we are right and that we know what we're talking about more than our partner does? How will it make them feel if this is the approach we take, and what will be the cost for our relationship? We may 'win' in the short term – being right keeps us 'safe' because it seems to imply to us that we can stay as we are without having to make changes – but in the long run we shall be huge losers because we shall lose the confidence, trust, respect, love and friendship of our partner and will instead earn their resentment because of our bullying self-righteousness. We may seek to claim our pound of flesh for our partner's error or ignorance but in the end we shall find as Shylock did that it will do us more harm than good. It is often better to be happy rather than (what we perceive to be) 'right'.

All this being said – and we've spent quite some time considering differences and disagreements by this point – while we should expect difficulties, we should not obsess over them or make more of them than we need. There will be disagreements; issues such as money, personal habits (tidiness), children, housework, sex, parents and friends do indeed bring differences of opinion but they are an opportunity for learning to live together and be united despite our differences.

At one level marriage means two sinners living together trying not to be sinners. It is the last part which is key – if we are both making a real effort to fight our unhelpful inclinations then with God's help and prayer we should be able to handle our differences and our faults and grow towards each other, and, even more importantly, towards Christ.

Isaac and Rebekah

Topics: A good start; Disunity and favouritism – a family divided; Failure to communicate.

The glimpses we have of the marriage of Isaac and Rebekah are a real mixed bag. There are certainly strengths (and this in what was effectively an arranged marriage), but there were also some serious issues which serve to highlight the importance of oneness in a relationship. We'll begin with a brief review of the positive scenes before a more in-depth examination of the more troubled side.

IT was Abraham's loyal servant who, at his master's behest, negotiated the marriage of Isaac and Rebekah. It was a calling she was willing and perhaps eager to accept and one which brought Isaac immense joy, a comfort which contrasted powerfully with the loss he had felt on the death of his mother. Isaac's taking her into his mother's tent speaks of shared intimacy and also the support and emotional closeness he hoped to enjoy with his wife. The action also hints at the family they would one day become, the first family to have the Abrahamic promises passed on to them for safekeeping.

There is another scene of intimacy, much later in their marriage when the Philistine king spots Isaac "sporting" with his wife, as the King James Version delicately puts it. The English phrase, though quaint, suggests two possible interpretations. One is that it portrays the mysterious dance-like aspect of a couple's physical attraction, or, as Solomon elsewhere put it, "the way of a man with a maid". Isaac and Rebekah were youth and maid no longer, but the affection and physical closeness they shared was such that they in some measure could not keep away from each other even in these clandestine circumstances. Alternatively, their "sporting" may be a reference to laughter: a shared joke or amusing happening relished by the pair, a knowing exchange which only comes from being acquainted with someone inside out and which told Abimelech there was more than met the eye about Isaac and Rebekah's supposed sibling relationship. A sense of humour shared between husband and wife is a wonderful asset in a marriage.

In yet another positive scene Isaac prays for his wife because of her childlessness, a touching illustration of one partner interceding for the other in a matter that would have been a big emotional burden for her to bear alone. His prayer is effective; even though her time of barrenness was long in human terms, the narrative tellingly juxtaposes the account of Isaac's prayer with the words, "And the LORD granted his prayer, and Rebekah his wife conceived" (Genesis 25:21, ESV). It is ample proof that our prayers on behalf of our partners do make a difference; all that is needed is for us to bother to offer and mean them. We might pray for our wife or husband when they are ill or going through some particular trial or stress, but our prayers are no less necessary when this is not the case.

The episode amongst the Philistines does have its negative side also. It was here that Isaac asked his wife to say she was his sister, just as his father had twice done. But when the scriptures quote the expression on Isaac's lips, "lest I die because of her" (26:9) an ominous note is struck. He was her husband, after all, so he was meant to be prepared to die for her, exactly as Christ would later do but specifically what he is reluctant to do here. Isaac's whole scheme here is one of self-preservation, saving one's own skin at the risk of the safety and integrity of one's wife. Isaac's behaviour provides a good counter-example to what a husband ought to do, seeking above all things the salvation of his wife even to the point of potentially laying down his life in the ultimate act of self-sacrifice.

But Rebekah loved Jacob

The breakdown of unity between Isaac and Rebekah really begins with the account of the twins. Isaac loved Esau because he ate of his son's venison – a rather shallow basis for favouritism and one in which it is hard to think the scriptures are encouraging our sympathy; Rebekah, on the other hand, loved Jacob (Genesis 25:27,28). In Rebekah's case no reason is given at all (though perhaps there is a resonance between her preference for Jacob and the Lord's, "Jacob have I loved but Esau have I hated"?); the record only leaves us to wonder.

Whatever the causes, the favouritism they allowed would drive a wedge into the family unit, no doubt exacerbating the tension that would have already existed between the two boys. This is seen in the episode of the sale of the birthright and in the thwarted blessing of Esau; this latter event will reveal all we need to know about the consequences of favouritism.

Clandestine operations

Oneness is central to what God wants from marriage because it is to be a reflection of His own oneness, the very essence of His nature. No one said that being one when you are in fact two is easy, but it remains what God wants, the journey of striving to attain it being one of the most educational and potentially rewarding paths that a man and a woman can take. In Isaac and Rebekah's case the problems of *not* being one are plain: the momentous occasion of the blessing of the firstborn seems to be planned by Isaac without his even discussing it with his wife; his action is high-handed, especially given his knowledge of what the promise of God had declared concerning the elder serving the younger. For her part, she clearly suspects something is up, listening at the keyhole to see what Isaac and Esau are up to.

When she discovers Isaac's plan she doesn't raise the matter with her husband, she instead plots and executes a whole clandestine operation which has interesting echoes and contrasts with the account of the Fall:

- The woman commands the man (this time her son rather than her husband: 27:6,8).
- The woman gives food into the hand of a man which becomes a trigger for sin.
- The deception.
- The closed eyes of Isaac and the moment of their opening.
- The coats of skins for clothing.

Each one of these details echoes the record of Genesis and sounds a terribly ominous note.

For her part Rebekah is certainly discerning and able to read the situation correctly; she is proactive and creative in coming up with a plan, and she is brave. All of these can be great attributes, but they are misused and misapplied in this sorry scene, this re-enactment of the Fall of the Edenic family. How much harder unity would be to achieve after this! Imagine how awkward it would have been at the dinner table that night, the stony tension, perhaps, between Isaac and Rebekah after this had gone down. Their marriage would never be the same.

They would both pay the price for their actions – Isaac's great trembling as he realises his foolish blindness and what he has almost done; the loss of one of their sons for years and years; the resentment and sorrow of the other; the deterioration of Isaac's relationship with Rebekah which would take much time and effort to rebuild. For Rebekah it would have been even worse given the closeness that she shared with Jacob. The dark shadow hanging over their marriage would be hers to bear too, but far worse, perhaps, the loss of her son. Much like her son she thinks she can organise, manipulate and orchestrate affairs the way she thinks they should be, bending circumstances to her will, but when she says, "Upon me be thy curse, my son" (27:13) she doesn't realise just how painful that burden will turn out to be across the years that lie ahead. When she encourages Jacob to flee to Haran for "a while", promising that "I will send and bring you from there" (27:44,45) she does not know that such a day will never come and that in this life she will never see her son again. We have to lie in the beds we make even though we are forgiven for our mistakes.

Communication breakdown

How can such an unfortunate sequence of events arise, and more importantly, how can it be avoided? The essential issue seems to be a failure to communicate, their inability to share with one another their views and plans and to come to a course of action. This must not be allowed to happen because communication is *essential* to oneness. Why is Isaac even *thinking* about blessing his son Esau without talking to Rebekah and involving her in the process? We can only guess that it's because he knows she won't agree and possibly because he even knows himself that what he is doing is wrong. It could be that he has already talked to her and they have reached a stalemate. If so they haven't communicated well enough and they need to go back to the table and try again.

Turning to Rebekah, even if we accept her clandestine spying, why does she not then talk to her husband instead of concocting her elaborate scheme of deception? As courageous as she evidently is, shouldn't she then have approached Isaac to bring the matter up, even if in a tangential way (if she thinks, for instance, that to confront him directly would be counter-productive)? Does she consider the consequences of her betrayal and think them a price worth paying, perhaps because she knows the whole question of the firstborn blessing and who should receive it is an issue they can't communicate about any more? Tragically it seems that she has stopped believing in their power to communicate and in their ability to be one.

Cross purposes

It's absolutely key to do all we can to try not to live at cross purposes with our partners on important issues in this manner. Isaac and Rebekah have come to live in separate worlds on this matter at least, working against each other in a climate of suspicion rather than in harmony and love. What they need to do is build bridges of communication back towards each other once more so that they can act as one in their family. It may well be for every couple that there are certain areas that are difficult to discuss – it is okay to accept that we shall not agree on everything and to make peace with that fact rather than constantly to pick at sores. We do, however, need to be able to express ourselves and to understand in some measure what our partner thinks and holds dear, even if we do not always share those feelings and views; our marriage covenant with them owes them at least this much.

Good communication requires a lot of investment; it doesn't come easily, especially if there are tricky matters to talk about where different opinions are held but it is essential to oneness, carrying the power to hold us together through disagreements. The alternative is to retreat into the isolation of separate worlds and to fight against one another as Isaac and Rebekah did.

The hard topics of communication are made easier when we take care of the more mundane matters. If we can be friendly towards one another by speaking respectfully and showing interest in what the other is saying over the small things then it will build a connection and strengthen a friendship bond which will stand us in good stead when the harder topics must be dealt with. If our communication has been reduced to vague grunts when our partner is speaking, or if we are always looking at our phones when our partner is trying to tell us about their day then that bond won't be there and frustration or hurt will take its place. We have to get the everyday right in communication before we can expect to be able to tackle the big things effectively; we have to invest. If we don't we can look forward to a taste of the isolation, manipulation and suspicion that Isaac and Rebekah experienced at this point in their married life.

Hannah and Elkanah

Topics: Family worship; Unsolvable problems – it's no one's fault;
Defensiveness; Taking problems to God; Giving one's partner space to deal
with their issues.

Elkanah chose to put first things first, structuring his family
life around the regular worship of God as the core component
of what their family was about. Introduced with the testimony
that "this man went up out of his city yearly to worship and to
sacrifice unto the LORD of hosts in Shiloh" (1 Samuel 1:3), the
scriptures follow this up with at least a further five references to
the family's worship, offerings, and yearly pilgrimage in the two
chapters the story takes to tell. Such a structure is the perfect
non-negotiable in family life because it involves putting God
in proper place and building the rest of life around Him. No
debate for Elkanah, then, whether worshipping God was taking
too much from family time; the two things were integral to one
another.

BUT even such a tremendous backbone to their family life,
as undoubtedly correct as it was, did not guarantee marital
bliss. The polygamy of the age provided a ready fuel for tension,
but there was another issue as well, one which was nobody's
fault:

> "And when the time was that Elkanah offered, he gave to
> Peninnah his wife, and to all her sons and her daughters,

portions: but unto Hannah he gave a worthy portion; for
he loved Hannah: but the LORD had shut up her womb. And
her adversary also provoked her sore, for to make her fret,
because the LORD had shut up her womb. And as he did so
year by year, when she went up to the house of the LORD, so
she provoked her; therefore she wept, and did not eat."

(1 Samuel 3:4-7)

Even the successful relationship that Hannah and Elkanah
seemed to share was not devoid of tears, then. Some of this
was avoidable (the polygamy-induced rivalry), some of it (the
childlessness) was not; it was just *there*.

Better than ten sons

Whatever the cause of sorrow in marriage, the issue has somehow
to be processed and often needs to be explicitly acknowledged
and addressed. It is the manner in which Hannah and Elkanah
do so that is instructive, furnishing some great lessons both
positive and negative for couples of every age:

"Then said Elkanah her husband to her, Hannah, why weepest
thou? And why eatest thou not? And why is thy heart grieved?
Am not I better to thee than ten sons? So Hannah rose up
after they had eaten in Shiloh ... and she was in bitterness of
soul, and prayed unto the LORD, and wept sore."

(verses 8-10)

Elkanah asks four questions, the first three of which are
about her ("Why weepest *thou*? Why eatest *thou* not? Why is *thy*
heart grieved?"), and a final one which introduces himself ("Am
not *I* better to thee than ten sons?"). This is a very interesting
transition. His overriding concern is with *her* (hence the first
three questions), but he ends up defending *himself* (implicitly,
'What more can I do here? It isn't my fault we can't have any
children together.') It is sometimes observed that men have a
tendency to look for solutions to problems when women just
want their husbands to listen, sympathise and understand.
Elkanah wants to help and there is nothing he would love more
than to be able to solve this situation but at the end of the day he

can't. Given that he can't – given that he has nothing to bring to the table as far as this problem is concerned – he feels inadequate and thus retreats to self-defence ('I'm doing the best I can; aren't I already the best husband I can be?!').

It has been somewhat dryly observed, "There is nothing so pleasing to a man as the happiness of his wife – he is proud of himself as the source of it!" What we have here is the truth of that little aphorism being illustrated in reverse. Faced with a situation where his wife is upset about something he is powerless to change, he moves from concern for her to defence of himself. He feels bad because of the sadness of Hannah and protects himself from any negative implication this might have for him as a husband by building a self-defence ("Am not I better to thee than ten sons?"). Elkanah never intends his questions to come over defensively in that way (and she has never once suggested that she thinks the childlessness his fault); indeed, as Elkanah starts out (the first three questions) self-defence is not his main motivation at all. But it is very interesting that this is nevertheless where he implicitly ends up. It is a very human trait: we are often inclined to jump to self-preservation mode under pressure or when we wish a situation to be other than it is.

It's much easier to see this transition from helping someone else to defending oneself when we witness it as a third party to someone else's conversation. It's much harder to spot it when it's in our own relationship, when *we* are the ones who are emotionally invested and whose honour or ego is at stake. Yet there is no need to be defensive when we are trying to resolve an issue in marriage or when we are trying to help our partner in a circumstance they face. Some difficulties in marriage are not anyone's fault (illness, unemployment, differences in schedules, interests, temperaments, opinions, feelings); it's just the way things are, and nobody is in the wrong. But this observation, while true, doesn't make those problems go away; they still have to be addressed in a spirit of love without any blame being implied or felt in either direction.

True and not true

Elkanah's words in his rhetorical fourth question ("Am I not better to thee than ten sons?") are both true and not true, as is often the case in what is said when couples are under pressure. In one sense Elkanah is right: he was a wonderful husband and she couldn't reasonably have asked much more of him than what he was already giving. But this fact, while true, is beside the point. The problem is that she yearns for a child and from that perspective it could not possibly be true that he is better to her than ten sons. He is a *husband*, after all, and no matter how many times we multiply husbands, it does not turn them into sons! He can never fill the role of son in her life, and he has to come to terms with that as much as she: she is still sad about her lack of children without thinking any less of him. What he has to do is to help her as she works it out with God.

When faced with such circumstances ourselves, we too may need to remind ourselves that this isn't about us and we should not make it so – it is about trying to help our partner. In a modern marriage one partner may suffer from depression, for instance; it is no one's *fault* in all probability, yet the depression is still there and has to be faced. Both partners may blame themselves; both may defend themselves – but neither of these behaviours will particularly help. What they have to strive to do is live and love *through* it in faith together. One partner may have an illness whose burden the other can never truly enter into or understand; they only suffer the indirect consequences of it. It is not the fault of either, and no one has a need to defend themselves. One partner may be having a real struggle in their work, or be working through a dysfunctional relationship with one of the children or with a colleague or boss at work – there are any number of examples. The one suffering in this way must be careful not to transfer blame or mistreatment onto their partner because they happen to be near at hand and the easiest ones to attack. Equally, the partner can only offer help and support, they probably cannot solve – and neither must they blame themselves nor feel the need either to defend themselves or attack their partner because the situation exists.

Involving the Lord

So does Elkanah help in what he says? In one sense, not very much. Pointing out that he is an excellent husband, while true, is most definitely *not* the point. Elkanah can never fill the void Hannah feels because of the absence of a son, and though this may be a sad reality for him to face, face it he must.

Yet paradoxically he does help. Though what he says certainly doesn't answer Hannah's question, it triggers a course of action in her which is absolutely the right thing for her to do. The most powerful lesson of all here comes from Hannah.

What she does is to take her problem to the Lord. She doesn't answer Elkanah's question; she doesn't ask him how he can be so foolish as to think that he can fill the hole that she feels in her heart. There is no helpful answer to his question of how he measures up against ten sons, so she does not pursue this line of reasoning. Instead, she makes up her mind that the only thing she can do is take her problem to the Lord. It is no use to sit at the table weeping any more and refusing to eat. It is no use, either, to sit there with her husband discussing it, since there is nothing he can do either. Perhaps she realises from his response that her continued free expression of the way she feels in tears and fasting will do more harm than good in her relationship if it continues. She has come to the end of the line; there is nowhere to go but to the Lord. Not, I think, that she hadn't prayed about the issue before. But not with *this* intensity. Now she stands at a crossroads in her life.

What this shows is that even through her tears she is listening to what her husband is saying. Not to the literal level of his question, but to what he *means*, and to the feelings which must undergird what he says. This is emotional intelligence of the highest order – tuned listening. Even in her distraught state she realises that this must now be between her and God alone;

she must leave it in His charge and then move on. This is very, very wise.

Consent

At this point in the narrative we must hit 'fast forward'. The rest of the story turns out well for Hannah – she has done the right thing in casting herself upon the Lord, and He has responded with overflowing grace. There is one more detail, though, which permits another glimpse of the strength of Hannah's relationship with her husband:

> "And the man Elkanah, and all his house, went up to offer unto the LORD the yearly sacrifice, and his vow. But Hannah went not up; for she said unto her husband, I will not go up until the child be weaned, and then I will bring him, that he may appear before the LORD, and there abide for ever. And Elkanah her husband said unto her, Do what seemeth thee good; tarry until thou have weaned him; only the LORD establish his word." (1 Samuel 1:21-23)

We often think of Hannah's sacrifice when she gave up Samuel to the Lord's service, but Elkanah made an enormous sacrifice too, doing so apparently without having been consulted, for Hannah makes the promise to the Lord in Eli's presence when her husband is absent. It's possible to imagine that he might have been outraged by this: it is his firstborn son through Hannah, after all – he is at least fifty per cent invested and firstborn sons were extremely important, perhaps particularly to fathers. But he is wise enough to give Hannah the space and autonomy she needs to make her decision. He does not need to make a point about his headship here, for he can trust his wife to make a good spiritual decision, and he will live with the consequences. He understands the wrench it will be for her to give Samuel up, and in the context of that he puts aside his own feelings on the matter, whatever they might have been.

Thus it is, in the verses just quoted, that when Hannah decides to remain behind to wean Samuel and spend her last precious days with him rather than participating in the usual

Shiloh pilgrimage, Elkanah can say: "Do what seemeth thee good ... only the LORD establish his word." As long as God's word is paramount in his family (this is the crucial rider, the "only ..." at the end of his speech), then Hannah has the freedom to make her choices even in matters which deeply concern him. He gives her space; he understands and makes room for her to 'do what she has to do'. He understands that this is her issue and that she has finally found a way, in God's mercy, to address it. And so he adopts a beautiful lightness of touch, lending his wife a supportive freedom within which she can serve the Lord as she has promised.

Jacob and Leah

Topics: Making peace with inadequacy and surviving disappointments; The most important relationship is with God; Times change and sorrows pass.

Few modern wives would envy Leah, foisted as she was upon Jacob by an over-eager and scheming father, locked in a relationship where she was clearly and repeatedly the second choice and forced to negotiate with her sister for the sexual favours of her husband. What is remarkable about her is that somehow or other she makes her peace with this and finds refuge and even joy in God. It may just be that in the end, when the distraction of Rachel is taken away, that Jacob comes more fully to appreciate and love her as well.

IT was not that Leah was unattractive. Her 'tender eyes' that King James' men refer to are also said to belong to King David in a context which is likely not derogatory. But she is not the devastating beauty that Rachel is, the one to whose charms Jacob seems inexorably drawn (Genesis 29:16-20). With the lights off Leah is the equal of her sister (what an exquisite condemnation of the human preoccupation with the sight of the eyes this is!), for Jacob does not discern his duping until the dawn. Once the light has returned, however, Jacob can't take his eyes off Rachel again and Leah is neglected:

"And Jacob went in also unto Rachel, and he loved also Rachel more than Leah, and served with [Laban] yet seven other years. And when the LORD saw that Leah was hated, he opened her womb: but Rachel was barren."   (Genesis 29:30,31)

Evidently Jacob and Leah did have periodic relations or there would have been no children at all, but the preference for Rachel was clearly known and understood by all. A glimpse from the later quarrel over the mandrakes perhaps suggests that Leah predominantly suffered in silence with this only occasionally flaring into a portrayal of her true feelings ("Is it a small matter that thou hast taken my husband? and wouldest thou take away my son's mandrakes also?", Genesis 30:15).

Less than the best

Before we examine the redemptive process through which Leah comes to move ahead in this awful situation, it's important to consider what parallels there might be, if indeed there are any, in a modern relationship. The polygamy and favouritism of Leah's actual and specific circumstance will not be ours but her discovery that her marriage is turning out to be rather less than she had hoped may well be very relevant.

Why might we be disappointed? One reason might be because of wrong or unrealistic expectations of marriage, something which we addressed in chapter 1. But let's suppose that this is not the case; the fact is that we can *still* be disappointed. Why? Because people let us down; because we let ourselves down; because people sometimes change in their interests and behavioural patterns, and occasionally in their characters. We are human beings, after all, and it's likely that even with the best will in the world, we won't have made enough allowances for the fact.

We do need to distinguish between the trivial and the more fundamental in terms of such misgivings. There are little disappointments which show up from time to time when our partner annoys us or reacts badly to a situation; there are disappointments, too, of a more nagging kind – but both can be put down to the foibles of human nature – foibles which through the virtues of love, forbearance and forgiveness, we can work around. But there is also in some cases a disappointment of a more fundamental kind which gnaws at the soul and causes the heart to ache, as it must have ached for Leah. There can be deep issues in a relationship which one partner wants to address but the other is not prepared even to recognise let alone work through and which consequently mar the relationship on a daily basis for one of the pair. What can be done then? People can find themselves in marriages where their partner no longer seems to feel they or their opinions matter, where love seems all but lost, and interest, effort and commitment long departed. While it is sometimes said that you can never really change your partner, sometimes partners *do* change all by themselves. They may lose their faith; they may develop a whole new set of interests and behaviour patterns which are at best disconcerting and at worst destructive; they may have an affair which forever changes the landscape of the relationship, or there may be yet other circumstances which seem to change fundamentally the type of person they are and the way they behave. This is something that as the partner you can certainly influence, but you cannot control; they must answer for themselves as you must answer for yourself.

How, then, can one survive traumas such as these? How can one live with this level of disappointment and find the strength to carry on? Perhaps it is here that Leah provides us with the most powerful exhortation.

Better than all the rest

We see it best in the passage in which Leah consecutively bears four children:

"And Leah conceived, and bare a son, and she called his name Reuben: for she said, Surely the LORD hath looked upon my affliction; now therefore my husband will love me. And she conceived again, and bare a son; and said, Because the LORD hath heard that I was hated, he hath therefore given me this son also; and she called his name Simeon. And she conceived again, and bare a son; and said, Now this time will my husband be joined unto me, because I have born him three sons; therefore was his name called Levi. And she conceived again, and bare a son: and she said, Now will I praise the LORD; therefore she called his name Judah; and left bearing."

(Genesis 29:32-35)

In total, Genesis lists seven children of Leah in this passage and in 30:18-21, six of whom (all the boys) have their names expounded by Leah after she has given birth. In no less than five out of those six name explanations Leah puts God front and centre:

1. "The LORD hath looked ..." (Reuben).
2. "The LORD hath heard ..." (Simeon).
3. "Now will I praise the LORD ..." (Judah).
4. "God hath given ..." (Issachar).
5. "God hath endued ..." (Zebulun).

This focus on the Lord and what He is doing for her in her family despite the huge inadequacies of which she was all too painfully aware shows Leah's high spiritual calibre. Rachel's naming of Joseph did refer to the Lord, but in such a way as to presume that she could control or predict His actions (Genesis 30:24) – which seems to be a far less spiritual approach (God is not named when Benjamin is born, so Rachel appears alone in her sorrow). Leah might have blamed God for her marital misfortune, but no, she finds solace in His grace in giving her children, and she is delighted to admit it. It may be that in the shortcomings in our relationships we may be able to find comfort in the closeness of the bond we can have with our Heavenly Father and with His Son which helps us through as seems to have been the case with Leah.

It is perhaps the case that there is a progression in the naming of the first four children, which illustrates the way in which Leah gradually comes to terms with her situation. The first son she recognises as an expression of God's concern and love for her, going on to express the hope that now her husband will love her. If only it were that easy! Sadly her enthusiasm proves a little naive, as she recognises when Simeon is born. She rejoices that God has heard her, seeing Simeon as a counterweight blessing to the reality of her husband's 'hatred' of her (admittedly a Hebrew idiom, but a striking contrast with the love she had hoped for when Reuben was born).

The third son Levi is the exception in Leah's naming scheme because it does not mention God: this time she states that now her husband will be joined to her.[1] Once again, this is probably aspirational rather than prophetic; so far the names of all her sons, whether they include a reference to God or not, centre on the room for improvement that exists in her relationship with her husband.

Most telling, though, is the birth of the fourth son Judah upon which she says, "Now will I praise the LORD!". For the first time there is no reference to her husband. It is as if she has at last found contentment in what she has rather than hoping for more. Perhaps now she can somehow accept her life for what it is to some extent and so move forward in praising God. Her praise of Him and the birth of this son is not now associated with or contingent upon any improvement in her relationship with Jacob. No doubt she would still like improvement, but she can celebrate this moment of joy in her life purely with God. Perhaps the achievement of a certain level of acceptance of her marriage and also a sense of self-sufficiency in her relationship with God enables her to feel complete in herself with the Lord. She ceases childbearing and perhaps, for the time being at least, ceases trying to catch up with her sister in the pursuit of Jacob's affections.

It is a hard thing for anyone to have to swallow, but Leah seems to achieve a level of spiritual maturity here which is powerful. Her marriage is what it is with all its inadequacies, but

---

1   Interestingly, Levi becomes the forefather of the priests and Levites who are themselves 'joined' to the Lord in service and through whose work other men and women can themselves be 'joined'. Even if in the first instance she was speaking of a natural joining with her husband, Leah's naming did become prophetic of a more important work of bonding.

this needn't spoil her relationship with God – in fact it may even make it stronger because her need for God is so tangible. Her acceptance bespeaks a maturity and a realism, certainly, but it also is the hallmark of a deep faith and spiritual connectedness. Her marriage will still have its issues: she will still quarrel with her sister, she will still feel pain, and she will still hope she can draw closer to her husband – but for now in this calm moment of joy she can find peace and contentment in praising God.

Times change
Perhaps it is wishful thinking, but there may be truth to the suspicion that as the years went by Jacob came to have a higher and higher opinion of Leah. The testimony of the scriptures to Leah's concern for God contrasts with Rachel making off with her father's household teraphim; over the years Jacob may have realised there were other differences between his wives beyond the irresistible physical attraction of Rachel, itself perhaps now diminishing with the passing years. Perhaps it was not until Rachel's passing that Jacob was finally able to focus on his relegated wife, the testimony of his last words recorded in Genesis 49 standing tall as a strong tribute in her favour:

"And [Jacob] charged them, and said unto them, I am to be gathered unto my people: bury me with my fathers in the cave that is in the field of Ephron the Hittite, in the cave that is in the field of Machpelah, which is before Mamre, in the land of Canaan, which Abraham bought with the field of Ephron the Hittite for a possession of a buryingplace. There they buried Abraham and Sarah his wife; there they buried Isaac and Rebekah his wife; and there I buried Leah."
(Genesis 49:29-31)

In the very next verse Jacob gathers up his feet into the bed and is gathered unto his people, meaning that the very last words on his lips in the scriptural account are of his wife Leah.[2] She had stuck with him through thick and thin – mostly thin –

---

2   This comment assumes the words, "The purchase of the burying plot was from the children of Heth" are a note from the narrator rather than the words of Jacob. Even

and now finally he gives her the place she deserves. Jacob places great store in being buried in the Promised Land where his fathers and their wives were buried. Rachel is buried along the way but Leah makes it to the end and is buried alongside Jacob awaiting the day of resurrection. Sometimes relationships are slow in realising their full potential, but with God's grace there is always hope that we may get there in the end.

---

if they are the words of Jacob, the fact remains that the final person of his family that Jacob lists is his wife Leah.

Nabal, Abigail and David

Topics: Why were Nabal and Abigail married?; Surviving a marriage to a fool;
Refusing to 'opt out'; Abigail's tact and decisiveness on behalf of her family;
How to speak to one's partner.

When the strange pairing of Nabal and Abigail are introduced
it is by way of stark contrast: "Now the name of the man was
Nabal ('fool'); and the name of his wife Abigail: and she was a
woman of good understanding, and of a beautiful countenance:
but the man was churlish and evil in his doings; and he was of the
house of Caleb" (1 Samuel 25:3). She is the perfect combination:
a spiritual woman (notice that this is put first) *and* really good
looking; what more could a man want than these two? But if
that is the case what is she doing with *him*? Nabal, by contrast,
is "churlish and evil in his doings", and his name, either by
unfortunate coincidence of sound or because he was given the
tag as a nickname, is 'Fool'.

S O how come these two are together? – there would scarcely
seem a more ill-matched pair, a more fateful juxtaposition.
The scriptures give no hint of an answer to this question but it
is interesting to think through the possible options. We might
speculate that the marriage was an arranged match or that
circumstances (social pressures or economic factors impacting
the families in some way) compelled it. In this case Abigail may
well have had little or no option in the matter, and kudos to her

for enduring him in faithfulness to her marriage vow. Perhaps this is the most likely explanation, and if so it is an illustration that even bad marriages can be survived if there is a will (Abigail seems no less of a person despite her ill-fortune).

Marriage gone awry?

It need not *necessarily* have been that way, however. It is possible that it was originally a love marriage even if little of that seems left by this point. Could it be that the marriage originally began on a stronger footing and that priorities and character have shifted for one or both of them as time has gone by, he for the worse and she for the better (could it be that it is essentially drink that has made a fool of him?). This is by no means impossible nor unknown: there are genuine cases where people change in a way that simply could not have been anticipated when the relationship began. If this is the case in a marriage the consequences have somehow to be absorbed and it will not be easy – though it is possible, as Abigail's example shows.

If this is the right interpretation we may observe that Nabal is too busy being surly and drunk to pay too much attention to his marriage, but we are left to sorrow for Abigail for the emotional pain and sense of spiritual compromise that she would experience on a daily basis because of what her husband had become. Still, though, she sticks with him – while we do not know whether she had any other options from a social or economic perspective (irrespective of the more important spiritual considerations), her doing so remains an act of covenant faithfulness to her marriage vows and in that sense a tribute to her spirituality. Her remaining in the marriage whether by choice (as it would be in the West today) or compulsion (as it may well have been then) presents her with an opportunity to exercise, in one of the most poignant ways imaginable, the godly virtues of longsuffering, forbearance, and faithfulness in the face of foolishness. Her life has become a living sacrifice of a kind that a more typical modern-day attitude devoid of spiritual considerations would scarcely begin to contemplate ('you only live once so you owe it to yourself to move on as fast as you can').

A bad choice?

A third rationale for Nabal and Abigail's relationship might be that she *did* have a choice but made an alarmingly bad one when she agreed to marry her fool, one that she now regretted almost every day. Could it have been that she had been attracted to some aspect of his personality, a sense of humour perhaps, a carefree attitude not yet spoiled by drink, or even some boyish charm or good looks? The fact that she is a "woman of good understanding" might make this explanation seem less likely, but wisdom and understanding do not preclude the making of occasional terrible mistakes, even such a big potential mistake as this. Whether or not it is so in this particular case (we simply cannot say), it is nevertheless worth considering what the implications of such a scenario might be.

The headline message would be blindingly obvious: 'Don't marry an idiot! Be really, really careful that you're making a good choice.' But while this is an obvious point it may still need making from time to time. Where the heart is concerned (and when infatuation kicks in) the head can be in danger of being overruled, particularly in a culture that esteems the cupid effect so highly. We can overweight a person's physique, background, status, humour, wealth, boyish smile, tempting curves, sporting prowess, sultry voice or turn of phrase – whatever it is that catches our imagination and has us spinning – and underweight the more important matters of spirituality, objectives, and whether or not a person is *godly* and whether or not they are *kind*. We are not saying that Abigail did this – it is but one of three possible explanations why she is married to Nabal. But the very fact that she *is* married to him and that they are such obvious misfits is good occasion to ask the wider question of how it can be that mismatches can happen, and how they might be avoided.

The problem of marrying a fool is that its consequences have to be endured every day; they never go away. If we strive to be godly ourselves and yet choose to marry someone who isn't then we shall have to lie in the bed that we have made with all the challenges it brings. The best policy here is not to be in the situation in the first place, to make sure we are thinking with our heads and that we are measuring a potential partner against a spiritual yardstick and not one from a glossy magazine or a cultural norm. Paul knew what he was talking about when he cautioned about being unequally yoked with unbelievers. It is a strongly worded passage which grabs us by the scruff of the neck and tells us to wake up if we are falling under the illusion that it really doesn't matter all that much.

Coping with a bad marriage

Assuming, then, that Nabal and Abigail's marriage is an unhappy one as seems most likely, what does Abigail's example within it demonstrate? Given the situation that she is in, what can we learn from her about how to survive such a marriage? Two aspects seem to jump out of the text here.

One is that she does not absolve herself of responsibility for her own behaviour and the care of her family; she does not resign herself to a 'come what may' failure compelled by his awfulness. Instead she is fully engaged in protecting and providing despite all her frustration with her husband. If he will not act in the right way for the interests of the household then she will because the family is her responsibility too (notice how the servant knows to come to her when there is a serious matter: 1 Samuel 25:14). Although "he is such a man of Belial a man cannot speak to him" she can still find ways to accomplish what she needs to for her family as she ably demonstrates when she saves them all from David's vengeful hand. Would it have been easier if he had been supportive, considerate, and someone with whom one could communicate? Absolutely. But though he was none of those things she still faithfully discharges her responsibilities to the household, growing into a bigger person for all his lack. It certainly wouldn't have been easy; most likely it brought some moments of intense sadness for her and perhaps a dull background ache every day. But she managed to do it, and her faithfulness within her house was rewarded.

The second aspect is her knowledge of her husband and her smartness in working around him. When she returns from visiting David to find Nabal bingeing on alcohol again she knows better than to say anything to him. She might well have picked a row on this or many another occasion. Instead she waits for a better moment the following morning. She knows how to keep her counsel and it is after this display of patience that God seemingly intervenes to take the fool away.

Swift action

When danger looms Abigail has the perception to see the significance of the issue and to take speedy and decisive action, doing what she has to do for the safety of her family and goods:

> "Then Abigail *made haste*, and took two hundred loaves, and two bottles of wine, and five sheep ready dressed, and five measures of parched corn, and an hundred clusters of raisins, and two hundred cakes of figs, and laid them on asses."
> (1 Samuel 25:18)

Although her husband was not about to provide any help she takes stock of the assets she has at her disposal (physical goods and her own personal charm in this case) and immediately puts them into action. The record states that she "made haste", proactively and decisively stepping out on what could have been a suicide mission. She sees a window of potential opportunity to avert disaster and she courageously takes it.

The record repeats the point about her speedy and decisive action only a few verses later:

> "And when Abigail saw David, she *hasted*, and lighted off the ass, and fell before David on her face, and bowed herself to the ground ..."
> (1 Samuel 25:23)

And then again towards the end of the chapter when Nabal is dead and David sends for her to become his wife the same note is sounded:

"And Abigail *hasted*, and arose, and rode upon an ass, with five damsels of hers that went after her; and she went after the messengers of David, and became his wife."

(1 Samuel 25:42)

Not hers, then, the tendency to mope or bemoan her lot, tough though it was in the first half of the narrative. Like the virtuous woman of Proverbs she makes appropriate preparations and then steps up to the plate, saving her family in the process. When she meets David there is no standing on ceremony on her part as the prosperous wife of a wealthy and powerful man; instead she prostrates herself before David and shows immense humility, carefully choosing her words and line of argument to influence him to do the right thing. For his part, he fully appreciates the distinctive bravery that she has shown, recognising behind it the hand of God at work:

"And David said to Abigail, Blessed be the LORD God of Israel, which sent thee this day to meet me ..."   (25:32)

The story has a happy ending and Abigail's longsuffering is rewarded. Later on David realises that Nabal's death is a reward for his sinfulness (and perhaps for Abigail's righteousness too though this is not stated), the Lord having used Nabal's folly and Abigail's understanding as part of His larger purpose. If we are in an unhappy marriage in which we are treated unreasonably and where our partner's behaviour is either sinful, foolish in the way that Nabal's was, or simply unkind and inconsiderate, we can be assured that God sees our struggles and is there to meet our need. While there may not be a solution of the kind that presented itself for Abigail when her husband died and David stepped forward, our patience and faithfulness in our pain is seen and will be rewarded. We have another and greater marriage partner in the Lord Jesus, a comfort and a hope that no one can take away from us. In the meantime Abigail's example and proactiveness to do what she could in the difficult circumstances she found herself in can be a source of encouragement and inspiration.

42

Hosea and Gomer, God and Israel

Topics: A living parable of unfaithfulness and forgiveness; Marriage, breakdown & reconciliation; Judgment and punishment; Mercy and forgiveness; God's five-point plan; Listening and reciprocity.

Hosea's relationship with his wife Gomer is a unique parable of God's relationship with His bride Israel. While we should be cautious about extrapolating from the specifics of this very particular parable into general rules about marriage conduct, there are certainly some interesting lessons to observe.

H OSEA'S marriage was carefully controlled by God and used as a living sign and witness to the people of Israel and Judah. In that sense it was highly particular, much like the termination of Ezekiel's marriage: his wife died at God's behest as a symbol of the 'death' of God's kingdom. In both of these instances the role of God's prophet takes on a very personal dimension – it is not just that they speak God's words; they also have to live with the anguishing emotional implications. The point of this is not that God is cruel but that the emotional trauma that His prophets experience is an analogue to the emotional pain that God Himself feels when Israel and Judah treat Him as they do. The nearest we can come to understanding what God goes through here in the failure of His own marriage is to analogise what it would be like to suffer this in a human marriage. For Hosea and Ezekiel this is not a theoretical exercise; the pain is sickeningly real.

Hosea is commanded by God to marry a "wife of whoredoms" – perhaps a woman who is known as a professional prostitute or a woman who was simply known to have been 'loose' and unfaithful in the past. Hosea therefore finds and marries Gomer, only to find that her unfaithful ways persist into the marriage.

While there are not quite enough details in the Hosea text to reconstruct precisely the timeline of his personal life, if we are prepared to 'join the dots' a little it appears that the marriage breaks down because she takes off and goes to live with other lovers. While no formal termination of the relationship is noted on Hosea's part, the words God commands Hosea to speak in chapters 1 and 2 imply that the relationship has terminated, much like God's relationship with Israel. Of course knowing the bigger picture we as readers know that God will restore it and that God has not permanently cast off His people, but language like "they are not my people and I am not their God" (1:9) and "she is not my wife and neither am I her husband" (2:2) suggests that for the time being God has divorced Israel and perhaps Hosea has divorced Gomer.

There is some debate in Hosea 3 about whether the woman in question is Gomer; without going into the details of this, let us assume that she is (this seems to make most sense in terms of reading the narrative and message of Hosea as a whole). If this is so it appears that Gomer has got herself into serious emotional and financial difficulties, perhaps resulting in her having to sell herself into 'slavery' as a prostitute. Her lovers have not really been there for her when she needed; their only interest was to exploit her for their own ends. At God's behest (and having suffered the trauma of her previous infidelity and the breakdown of their marriage) Hosea forgives her and buys her back, becoming her husband once again. This is a moving picture of God's willingness to redeem His people to Himself and marry them again despite all that they have done. There appears to be no resentment, no extracting of payment or lesser status for her because of the trouble she has caused. This is pure grace, and chimes with passages like the Isaiah one in which God asks: "Where is the bill of your mother's divorce?" (Isaiah 50:1). The implication of this rhetorical question is that there isn't one any more because God has torn it up, completely and utterly forgiving His people and reconciling them to Himself. Now that the circumstances are right for her forgiveneness and their delightful reunion, God does not keep score.

Judgment and forgiveness

Two clear lessons emerge from all of this which must be carefully balanced: lessons relating to judgment and forgiveness. We can reflect on these both in relation to the Hosea narrative and what it reveals about the character of God, and also in relation to its relevance for marriage difficulties today. First, let us consider judgment. It is not the case that Gomer (or Israel for whom she stands) is simply able to do whatever she likes and God will overlook it. There is no way that it can be said she 'gets away with it' – that God just turns a blind eye to her gross unfaithfulness. This comes out clearly in a passage like the following:

"Say ye unto your brethren, Ammi ('my people'); and to your sisters, Ruhamah ('mercy'). Plead with your mother, plead: for she is not my wife, neither am I her husband: let her therefore put away her whoredoms out of her sight, and her adulteries from between her breasts; lest I strip her naked, and set her as in the day that she was born, and make her as a wilderness, and set her like a dry land, and slay her with thirst. And I will not have mercy upon her children; for they be the children of whoredoms. For their mother hath played the harlot: she that conceived them hath done shamefully: for she said, I will go after my lovers, that give me my bread and my water, my wool and my flax, mine oil and my drink. Therefore, behold, I will hedge up thy way with thorns, and make a wall, that she shall not find her paths. And she shall follow after her lovers, but she shall not overtake them; and she shall seek them, but shall not find them: then shall she say, I will go and return to

my first husband; for then was it better with me than now."
(Hosea 2:1-7)

God's standards and righteousness must be upheld and His truth will out. One cannot look at Gomer or Israel's behaviour and say that it does not matter or that there was no price to pay. The language of judgment is prevalent here – there must be and there were consequences for the terrible way she behaved. Similarly in a marriage today in which there is misconduct and serious difficulties of the type encountered here, the message is not that whatever is done to us and however we are treated we must simply grin and bear it. The example of God and Israel does not support the view that we should not respond or take appropriate remedial action if we are mistreated or are the recipients of repeated unfaithful behaviour. It was the consequences of Gomer's sin and the separation which ultimately brought Gomer (and Israel) into a position where Hosea (and God) could take her back. While a willingness to forgive and an understanding of the weaknesses of human nature is clearly important, people are much more likely to change and to realise their behaviour is unacceptable if there are consequences. That is clearly the approach God takes with Israel, and while we are not in God's stead as judges it's important not to think that a Christian faith impels us to have no standards and demands that we accept however evilly our partner treats us or our family.

The second lesson though contrasts with this point about judgment and centres instead on forgiveness. Ultimately, when the time was right, God was prepared to forgive His people (as Hosea did with Gomer) despite the despicable nature of their sin. This then tempers the principle of judgment and reminds us what is unique about the Biblical position. God forgives and takes back in a situation where perhaps most professional marriage counsellors might tell Him it makes no sense – that the situation is too hopeless for resolution. It is a very powerful thing that even in Hosea 1-3 when there is so much written about judgment God cannot help Himself (as it were) from speaking about the glorious possibility of reconciliation and His willingness to bring it about. This means that through all our failings in marriage – and in particular here we are talking about the failings of our partner – we should be looking for opportunities not to extract our pound of flesh or 'teach them a lesson' but to show the mercy of God and His drive to heal the breach and be reconciled so that unity will prevail. There must be judgment in a marriage at a certain level – but it is not this which will distinguish a Bible-based marriage from any other; it is the willingness to show mercy and forgiveness which will do that, the willingness to pick oneself up and try again and again and again because the drive to be one with our partner and so demonstrate the unity of God is so strong.

It is the balancing of these two aspects which is the great challenge, and of course there are no easy answers here. Studying Hosea's marriage does not tell us what to do if our own marriage is in difficulty (as we mentioned at the start, we need to be careful about extrapolating from a highly specific parabolic example of a marriage), but it does put before us two principles which we must think through and which, if we can balance them out, can help us immensely. If our partner is behaving unreasonably in our judgment then it is something that needs to be addressed, and there may need to be consequences if they are ever going to change; being a doormat for our partner is no good for either them or us. But at the same time we have a calling and a duty to be tirelessly forgiving, to be people who love mercy and kindness, and to forgive as our Father in heaven has forgiven us.

God's road map for marriage
One of the most beautiful of the many beautiful passages in Hosea occurs at the end of chapter 2 once God has made plain the judgments that His unfaithful wife must suffer. His ultimate plan is not to leave her there stewing in the juice of her own evil, but to bring her to Himself again, to cleanse her and to make her glorious. This ultimate purpose of God in His marriage to His people (both natural and spiritual Israel) is expressed like this:

"And I will betroth thee unto me for ever;
Yea, I will betroth thee unto me …
    in righteousness,
    and in judgment,
    and in lovingkindness,
    and in mercies.
I will even betroth thee unto me
    in faithfulness:
And thou shalt know the LORD."   (Hosea 2:19,20)

These five attributes are a very helpful summary of attributes which are characteristic of God's own marriage and which will be extraordinarily helpful in a human marriage also. They are attributes which we should look for our own marriages to uphold and express, and which we each individually must try to display towards our partner. They involve being fair, honest and true, speaking what is right rather than what is convenient or easy. They involve us in an exploration of the very character of God Himself, seeking to show forgiveness and covenant mercy and faithfulness towards our partner as we have been shown. They are attributes which, if we can only inculcate them and make them part of ourselves, will enable us to know and experience the divine.

Listening

Immediately after this five-point plan God enumerates some further blessings which will flow from this wonderful marriage. They all revolve around the concept of *hearing* or *answering* (the same Hebrew word can have both meanings), repeated five times (it is worth reading the passage twice, once using the word 'hear' as below, and then again substituting the word 'answer'):

"The LORD will hear;
The LORD will hear the heavens;
    The heavens will hear the earth;
        The earth will hear the corn and wine and oil;
            The corn and wine and oil will hear Jezreel."
(Hosea 2:21,22)

It all begins with listening, and once one listens one can answer (of course the passage speaks about that too). The great power of this marriage is that everybody is listening to everybody else – God especially so because He is stated *twice* to be listening. Every item in creation is responsive, hearing or answering, in tune with every other element. It is just how it should be in a marriage – not a one-way street but something which starts with partners listening to each other – really listening – and answering by meeting each other's needs. We can't meet those needs, the needs of our partner, if we have never bothered to find out what they are. And we can't answer them or meet them if we weren't listening when our partner told us. Listening is key, and from it comes answering and fruitfulness and reciprocity. This is what Hosea also describes in the same passage:

> "And I will sow (here is the industry and fruitfulness that can grow from marriage)
> And I will have mercy (mutual listening leads to mutual kindness)
> And I will say, 'You are my people'
> And you will say, 'You are my God.'"
>
> (reciprocity) (Hosea 2:23)

This is true communication, and it is a wonderful template for fixing a struggling marriage.

Postscript: when times are bleak

Topics: Recognising a problem and seeking and offering forgiveness; Taking responsibility for one's own part in the situation; Going back to the recipe and the Bible's commands; Being an initiator of good in the marriage; Reversing the pattern – starting with self-sacrificial love.

W HAT can be done when a marriage is in real difficulty? We exclude here cases that require specialist help such as addictions, physical violence, sexual abuse and repeated unfaithfulness, focusing instead on what may help when there seems to be constant antagonism or when a marriage has gone cold and partners retreat into separate domains. We shall be dealing with what can be done potentially to improve a marriage (not the question of divorce which has been dealt with elsewhere in our literature), what we do when we seem to be stuck in a rut of increasing volatility or isolation, when minor hurts build up over time into a big problem, when, as one writer put it, "selfishness and laziness replace loving deeds, when kindness is met with ingratitude, when an attempt to hug is met with 'Can't you see I'm busy?'"

It will usually be a prerequisite to recognise the problem, talk about it, ask for forgiveness for the part one has played in the situation, as well as being ready to forgive the other. Without these elements it will be tough to make progress because too much hurt and resentment has already built up. It is possible that your partner doesn't even recognise that there is a problem or that they refuse to discuss it even if they do. This makes for a challenging and traumatic situation, perhaps like the one

Abigail faced with Nabal (one can scarcely imagine someone like him agreeing to go to marriage counselling or sitting down with Abigail for some introspection on how to improve their relationship). Even in these difficult circumstances, however, it is possible to make a difference – hard though it may be – by working on oneself and by allowing oneself to forgive one's partner for how they have wronged you.

Taking responsibility

A critical step here is, as one well known psychologist put it, to 'own' one's relationship – to recognise that you are a part of what it is like as well as your partner, to take responsibility for your part in allowing it to get to where it is. He put it very frankly like this:

"You set (your relationship) up the way it is by actively, consistently, and efficiently designing, programming, and choreographing your entire lifestyle to generate and then support a bad relationship ... I cannot say this too many times in too many different ways. Owning your relationship means that you accept responsibility in creating your own experience. You are the architect of your thoughts. You choose the attitudes that you bring into the relationship. You choose the emotions and feelings that will control your thoughts in the relationship."[1]

He makes an analogy between a poor relationship lifestyle with its unsatisfactory emotional implications and a poor physical lifestyle. We make choices about our diet, whether or not we shall exercise, get enough sleep, engage in unhealthy activities and so forth; similarly we make choices about how we shall behave in our relationships and must take responsibility for these choices. We have come together consciously or otherwise with our partner to define our relationship in the way that it is – we have negotiated it into its current condition and if there is a problem with the state it is in then we are the ones who must

---

1   Philip McGraw, *Relationship Rescue* (New York: Hyperion, 2000, pages 10,14).

do something to change it. We must start with ourselves and not our partner.

This, then, is the starting point – that I myself must take action and be the person I should be in my relationship, not point my finger at my wife or present her with a list of demands. We must inspire our partner to change, if necessary, by the quality of our own example, not by nagging, abuse, carping criticism or some other method.

Back to the recipe

The fact is that Bible values, if really believed in and applied, have the potential either to solve or at least significantly improve many of the common difficulties that arise in marriage. We personally can control the extent to which we shall try to bring these virtues into our half of the relationship. It is *always* worth going back to the core elements of character and godly virtues that the Bible advocates to ask how these can be better and more systematically applied within one's marriage. The lists of virtues – these fruits of the spirit – are there to be reflected on, absorbed and applied, not skimmed over and left on the page. There is no better place to work at trying to apply them than in marriage. Think of it as a daily personal challenge: pick a godly attribute such as patience or gentleness and resolve that you will try to demonstrate it in your behaviour towards your partner at some point in the day – and without telling them that you are doing so! This sort of thing, consistently applied, can make a real difference to both you (as you become more like Christ) and your marriage.

Similarly, we must return again to the spiritual model of Christ and his bride. This is God's recipe for marriage, a unique gift bestowed by God upon His children regarding the best way to be a married couple. Of course you know it already, you've thought about it before as every believer has; but there is always more room to apply it. What about those words to husbands: 'seek above all things the salvation of your wife'? Is that what you do? *Really*? At this point it's not about what *she* does and how she may annoy or frustrate you, it's about what *you* do and whether or not you are making an effort to practise this commandment. 'Love her as Christ loved the church and sacrificed himself for it' it says – this is the standard, and before we start complaining to ourselves about this or that inadequacy in our wife we ought to think again about how much of an effort we are really making to love her to that measure. Remember the fourfold injunction from Ephesians 5 ("Love her ... love her ... love her ... love her") – there's bound to be room for improvement here for all of us men.

So, too, for a wife: 'let the wife see that she respect her husband' it says; what evidence would there be, over the last week of your marriage, say, that would demonstrate your fulfilment of this command? How could it be different? Does your husband know you respect him (because you are behaving towards him as you would towards Christ), and how does he know it? Thus we could go on through all the New Testament passages that centre on God's pattern for Biblical marriage: these passages are there to be used and applied; there is always more that we can get from them, safe in the assurance that God really does know what is best for us.

Focus on the symbolism, then. If you are a wife, try to love and respect your husband as if he were Christ, hard though it may be. If you are a husband, try to show the saving love of Christ to her. You may not be able to find it within yourself to come up with your own strategy for improving your marriage – but Christ has already shown a strategy more powerful than any other in the example that he gave. We all need to fight against our own hard hearts, moved by the power of that example.

Control

It's important to recognise that you can't control what your partner does or how they think and behave. You can influence it, certainly, but you cannot control it. The best influence is your manifestation of the character of Christ, not a list of all the ways in which you are wronged and not appreciated. Although you can justly have certain expectations of your partner which are scripturally derived and which you should at an appropriate time and in an appropriate way discuss with them, it will ultimately be to God that they will answer for their behaviour with respect to their marital responsibilities, as you will answer for yours. The secret here, then, is to focus on what you can control and not on what you cannot. The temptation is all the other way: if only *they* would change this or that annoying thing that they do or unreasonable attitude that they have then the marriage would be so much better. It may very well be true – the marriage may indeed be much better and it would be much easier for you to respond in a Christlike way to your partner if only this were the case. But the fact remains that you cannot make this happen; you cannot control or be ultimately responsible for what they do – that is what free will necessitates.

But this does not mean you are stuck or that the marriage is at an unresolvable impasse. The point is that you are still in control of yourself and what *you* put into the marriage, and even if your partner appears to have stopped trying in some respects, this doesn't stop you trying. It may very well be that your partner ought to bring more to the marriage, but that doesn't stop *you* bringing more which is the Christlike thing to do. The whole basis of our salvation is not that we deserved to be treated a certain way (that Christ *should* have given himself for us because we had brought so much to him), but that despite our lack he gave himself. Our partner's deficiencies, viewed from this perspective, are the perfect opportunity for us to exercise ourselves in truly Christlike behaviour. What is more, the good news is that if we endeavour to do so – to put more into our marriage even when it seems to be flagging – there is always the possibility that our partner will respond and that there will be the beginnings of a virtuous cycle.

At stressful times and in times of frayed relations or dissatisfaction we need to prioritise the marriage. It might be natural to want to shrink from it, to retreat into care for the children, to retreat into work or some side activity, to put up emotional walls because it's too upsetting to think about the marriage – but it's important to try not to let this happen. We may feel wronged and aggrieved and consequently draw in to protect ourselves and reduce our emotional pain, but unless we try to invest in the marriage rather than retreat from it then it is unlikely to improve. Make time to talk, and try to talk without blame – a list of accusations is no conversation and is likely to engender the wrong response; make time *not* to talk also, time just to do fun things together of the kind you would have done in easier times. Look for ways to try to rediscover what it was about each other that once provided such strong attraction.

Be patient. Tough times, particularly those caused by difficult circumstances and the pressures of life, will pass – sometimes all that is needed is the tenacity to hold on and not give up until circumstances begin to ease.

And pray. The psalms show beyond any doubt that *all* circumstances and most feelings (even if they are not 'right' in the absolute sense) can be brought before God in prayer. He does care; He does understand; and He is able to help.

Reversing the pattern

The most helpful advice I have come across as a strategy for attempting to reverse serious marriage difficulty and dysfunction comes from Selwyn Hughes in a piece he called, "When the wine runs out" (a reference to Jesus' first miracle of the wedding in Cana). There may be times when professional counselling, self-help books and other tools are helpful in trying to understand and improve the dynamics of one's relationship or when it is helpful to seek advice from a close friend or relative or from other believers you respect, but the best strategy of all comes from applying the principles of scripture. Hughes gets to this by drawing attention to the different types of love that are spoken of in the scriptures and suggesting how they should be thought about in the context of a relationship. We'll begin, therefore, with what might seem a bit of a digression into different types of love, but this will in due course come back to the question of resolving marriage difficulties.

Human languages often have several different words to capture the various different facets of love: in English, for instance, we have words like 'affection' and 'infatuation' which can be aspects of love, or we might differentiate between 'romantic love' as against 'brotherly love' or philanthropy. In Greek there were at least three different words. *Eros* referred to sexual love (from whence the English term 'erotic'), whereas *phileo* referred to the love of companionship, a love according to which a person carries out an activity with someone else simply because they enjoy their company or because they care for them. Then there is *agape*, a predominantly New Testament term which refers to sacrificial love, a love whose pattern is set by the love of Christ in dying for the sins of the world.[2]

There are probably other ways of slicing and dicing the concept of love and its vocabulary, but this basic three-way distinction in Greek is a helpful one for our present purposes. In a good marriage all three of these aspects should be present:

- A *companionship love* (*phileo*) which delights in being together, doing things in each other's company whether for the sheer enjoyment of doing so or simply because they have to be done and because companionship in such chores can be both more enjoyable and more effective than going solo. *Phileo* finds its place in both tasks and free time shared and enjoyed.
- A *sexual love* (*eros*) which brings a husband and wife together as one both physically and emotionally in a way that no other activity can.
- A *self-sacrificial love* (*agape*) patterned after the love of Christ which considers the needs of others before one's

---

2   There are some occasions where the terms *agape* and *phileo* are used more interchangeably as synonyms and the rigid distinction does not seem to hold and should not always be pushed *too* far. The word *eros* and its cognates do not occur in the New Testament; this should not be taken to imply that sexual love is not important (it is dealt with in the scriptures even if the specific term is not used), but it does not seem to be defining of the New Testament's concept of love in the way that it has come to be almost first base in modern culture.

own, a love which gives and expects nothing in return, putting itself out purely for the sake of the other person.

It is very important to keep these three aspects in balance. A marriage in which partners do not bother to make or take time to be together as friends will quickly grow cold and distant – the sheer power of sexual chemistry may keep everything together for a while, particularly in the early days when feelings of infatuation are strong, but this is unlikely to be sufficient on its own to carry a marriage through. Conversely, a marriage which is all friendship but no or insufficient intimacy – no *eros* – is likely over the longer term to leave one or both partners with unmet needs, disappointment and frustration; ultimately this will spoil the friendship, hamper the self-sacrifice, and harm the marriage.

Similarly a marriage which has companionship and sexual love but insufficient sacrificial or *agape* love will ultimately struggle. The striving to make one's own marriage godly is probably the best antidote to selfishness that there is; few would deny that self-sacrifice and the willingness to prioritise the needs and desires of others as well as one's own is essential to a successful marriage. Consequently, if we do not work to ensure that self-sacrificial love is present in our marriage we are denying it one of the most powerful ingredients God has shown us. One way to think about it might be this: if we take out self-sacrificial *agape* love after the pattern of Christ our marriages become much more like those of unbelievers and we thereby reduce our odds of success to something much closer to those of society at large – around fifty per cent in most Western countries, and hardly good enough. Self-sacrificial love is essential; it is what is supposed to make us different, and to show it to our partner is to live the Truth.

Let's think about what happens when the mix is wrong. As sex is exalted and deified within human culture then people start to think it is the most important thing there is within a relationship. When difficulties come and there isn't either the quantity or quality of sex in a relationship that one or both parties would like, then to that way of thinking it quickly becomes time to start considering moving on (why would you show sacrificial love to someone who is not meeting your sexual needs?). Similarly, if you no longer enjoy the companionship love you once did with your partner, then why stay around? If being with them doesn't bring the thrill or the warmth that it once did, why put yourself out to sacrifice on their behalf?

The thinking can affect Christian marriages too. When a marriage is experiencing difficulties or losing its shine often erotic love takes a back seat or even disappears completely. But this only deepens the problem, and before long companionship love is affected too. Once both of these are diminished then it becomes much more challenging to show the self-sacrificial *agape* love which is so precious within a marriage and which can really differentiate a believer's marriage from a marriage which does not have a foundation of faith (after all, the whole Christ-bride parable which a believer's marriage is meant to evoke is based on self-sacrificial *agape* love).

What needs to be done if these times of marriage difficulty emerge is to reverse the process. Instead of thinking that the first part of a relationship is physical attraction, that this grows into friendship, and then – if you are lucky – some self-sacrificial love might start to be occasionally displayed, we need to think precisely the other way round. We need to think about what is defining of Christian marriage and begin with that. It is no use (for example) expecting the repair of a strained and crumbling relationship to begin in the bedroom – that will probably be the last aspect to improve. We have to begin with what we can choose to be responsible for – what we can voluntarily and willingly do rather than what we feel like.

There is a clear differential between the three types of love we've considered in terms of the amount of will power required to show them. Of the three, sexual love is the most involuntary – it is instinctive, a drive, and it is very hard to make yourself love in that way if you don't feel like it, particularly for a woman. Companionship or friendship love comes next – we can feel like it and it can be instinctive (you either like someone and want to spend time with them or you don't), but there is more of an element of choice and will power involved here – it is possible to make yourself spend time with someone to do things together because you think it is the right thing to do even if you don't particularly feel like it; it can be a feeling but it is also a choice. *Agape* love, by contrast, is by definition all about a choice. It requires the exercise of the will to sacrifice oneself for another, and while we can feel more or less like making that choice at any particular point depending on how we feel about the other person, choice and the exercise of will will always be required. As Hughes put it, God does not hold us responsible to produce loving feelings but loving actions. Or again, from the Dalai Lama this time, "Be kind whenever possible. It's always possible".

The advice in times of difficulty then is to begin with what we can control (our ability to choose to show sacrificial love towards our partner). As we do this (not once but repeatedly as an expression of who we are) then it will have an impact upon our partner – it will be very difficult for them not to realise that something has changed and not to respond. Of course it is possible they may not – in which case we have still done the right thing and learned much from following the example of our Lord. But if, as might usually be the case, they do notice a change in our approach – that we are giving without expecting a return – then gradually, over time things can start to improve and the relationship can start to breathe again. If someone repeatedly sacrifices themselves for us in words of respect where tension was once the norm, in acts of kindness even though there are frustrations and areas of disagreement, then we shall be drawn to respond ourselves in a similar way. We shall start to want to be with that person and step by step the friendship type of love will begin to return – we shall want to spend time with such a person and rediscover the things that we used to love doing with them. As this aspect of love gradually begins to return and the relationship continues to heal in due course there will be scope for the intimate side to recover also – desire will start to be rekindled where once the instinct was to recoil. It will be a slow process with setbacks and disappointments along the way from time to time, but a process will have begun which is heading in the right direction. It begins not with our partner but with *us* – we are in control of our side of the relationship and it is up to us to take the initiative to start to put it back where it ought to be by the way that we behave.

Part 8
Oneness and true partnership

Introduction: how to be united

Topics: Jesus' prayer for unity; Avoiding dividing 'walls'; The importance of
listening and communication; Pitfalls of poor communication; Love languages;
Being good friends; Making time and prioritising the marriage.

The Bible starts and ends with marriage, its story spanning
from the historical beginnings of Genesis 1 and 2 and stretching
towards the wonderful future of Revelation 21 and 22 as New
Jerusalem descends like a bride adorned for her husband.
Marriage presents unparalleled opportunity for learning and
practising Christlike qualities of unity, peace, patience, love,
forgiveness and understanding. On a similar vein Martin Luther
is said to have remarked that there were two ways of becoming
less selfish and more like Jesus Christ: one was to enter a
monastery, the other to embark on a marriage.

AS we have seen during the course of this book, a marriage
needs to have a model or a recipe, something larger than
itself for it to aspire to. The objective of marriage is centred in
the very nature of God Himself – in His unity, in the unity He
shares with His Son, and in the unity He desires with all that He
has created. Considered from this perspective the prayer of Jesus
in John 17 is also remarkably powerful when read as a prayer for
marriage. The words below are primarily about Jesus' wish for
the unity of believers, but read them again as Jesus' prayer for a
married couple and they come across very powerfully:

"Neither pray I for these alone, but for them also which shall believe on me through their word; that they all may be one; as thou, Father, art in me, and I in thee, that they also may be one in us: that the world may believe that thou hast sent me. And the glory which thou gavest me I have given them; that they may be one, even as we are one: I in them, and thou in me, that they may be made perfect in one; and that the world may know that thou hast sent me, and hast loved them, as thou hast loved me." (John 17:20-23)

We can derive a mission-statement for marriage from this passage. We should be doing all we can to strive for unity centred on the Lord Jesus with our husband or wife, some of the partnerships we'll consider in this section (Zacharias and Elisabeth, Priscilla and Aquila, Abraham and Sarah) providing a great example of how this can work in practice. If we can abandon the prevailing 'consumer' approach to marriage that prioritises our own selfish needs (chapter 17) and instead adopt a 'covenant' model which focuses on the marriage and our faithfulness towards the promises we have made it will help us tremendously. There is a wonderful model for us in the symbolism of Christ and his bride which God has asked us to demonstrate in our own lives while the unique responsibilities He has given us as male and female arising out of Genesis (chapters 2-4) and demarcated in Ephesians (chapter 5) further help us to fulfil this objective. This is the recipe God has given us for marriage and our confidence in His abilities as our Maker give us strong reason to believe that He knows best.

In striving to meet this goal of being a strong and united partnership we can single out four areas of focus. One is our need to understand and cope with difference – the differences between a man and his wife in terms of gender, genes, physical make-up, history, thought patterns, emotional and spiritual perspective and so forth. We considered this in detail in chapter 37 but it is important enough to mention it again; being united does not mean being identical, and the sooner we can stop trying to fit our partner into our mould and learn that our differences are very often strengths the more successful and the more united we are likely to be. God doesn't want us to be clones of one another, but rather to be a wonderful combination of attributes and abilities, the one complementing the other.

The three further aspects of unity to be considered in more detail now are communication, friendship, and the importance of prioritising the marriage.

Communication and connectedness

Communication is fundamental because it builds connection and understanding which are essential to unity. It is the antidote to the marriage which becomes increasingly cold and isolated, one in which two partners retreat into two separate worlds. The following extract from an anonymous poem called "The Wall" quoted by Nicky and Sila Lee shows what this can look like in a modern context:

> Somewhere between the oldest child's first tooth
> And youngest daughter's graduation
> They lost each other.
> Throughout the years each slowly unravelled
> That tangled ball of string called self
> And as they tugged at stubborn knots Each hid their searching from the other.
> Sometimes she cried at night and begged
> The whispering darkness to tell her who she was
> While he lay beside her snoring like a
> Hibernating bear unaware of her winter.
> ...
> She took a course in modern art trying to find herself
> In colours splashed upon a canvas
> And complaining to other women about men
> Who were insensitive.
> He climbed into a tomb called the office
> Wrapped his mind in a shroud of paper figures
> And buried himself in customers.
> Slowly the wall between them rose cemented

By the mortar of indifference.
One day reaching out to touch each other
They found a barrier they could not penetrate
And recoiling from the coldness of the stone
Each retreated from the stranger on the other side.

It is a chilling and desperately sad scenario, and, again, the solution is real communication which builds intimacy and a sense of togetherness.

Communication takes effort – we need to take the time to do it in a proactive way and we need to make the effort to be interested and interesting. There's nothing worse than one partner reaching out to the other to build a connection, hoping for their interest and attention but finding their partner unresponsive.

For communication to involve real sharing it has to move beyond the mere exchange of facts ('I won't be home until 8 tonight'; 'Bob got fired') and into the realm of meaningful exchange whether in terms of sharing feelings and responses, enjoying each other's sense of humour, or a discussion of hopes and goals, disappointments and frustrations. There are times to discuss the relationship itself: how things are going, what growth there has been, whether there are any improvements to be made, the volunteering to make changes oneself if that would help the other.

We need to confide in one another rather than doing so outside the relationship to friends, parents or siblings. We should share our thought life with our partner and seek to have some awareness of theirs; this is what partnership and sharing are all about. Couples in counselling sometimes find themselves telling a complete stranger (the counsellor) things that they have never told their partner, the partner being taken aback to learn that a certain thing happened or that their partner saw things that way. If communication in the relationship is strong, this sort of scenario would tend not to arise because a couple would already have talked about it.

Improving communication

Regarding the 'how' of communication – the things that it's helpful to say and those it's best to avoid – there are some people who seem to have a very special skill of being able to say just the right thing in any given circumstance, and there are others who, well, *don't*. There's a need to be careful that we don't take the other too much for granted and be too lazy in our approach to communication. To our marriage partners we are ourselves – we have no need to put on social airs or to fabricate an image, we can relax at a certain level and be who we are, say what we want to say. This is a wonderful thing in many senses, liberating us to an intimacy and a connection with another person that we don't share with anyone else. But there is a danger in this ease: what we 'naturally' are, our unvarnished self, probably has some not very attractive features to it; if we utter our spur-of-the-moment natural thoughts either about our partners themselves or about certain sensitive topics then some decidedly unconstructive and hurtful things might come out. To say what might first come into our head may not be very helpful at all.

A good test, therefore, before saying anything which might stray into such an area is to ask oneself questions of the kind, 'Is what I am about to say –

    a. true?
    b. necessary?
    c. helpful?
    d. kind?'

Not everything can pass all of these tests; there are occasionally times when difficult things which will cause hurt have to be said but in that case careful thought needs to go into crafting the message, depersonalising it as far as possible, and taking effort to ensure we are not misconstrued.

Communication is not just about what we say, of course. It is also about the tone and body language we use. The tricky thing is that the body language aspect is usually entirely automatic: we're not even consciously in control of it. Tone fares little better – we *do* control it, of course, but usually don't think about it: it has already made itself known before we have taken the step to apply a regulator. Sometimes we talk to those we don't know in a much more pleasant manner than those we love the most; this makes no sense at all, yet it often happens. Speaking with a spirit of love and respect appropriate to the one who is our life partner and gift from God is critical.

Listening is a key component of good communication. We can be so busy thinking about what we want to say next that we don't really listen to our partner – this is called ego-speak, and there is nothing good about it. Counsellors and psychotherapists have suggested the technique of listening, reflecting back ('so you are saying you feel that ...') and then checking that you've got the right end of this stick. While this can be a bit pedantic and contrived in a real-life conversation, there is certainly value in making sure that we are really listening and have heard our partner correctly. There is also value for them in being reassured that we have listened and understood. It is often not just the actual words spoken to which we must listen but also the feelings which underlie and motivate them; sometimes we have to listen for what is meant rather than what is said. One well known but useful piece of wisdom is to concentrate first on understanding your partner and where they are coming from, and only then to ensure that your own thoughts and views are understood; all too often we invert these and focus all our energies on getting our own point across.

Men often find the communication aspect of a relationship more difficult, preferring to work privately through things in their own heads rather than to use communication as a way of arriving at a solution. Understanding is needed on both sides here: a wife that her husband will have times when he needs to work things out on his own and doesn't want to talk, and a husband that verbal interaction is really important to his wife. If there are times when he feels he can't, that is fine – but he needs to ensure that at other times he makes himself available and makes an effort to engage with his wife at the verbal level.

It's worth looking at a few potential communication pitfalls to be avoided. One is to be the advice-giver (a particular danger for men – often a wife just wants to be heard, understood and sympathised with; she is not looking for her husband to provide the solution to her problems or be told that they are not really problems at all). Another is to deflect a conversation off at a tangent if something comes up that you are either not interested in, hits a nerve, or is otherwise difficult to discuss. It is not helpful to rationalise, dismiss or reassure too quickly. Instead what is important is to get a full grasp of the situation from your partner's perspective to understand why they are upset about it and to offer suitable comfort and support.

There are some forms of communication which can become habitual in a relationship but are particularly unhelpful and should be rooted out and avoided at all costs. One is to talk to our partner in a patronising way as if we are talking to one of our children. If our talk often involves phrases like, 'If I were you …', 'I would …', 'Why didn't you …?' or 'You should …' then we might have a problem. Overuse of sarcasm can be another danger – we can somehow work ourselves into a position where nearly everything we say to our partner involves sarcasm, or where we continually make put-downs to diminish or belittle their position or things they have done. This is ultimately a bullying tactic, and even if our partner doesn't pick us up on it, over time it will lead to bad feeling, antagonism and resentment. Verbal abuse is not just about losing one's rag and swearing at someone or about saying one particularly nasty and hurtful thing. We can drip-feed mild verbal abuse into a relationship over years and years, possibly not even realising that we are doing it. It happens by making little comments that are not respectful of our partner, which diminish their views and opinions, or which imply that they are just a little bit silly or less capable than ourselves. Any one of these comments might be relatively mild and unobjectionable on its own but they are hard to counter because it would seem over the top to make a big issue out of any particular one of them. But they can have a cumulative effect which is exhausting and demoralising and might well lead to a response of passive aggression even if not to an out and out row.

There are some classic examples of things that are often said by couples to each other which are best avoided. One of them is 'You always … (leave a mess when you've washed up, get upset unnecessarily', and the other its partner: 'You never … (think for yourself, pay attention when I'm talking to you)'. If we have a point to make, then it's potentially fair game for us to make it. But to dress it up in 'always' or 'never' language is almost always (!) an exaggeration. It simply can't be true, for instance, that our partner *never* listens to us, so we are not helping by making a false and exaggerated claim with loaded language which states that it is the case. Far better to say (for instance) 'Sometimes when you're busy with (xyz) it seems like you're not really listening when I'm talking to you, and it upsets me …', and perhaps even follow it up with a suggestion of how this problem might be avoided going forward.

Some other destructive phrases are ones like 'I don't care', 'Why should I?', or the dreaded 'So?' They project a detachment from the marriage, a lack of concern for the views of our life-partner, and an attempt to opt out emotionally from the implications of what it means to be married. If we say 'I don't care' it is actually very unlikely to be true, because we have invested a huge amount of our time, resources, and emotions into the person to whom we are saying it – so we actually *do* care very much indeed. In fact, then, we most likely mean something else (possibly even the very opposite, it's just that at the time we can't see a way out of the impasse we have got to in a particular point of disagreement). Better, then, to think about what we really do mean, and to think of the big picture context in which that should be set, not merely the heat of the current moment. We *chose* to be married, we *are* invested in it, and it *does* affect us so it's wise to choose our language accordingly.

Instead there are all kinds of wonderful, loving and positive things that can be said, with caring and open body language and in warm and open tones of voice. It's a wonderful thing to be able to look for the positive and to say *that*, to focus on what is right, on what is going well – to notice it, acknowledge it, say it, and enjoy it. There are some things which are better left unsaid and it takes great wisdom and skill to avoid them, but it is also important to say some of the many positive things that are in our power to acknowledge.

Love languages

Communication isn't exclusively about the verbal and its accompanying body language; we communicate also by our actions. The point was made memorably by Gary Chapman in his 1992 book *The Five Love Languages* (Chicago: Northfield Publishing). He pointed out that each of us has our own natural 'language' of love: the way we naturally tend to express our love for another person and the way in which we like to receive it. People feel loved in different ways – what makes one feel warm and content, assured by their partner's love, can be quite different from what works for the next person; that is, we respond to different love languages. Some women may appreciate receiving flowers or other gifts, for instance, while for others it's no big deal and they would much rather have a hug, say, or know that their husband will take out the trash or help with other chores. Some men enjoy the verbal affirmations of their wives, for others this may be a take-it-or-leave-it matter and they would prefer some other expression of their wife's love such as an in-depth conversation about one of his interests or going out together for the evening.

Chapman distinguished between five principle 'languages' which he defined as follows:

1. Loving words.
2. Kind actions.
3. Quality time.
4. Thoughtful presents.
5. Physical affection.

The point is that what works for you may not necessarily work for your partner and that if you want to show that you love your partner then you should think about what the most effective way of doing so would be – not for you, but for them. Sometimes we can make assumptions about what our partner would like which are completely mistaken. Just as it would make no sense to give someone a present that they don't particularly want or that would mean more to you than it would to them, so too it makes sense to understand what makes your partner happy, what their needs and hopes are from the relationship, and to try to ensure that as far as possible you provide them. If your partner needs verbal affirmation then make sure you give it, even if it feels awkward at first; if what really makes them feel loved is knowing that you are there to help out and get practical things done whenever needed then make sure you are; if they appreciate physical affection, then show it. It's about really getting to know them and they you so that you can be what is needed for each other.

Friendship
While it might seem obvious that it would be a good idea to be good friends with one's partner, this isn't always paid attention to, and I wonder if its importance is under-appreciated. Marriage is about sharing and cleaving, and these are so much more straightforward if you actually like the person you are living with and if they are your friend. There are countless decisions to be made in life, a myriad of things to be discussed and lived through – each one of them is easier and more enjoyable if your partner is your friend. The empty nest syndrome in which couples find their children have left home and there is now a vacuum with two people living together with not very much in common is not, sadly, altogether uncommon. The best way of working through it is to ensure that you have been friends in the meantime, not just flatmates, business partners or people living in the same house because it seemed like the convenient thing to do at the time or was necessary for the upbringing of the children. If you are still good friends when the children leave home, then you will be able to lean on each other and find comfort in being together

and enjoying each other's company even more than you had the opportunity to do before at this potentially challenging time.

Being good friends means delighting in being together, doing things glamorous or mundane in each other's company whether for the sheer enjoyment of doing so or simply because they have to be done and because companionship in such chores can be both more enjoyable and more effective than going solo. The love that the term *phileo* speaks of finds its place in both tasks and relaxation shared and enjoyed, in time and experience spent together and reflected upon.

How will this friendship be achieved? Only by believing in its importance and making the effort to *be* a good friend to your partner. It's hard for your partner to be your friend if you are constantly picking at them, if you have no interest in their opinions or interests, if you assume you already know what they think on every matter, or, conversely, if you don't share your own thoughts and feelings and invite them into your mental and emotional life. Marriage in which partners do not bother to make or take time to be together as friends will quickly grow cold and distant; it's almost impossible to be truly unified and achieve the spiritual goals of marriage unless friendship and thus sharing are in place.

Making the time

There is no substitute for setting aside time to talk, time when you can listen to your partner with full concentration and when you have the opportunity to be listened to in the same way. Unless you are retired (and perhaps even then!) the slower day in which you are not busy and will naturally have the opportunity to do this is probably never going to come, particularly if you are busy with work and children. You need to do it now, not put it off until some remote time in the future.

There is no substitute for quality marriage time, but that time has to be found, guarded, and made use of. Emotional deserts, if they have been allowed to develop, will only become fruitful ground again if the time is taken to water them.

Emotional connections have to be built (or rebuilt if they have been destroyed) and that takes time and effort. We must move beyond the mere exchange of facts and functional requests into something more enjoyable and fulfilling.

If one or both of us is working for most of the week we shall likely only see one another twice in the day and it can be a struggle to get that quality time. One of these occasions will be at the beginning: it's unusual to find that both partners in a marriage are great morning people, and even if they are there is just too much to be done showering and dressing and getting ready for the day ahead to have much in the way of meaningful connection. By the time it is evening and the chores and other duties have been done – taking care of children, eating, necessary paperwork perhaps – and we finally have time to interact properly with our partner we may well be exhausted. In other words, we get to interact with our partner most closely at precisely the worst times of the day. Unless we work at this it can take its toll on the quality of the interactions that we consequently have. We need to have active strategies to cope with this so that we continue to invest in the relationship.

Speaking of making an effort, think of all the thought, effort and sometimes angst that goes into dating – taking care of what you say, making sure you give a good impression and look your best. Yet once we are married so much of this can go out of the window. In one sense that is a huge relief, but in another something is lost.

Another way of thinking about it is like this. When relationships fail in society people often make a big effort to reposition and restart their lives. They may go to the gym, lose weight or take up new interests realising that they need to make more of an effort if they are to be attractive both to themselves and to someone else. If only all that effort had been harnessed and made in a more level and consistent fashion beforehand perhaps it could have made a difference? We must replace stagnation and apathy where it exists with concern and activity; we must require of ourselves that our relationships be better, our companionship more united, our marriage a better model of what it is supposed to be. We need to show our best side once again by reawakening some of the effort we made in earlier years. In short, we need to be investors if we truly want to experience unity in our marriage.

Ananias and Sapphira

Topics: The second conscience; Individual and combined responsibility; Using one another's strengths.

Like Ahab and Jezebel before them Ananias and Sapphira's relationship can definitely be put in the category of 'for worse' rather than 'for better', but this doesn't mean that there is any less to be learned from them. In fact their example presents some quite interesting points about unity. Let's take a look.

THE passage that tells of their deed and its consequence is a short eleven verses, but one which, for all its brevity, is devastating in its impact. The account opens like this:

"But a man named Ananias, with his wife Sapphira, sold a piece of property, and with his wife's knowledge he kept back for himself some of the proceeds and brought only a part of it and laid it at the apostles' feet." (Acts 5:1,2, ESV)

It is a deed agreed to and done together ("with his wife Sapphira … with his wife's knowledge") but one which seems to have been hatched initially by Ananias. This becomes clear when Peter addresses him in the next two verses:

"Ananias, why has Satan filled your heart to lie to the Holy Spirit and to keep back for yourself part of the proceeds of the land? … Why is it that you have contrived this deed in your heart?" (verses 3,4, ESV)

But if it is Ananias' idea, Sapphira is not let off the hook: "How is it that you have agreed together to test the Spirit of the Lord? Behold, the feet of those who have buried your husband are at the door, and they will carry you out."

(verse 9, ESV)

Three times, then, in the few verses we've examined so far, the text highlights their complicity ("with his wife … with his wife's knowledge … agreed together"). Togetherness can be a wonderful thing – normally something that we would think of as a virtue to be striven for in marriage – but not if it is togetherness in sin.

A second conscience

One of the great potentials that marriage opens up is the presence of a second conscience, a second chance to catch ourselves from falling into wrongdoing. The conscience is a very powerful sin-prevention device with which God has equipped us but it needs training by His word so that it conforms to His standards rather than our own (the alternative is a vague and woolly notion of what 'feels right to me'; hardly satisfactory). Sometimes our conscience is not as well trained as it should be, and even when it suggests the right choice, the power of the mind to wheedle around its voice, heeding instead some selfish inclination, is considerable. It is indeed a battle.

But suppose our partner, perhaps a little more detached from the particular situation than we ourselves, is able to bring to bear *their* conscience also, suggesting that we may be letting God down by the choice we are making, pointing out that there may be a better way in which to proceed. If this happens, and if it is done in the right spirit, we can potentially spare ourselves from sin and the pain and consequences that go with it. Any such intervention has to be carried out in the right way: it can be all too easy to put our partner's back up or to talk down to them as if they were a child, but assuming we are smart enough to manage this aspect of communication, there is a lot of positive potential to be unleashed. A wife's conscience may be more finely and more spiritually honed in some areas than a husband's, or vice versa. There is a real opportunity for preventative intervention and for discussion and advice-seeking about the most Christ-centred way to tackle a particular issue. So for example in my own case, it would probably be true to say that every e-mail that I have ever sent which I regret is one that my wife didn't check. When our combined conscience is operating we can avoid at least some mistakes that would otherwise have been made.

Unfortunately it can work the other way also, and in Ananias and Sapphira's case it certainly did. Ananias had the idea and she knew about it, but instead of questioning what he was doing or suggesting it might not be for the best, she agreed and they did it together. She became complicit in sin, her acquiescence perhaps even comforting him, spurring him on to silence any voices of conscience that were still playing in his mind. If our partner thinks it's okay it can lead us on, allowing us to persuade ourselves that a course of action is not so bad even when we know deep down that it is. We shouldn't agree with something just because our partner says so; Sapphira is not excused here on the basis that her husband is the head and that she is only going along with him. Both partners have a responsibility to uphold what is right and to save one another from sin.

Agreeing together

The text notes that Ananias and Sapphira "agreed together" in their sin. The concept expressed by this little phrase is one which is worth discussing and exploring between a husband and wife in marriage today. What are the marital sins that we commit *as a couple*? What do we stand for *as a couple*, and what have we implicitly voted for with united voice in the way in which we live? What are the decisions that we make together which set a direction for our families? What are the patterns of behaviour and the structures that we have put into our family lives that we both agree to and have signed up for as a couple? Are they what they should be? Are they the best we can do, or should we discuss them again, listening more carefully when the conscience of one or the other of us may suggest a better way?

United in death

Ananias and Sapphira can certainly be commended for togetherness – they had a unity, no doubt – but it was a unity in sin rather than a unity in righteousness. Fittingly, then, they share the same fate – in their deaths as also in their sin they were not divided. They had stood together side by side, presumably, when they had first married. For their sin they would now be together again: lying down this time, side by side, united in their deaths:

> "When the young men came in they found Sapphira dead, and they carried her out and *buried her beside her husband.* And great fear came upon the whole church and upon all who heard of these things."   (verses 10,11, ESV)

This is how high the stakes are. In our marriages we must find a better way.

Zacharias and Elisabeth

Topics: Prayer and (un)belief; Standing together in testing situations.

There isn't a lot of scriptural colour on Zacharias' and Elisabeth's relationship but the few phrases which are used are quite telling and merit a brief consideration.

THE couple are introduced by Luke as follows:
"There was in the days of Herod, the king of Judaea, a certain priest named Zacharias, of the course of Abia: and his wife was of the daughters of Aaron, and her name was Elisabeth. And they were both righteous before God, walking in all the commandments and ordinances of the Lord blameless. And they had no child, because that Elisabeth was barren, and they both were now well stricken in years." (Luke 1:5-7)

The pair are presented as a model couple: of Aaronic descent and united in their devotion to the ways of God, walking together (note the journey metaphor so appropriate for a marriage) blamelessly in all the commandments and ordinances of God. Their enthusiasm for their God was shared; they were equally yoked and on a quest for spiritual growth, their priorities in sync and well founded. It's a great starting point for marriage – and for them, advanced in years as they were, it was a great finishing point as well.

Prayer, unbelief and resolution

There was a problem, however: they had no child. At this point, even without knowing how the story proceeds but being aware of the Old Testament background, we would have a good feeling about where this was going. It's a type-scene – a repeated pattern in the scriptures in which a couple, unfruitful and unable to bear children are miraculously provided for by God. We have seen it with Abraham and Sarah, with Isaac and Rebekah, with Jacob and Rachel, with Manoah and his wife – and we are about to see it again. A later passage (Luke 1:13) informs us that Zacharias had prayed about this issue, perhaps fervently and often, and his prayers are about to be answered.

It is an encouraging thing that the God we serve today is the same God, powerful to help in our wider needs as well. There can be various areas of life in which a couple can be 'unfruitful' in a metaphorical sense – parts of the relationship that don't seem to work quite as they might hope, emotionally and relationally as well as physically. God is powerful to help in these areas too if it is according to His will. To engage Him in prayer as Zacharias had, therefore, is the right thing to do. He can work in areas we don't expect and where it might seem that things can't change.

It's ironic that when an angel finally appears to him in answer to his prayers he doesn't believe the message he receives! This means effectively that he has been praying without expecting that God would actually do anything about it! Perhaps there is a gentle barb here – if we are not going to believe in God's power to act when we say our prayers we might as well be dumb, the very fate which temporarily meets Zacharias because of his unbelief. It would be a powerful reminder to him never to distrust again!

Though the promise and instructions about the birth of John are given to Zacharias he is ironically unable to name the child when he is born, a defining moment for the father in those days perhaps, and one which recalls Adam's naming of the creatures in Genesis 2. This gives the occasion for another wonderful display of the couple's unity, however. Elisabeth insists that he is to be called John, but she doesn't really seem to be taken seriously – perhaps, in that particular cultural context, because she is a woman taking an unexpected approach. Though the couple hadn't been able physically to communicate in the normal way during the pregnancy because of his dumb state, they had found other ways to communicate and were intuitively united on the matter. The crowd turns to Zacharias to decide the dispute and he is right there with his wife writing down the words: "His name is John"! Sometimes a couple has to make a stand for what they and their family believe to be important whatever others may think and however it may flout societal convention; here is a great example of this in action. It's only at this point that the priest's tongue is finally loosed and he is able to utter his remarkable prophecy. First Elisabeth and now Zacharias are inspired by the spirit to speak on separate occasions of the salvation which their son would herald – what a joyful privilege to share these thoughts, especially after the long silence that Zacharias' punishment had entailed.

Priscilla and Aquila

Topics: Partnership; Hospitality and supporting others; Flexibility in different circumstances; Coping with change; An inseparable couple.

Priscilla and Aquila stand, perhaps, as one of the finest scriptural examples of a united couple. What is special about them is that they are always mentioned together; they are, in a word, inseparable.

IT was in Corinth that Paul originally met Priscilla and Aquila (Acts 18:2), the text noting that Aquila was born in Pontus, having found his way to Corinth via Rome. It is at this point in Acts 18 that his wife Priscilla is introduced to the narrative, the pair thenceforth never to be parted. Priscilla's home town is not mentioned, but evidently they were in Rome together, Claudius Caesar's expulsion of the Jews from his capital the catalyst for their evacuation to Greece.

These were likely not easy years; while it isn't uncommon to have to move home or city for one reason or other today, few will have done so because a racially motivated political power is forcing the issue. A trauma such as this is easier to bear when it is shared, the very experience containing the potential to draw a couple closer together.

It is not always easy to see things that way at the time, of course; circumstances take time to adjust to. Sometimes one partner finds it easier than the other to adapt to a new situation which can enable them to impart the extra strength to see all members of the family through. What is counterproductive in these sorts of situations is if blame is attached, whether or not this is verbalised ('I told you we should never have gone to Rome; we wouldn't ever have gone there in the first place if you had listened to me!'). Once a decision has been taken in faith – after ample discussion, exchange of views and prayer – it is the family's decision which they all must stand behind, whoever may have been the primary 'beneficiary' (whether it is for the husband's work, the children's school, the wife's family, or whatever it is). It is of no value to pick at the past when it cannot be changed, especially when we could not have known that things would turn out the way they have.

Daily rounds and common tasks

Priscilla and Aquila were certainly survivors following their experience in Rome, but they were also work mates: tentmakers, like the Apostle Paul:

"And Paul found (in Corinth) a certain Jew named Aquila, born in Pontus, lately come from Italy, with his wife Priscilla; (because that Claudius had commanded all Jews to depart from Rome:) and came unto them, and because he was of the same craft, he abode with them, and wrought; for by their occupation they were tentmakers."   (Acts 18:2,3)

Their shared occupation can be looked at as a metaphor for their role as co-workers in the wider sphere of life. They worked together in their 'day job', but this bespoke a wider companionship and sharing which traversed all aspects of life. Husbands and wives *have* to work together in that wider sense – pulling in the same direction and to the same goal, not to opposing objectives which will pull the family apart.

They were also a hospitable couple, not merely through the temporary commitment of, say, having given Paul a meal once or twice (significant though such acts of hospitality certainly are), but by sharing their home with him by having him to stay for an extended period, and by inviting him to share their commercial facilities as co-workers.

The closeness of Priscilla and Aquila is thus not an internally-focused, self-serving affair which concentrates only on themselves. Some relationships can be like that, so self-contained that they can border on the self-absorbed (perhaps we should say 'mutually obsessed' – concerned with each other, but no one else; whole families can sometimes operate in a very self-contained way of this sort). Blessings are to be shared rather than hoarded.

This willingness to share what they had is also seen in a later passage from Corinthians which tells us that they shared their home with the entire ecclesia:

> "The churches of Asia salute you. Aquila and Priscilla salute you much in the Lord, with the church that is in their house."
>
> (1 Corinthians 16:19)

This passage pays tribute to their natural warmth and concern for the brethren ("Aquila and Priscilla salute you *much* in the Lord"), and to their giving over their home for the use of the entire congregation for the purpose of worshipping God – there can't be a much better use of family resources than that!

Flexibility

When Paul leaves Corinth it transpires that Priscilla and Aquila decide to go with him to support him in his missionary work.

> "And Paul after this tarried there yet a good while, and then took his leave of the brethren, and sailed thence into Syria, and with him Priscilla and Aquila ..."   (Acts 18:18)

This speaks of their enthusiasm for Gospel preaching, their flexibility and willingness to change plans spontaneously as opportunities presented themselves – and also of the way they must have 'clicked' with the Apostle Paul both spiritually and personally.

Nor were they mere passive bystanders to his preaching. Only a few verses later the narrative tells of their active involvement in preaching as a couple:

"And Apollos began to speak boldly in the synagogue: whom when Aquila and Priscilla had heard, they took him unto them, and expounded unto him the way of God more perfectly."

(Acts 18:26)

No wonder that Paul calls them his "helpers in Christ Jesus" in Romans 16:3. His bond with them was unique, as witnessed by the fact that he refers to them in three of his epistles, the only couple of whom this is the case.[1]

Power couple

How could we sum up Priscilla and Aquila? There is so much about them that we don't know, but an indisputable thing that we do: they are always referred to together as a unit. Doubtless many other of the key male New Testament disciples were married, but their wives are not mentioned. There are sisters who are mentioned, but these sisters are not inseparably bound to their husbands in the way that is the case for Priscilla and Aquila in every single passage in which they are mentioned.

This indicates a particular closeness and a particular level of joint involvement as a couple in the Gospel work and in the life of their ecclesia. They were individuals, surely, but individuals that people always thought of together because they were indeed *united* as marriage partners: as friends, as lovers, as co-workers, as partakers in the same experiences, as helpers of the Apostle Paul, as believers, and as preachers of the Gospel message. They stand as a wonderful model of collusion for good.

---

1   This passage implies that in later years they found their way back to Rome, likely playing a key role in the life of the early ecclesias there. The other reference to the couple in the epistles is 2 Timothy 4:19.

Joseph and Mary (2)

Topics: Expectations, surprise and reality; Dealing with a partner's sins; Listening to God in trying circumstances; Supporting one's partner through thick and thin.

Everyone approaches marriage with a set of expectations, and for Joseph and Mary it would have been no different. Sometimes these expectations can be of a wedded bliss romantically naive and unrealistic, but the kind of shift in mindset that Jesus' parents had to undergo would have been on a much different level: for Mary, the massive responsibility of the angel's words set against the abuse she would take due to her pregnancy out of wedlock; for Joseph, the challenge of whether or not to believe her story coupled with the public shame that sticking by her would inevitably bring.

THERE are lots of unknowns in the narrative. We don't know when the angel appeared to Mary relative to his appearance to Joseph, when (or even whether) she told him – and if she did, whether he believed her. He certainly had times of doubt because he reflected on whether he should marry her at all, the narrative implying that at least part of him thought that the right thing to do was to "put her away". These ruminations would have been a far cry from the elated thoughts and hopes for marriage with which his engagement to Mary had begun. Now there would be talk and rumour targeted at both of them, perhaps even open insult. Gone, too, would be the prospect of having time to enjoy and learn about married life as a couple before the first child – not even his! – arrived on the scene.

Our expectations about marriage change all the time as we progress through it, but there are some events such as this which are transformational. Joseph and Mary would have had to completely reconstruct their concept of what becoming married to each other would mean and what their lives would look like going forward. The same thing can happen when there are big changes in circumstances (health, employment, conditions relating to children or parents) or even significant changes of behaviour within a marriage. It is here that the proper covenant basis of marriage in which the two partners promise to be there for each other whatever the circumstance is particularly important. We are faithful to our marriage promises because God is faithful to *His* covenant promises.

Of course Joseph's dilemma was different from this because he had not yet made his marriage covenant with Mary; they were only engaged. Given what he knew or seemed to know about his fiancé's pregnancy, should he go ahead with the marriage at all?

Two points are important here. One is that he thinks carefully about the matter, considering what the right course of action would be rather than making an instinctive emotion-based or pride / ego-based response. A second is that he communicates with God and listens to His advice. Let's take a closer look at how these two things come together.

Responding to sin

First, Joseph's internal thoughts. Rather than making a public scene that would have better protected his own honour, Joseph is minded to "put her away privily". Under the law he was entitled to make a public spectacle of her apparent lack of virginity, thereby defending his own honour by exacting his pound of flesh. Acting in self-defence and self-preservation is the instinctive thing to do when under pressure but Joseph does not go down that path.

Instead his interest is in protecting her from any such shame and potentially extracting himself quietly from the situation – a powerful tribute to his selflessness. Joseph is not blamed for his ignorance or his potential disbelief of God's promise to Mary; instead the account praises him for doing what to him must have appeared to be the right thing ("being a just man"), and the doing of it in a quiet way with the minimum of fuss. If he regarded himself, for a while at least, as the wronged party, he didn't see this as an excuse to self-justify, self-promote, or to take his revenge through the public humiliation of the one who had wronged him. He is righteous but not self-righteous.

It can be all too tempting, when we are wronged or when we catch our partner in error, to want to make a big spectacle about it – to make sure that they see just how wrong they have been. Sometimes we don't even stop there; it can even become about parading their sin before witnesses such as friends or family members so that all can see how unreasonable our partner has been, and what a martyr we are for having to live with them. God will be the judge of both ourselves and our partner, and it is not our job to turn them into a public example, even if it is supposedly in jest.

The incident also raises the question of how we behave when our partner has done (or is perceived to have done) something more seriously wrong, particularly if their action impinges on us and how *we* shall be perceived. While there can be marital sins in which both parties are responsible for a sin mutually committed by the couple (Ananias and Sapphira), generally speaking we are responsible as individuals for our own actions, not those of our partner. If a husband chooses to commit fraud, for instance, the wife is not guilty unless she has aided and abetted, and even in this case the crime may be of a different nature. But if she discovers her husband's sin or it becomes known some other way, how should she react? While there is no 'one size fits all' answer it's important that the response is a spiritually guided one, as Joseph's would turn out to be. It is important that our actions are not driven by fear of social stigma or concern about appearances, but rather by offering support to our partner in their need – not condoning their sin but helping them survive its consequences and learn a better way. We are not to blame for our partner's sins, but we are accountable for how we behave in their aftermath.

The angel

Returning to Joseph, it is while he thinks on his course of action that the angel intervenes in his life, the first of some four occasions recorded in the narrative.[1] This is the second of our two points about Joseph's response to his discovery of Mary's pregnancy. Just as his Old Testament namesake is associated with dreams and divinely inspired dream interpretation, so this Joseph, the surrogate 'father' of God's Son, is a man with whom God chooses to be close. This might seem to set him apart from our own circumstances when facing times of crisis in marriage (if only God would appear to *us* and tell us what to do things might seem a whole lot easier). The point though, at the big picture level at least, is that there is communication. Joseph has open ears to what God has to say, and he is prepared to act upon it. God may not tell us what to do in the highly specific way in which He does Joseph, but God is still speaking today through His word and through His activity in the affairs of our lives.

What we need to do is make ourselves available so that we can hear what He is saying. We do this through prayer and we do it through paying attention to His word and making sure that we read and think about it. God is still speaking, and what He is saying has bearing on every aspect of our lives – particularly the challenging parts when we would be unsure of ourselves what we ought to do. God kept speaking to Joseph and Joseph kept listening rather than second-guessing whether he was really hearing things correctly and whether some scheme of his own might not in fact be better. He immediately and instinctively did as he was bidden.

---

1   Matthew 1:20; the other occasions are Matthew 2:13,14,19-23.

As Joseph carefully considers how to handle the situation it preys deeply on his mind and impacts his subconscious also. This is exactly how big matters in life affect us and it is interesting how the text delicately shows this. The account of the angel's appearance begins with the words: "While Joseph thought on these things", but at the end he is "raised from sleep". This suggests that he either fell asleep (or was put to sleep) as he was deep in thought or that the thought he was having was taking place in his subconscious mind as he was sleeping, a natural continuation of the proactive thoughts he had been having during the day.

It was perhaps while his subconscious mind was at work, then, that he receives the vision from God. Though our own circumstances will not precisely match Joseph's, it is interesting how science has revealed more and more about the power of the subconscious mind and its impact on human decision making. The more we exercise our active minds in listening to God, the better we equip our subconscious to help us process difficult and stressful times of decision making.

Just do it

There is something delightfully matter-of-fact about Joseph's response to what was by any standards a life-changing message:

"The angel of the Lord appeared unto him in a dream, saying, Joseph, thou son of David, fear not to take unto thee Mary thy wife: for that which is conceived in her is of the Holy Spirit. And she shall bring forth a son, and thou shalt call his name Jesus: for he shall save his people from their sins ... Then Joseph being raised from sleep, did as the angel of the Lord had bidden him, and took unto him his wife: and knew her not till she had brought forth her firstborn son: and he called his name Jesus."   (Matthew 1:20,21,24,25)

Once he had received the guidance, there was no prevarication. He was concerned no longer about how others would react (if that was ever his concern); he would stand by and cleave to his wife whatever anyone else thought or said, taking her reproach on himself and jointly shouldering the blame others would choose to attach. Thus together they went to Bethlehem for Jesus' birth, Joseph being divinely delegated the responsibility of naming the child even though it was not strictly his. It must have been an amazing moment for him, to name God's Son on His behalf as Adam had once given names to creation – a worthy reward for his faithfulness to Mary and to God.

Changing plans

A final feature of the early scenes of Mary and Joseph with their young boy is the frequent upheavals they experienced: first to Bethlehem, then to Egypt for an indefinite period of waiting, then back again but to a different place from the one they initially planned. None of these steps would have been easy; the disruption and feeling of being unsettled would have been immense. Joseph is asked by God to lead his wife and son through all these adventures, taking care of them at each step and forsaking the previous plans he might have had. The birth of a new child is a disruption to family life at the best of times, but in these circumstances it must have been doubly hard!

Both parents – though in particular the text singles out Joseph to whom God repeatedly speaks as the head of the family – take seriously what God tells them, upping sticks and endeavouring to recreate a life for themselves quite contrary to the one they had envisioned. They first become strangers and foreigners metaphorically in society (because of Mary's unmarried pregnancy) and then physically as they head south for Egypt. The phrase that Joseph should "take the young child and his mother" is used on at least three occasions, but at the last he is expected to lead the family back from Egypt, the very reverse of the direction the other Joseph his namesake had taken the family way back in Genesis. We might guess that this wonderful irony would not be lost on him. At last a Joseph was not heading down to Egypt leading an old father (Jacob), but instead leaving Egypt behind with his young son with all that this portended.

What happens to Joseph in the end? The record does not say, though it is commonly speculated that he dies relatively early which is why later Gospel accounts speak of Jesus' mother and brothers but not his father. Whether or not this is the case, the scriptures portray a man who cared more about what God thought than his fellow man, a man who didn't seek to score points or demand his pound of flesh but who thought firstly of his family and their safety. He was quick to act whenever God commanded him, taking his duty to protect and provide for both his wife and his new child very seriously. He adjusted his expectations for his marriage admirably and on numerous occasions, and in all these things he is a great role model of a spiritual man.

Abraham and Sarah

Topics: Female respect; Tenacity to survive difficulties and changing circumstances; Hospitality; Bereavement; Seeking the salvation of one's wife.

Abraham and Sarah's is one of the few Old Testament marriages commented on in the New, Sarah's attitude towards her husband held up as model of loyalty and respect worthy of note and emulation. Genesis offers a wealth of material which showcases Abraham and Sarah's relationship as a couple in both its positive and negative aspects, providing fertile ground for enquiry. From this wealth of material we shall select just a few cameos for further exploration, culminating in the touching scene in which Abraham mourns his wife and devotes himself to securing her a burying place in the Land of Promise.

FIRST, though, let's take the lesson drawn in the New Testament:

"Whose (female) adorning ... let it be the hidden man of the heart, in that which is not corruptible, even the ornament of a meek and quiet spirit, which is in the sight of God of great price. For after this manner in the old time the holy women also, who trusted in God, adorned themselves, being in subjection unto their own husbands; even as Sara obeyed Abraham, calling him lord: whose daughters ye are, as long as ye do well, and are not afraid with any amazement." (1 Peter 3:4-6)

It's a familiar passage, one which argues that there are two kinds of adorning. There is the external which is a very high proportion of what preoccupies men and women, and there is the internal. Never was it clearer than with Saul and David which of these it is that God most cares about: He is a God who looks on the heart – and so should we.

As his example, Paul selects Sarah's interaction with Abraham. It is a good example to pick because we know from Genesis that Sarah was a very attractive woman (Abraham himself tells us so in Genesis 12:11, though not necessarily in a context which reflects particularly well on him).[1] It is not this which is her most important feature, however. For all her beauty she knew the godly way to behave towards her husband, and it is this that she chose. We do not see her using her physical appearance as leverage over him in order to manipulate him in some way. Instead she 'obeys' him and calls him "lord", *even when she is speaking to herself in private*! This shows that her submission to Abraham's headship was automatic and unforced: she naturally respected his role in the family and honoured him in her heart as well as in what she said and did. It can be tempting to spew words of annoyance, frustration, or perhaps even vitriol about one's partner when their back is turned on occasion (just occasionally one sees some of this exasperation from older women who have lived with their husbands a long time and have become all too familiar with their foibles!), but in Sarah's case she shows her high opinion of her husband whether or not he is present.

We get another glimpse of what Sarah thinks of Abraham when Isaac is born. Though she is undoubtedly pleased for herself, she expresses a wonderful delight about what this will mean for her husband: "And she said, Who would have said unto Abraham, that Sarah should have given children suck? for I have born him a son in his old age" (Genesis 21:7). She is so happy to

---

1   Abraham is not referring to her beauty to pay her a compliment, he's asking her to save his skin, using her beauty as a reason why she should put herself at considerable risk for his sake. Though she complies with his request, the text is ominously silent as to her view on the whole 'I am his sister' affair.

have brought this joy and fulfilment *to him*, a happiness which speaks volumes about her love for her husband. There is a selfless concern here which is delightful.

Tenacity

None of this means the relationship was all easy-going, of course. Abraham caused significant anxiety for Sarah (not to say putting her at huge physical and sexual risk) with his two "She is my sister" schemes. And she, in her turn, brought major disharmony into the family through her idea that Abraham have a son by her maid. When this doesn't quite work out as she had hoped it is followed by her mistreatment of Hagar and her insistence that Abraham banish the pair of them.

These events gave rise to significant potential for tension – more than mere potential in fact: it crystallised into very tangible unpleasantness once Ishmael was born. Sarah demands that Abraham "cast them out (mother and son)" and the text notes that "the thing was very grievous in Abraham's sight because of his son" (Genesis 21:11). Bible narratives don't generally say a huge amount about the emotional trauma of their characters, so this comment is noteworthy: Abraham was seriously distressed by the disharmony in his family at this time.

The fact is, though, that Abraham and Sarah managed to work through these difficulties and keep it together. These were *major* difficulties, easily grounds for divorce to a modern worldly mindset if either of them had had a desire to go in that direction. But their bond and commitment was strong enough to hold them through all these things. Sometimes it is an act of will, a grit and tenacity which is called for just to hold on through the dark times – but this is what Abraham and Sarah had. They *chose* to survive the tensions they faced, and they refused to buy the modern lie that if you aren't getting just what you want out of your relationship right now then you should leave. Abraham and Sarah's example shows that even the most major difficulties and disruptions can be survived if there is a will to do so.

   Significant credit should also be given to Sarah for what she has to put up with during the course of the marriage, the disruption and emotional stress that came her way. It was not just Abraham who had to leave Ur and the significant cultural attractions, comfort and familiarity that it offered. No word of complaint or disharmony is recorded over this; Abraham goes, and she goes with him – sacrificing as well as he, and trusting not only in the Lord, but in her husband as well. Several times they uprooted and moved on – it was inconvenient and disruptive no doubt, but she did it anyway. Of course it is true that they become extremely well off, seemingly living a good life with ample domestic help, good food and the like, which would have made the burden easier to swallow – but still their life is an itinerant one, something which is not in keeping with a woman's natural instincts. In another incident later in life she has to watch as the beloved son Isaac is taken off to Mount Moriah.[2] It is perhaps all three who are prepared to sacrifice in this scene, not just Abraham.

Hospitality
Another aspect of Abraham and Sarah's marriage was the hospitality they were able to offer as a couple, similar to what we saw with Priscilla and Aquila. This can be seen in the visit of the three angels in chapter 18:

   "And Abraham hastened into the tent unto Sarah, and said, Make ready quickly three measures of fine meal, knead it, and make cakes upon the hearth. And Abraham ran unto the herd, and fetched a calf tender and good, and gave it unto a young man; and he hasted to dress it, and he took butter, and milk, and the calf which he had dressed, and set it before them; and he stood by them under the tree, and they did eat."
                                                          (Genesis 18:6-8)

   There are two points to make here. First, as soon as the guests appeared on the scene Abraham was able to ask Sarah to

---

2   This is on the assumption that Abraham tells her; of course it is possible that he does not.

spring into action on the hospitality front and know that she would be happy to contribute. A husband should consider his wife and make sure that she is able and willing, with the other demands she faces, to down tools and quickly offer hospitality this way rather than issue invitations to all and sundry and then say to his wife, 'By the way, we have twenty people coming for lunch on Sunday; I hope that's okay?' It's not exactly easy for her to say 'No, it's not okay; ring them all up and tell them they can't come!' My suspicion here is that Abraham and Sarah had already agreed together that they would offer hospitality whenever possible, so when the opportunity suddenly and surprisingly presented itself, Abraham could count on Sarah that she would be with him in the hosting he was so eager to provide.

The second point is that Abraham too was deeply involved. Even though he had Sarah to help him and many, many servants (he gave one of them the task of preparing the calf, for instance), he didn't use this as an excuse to sit back and do nothing while others busied themselves at his command. He expected them to be involved but he himself also put in the graft to make sure that everything came together; he personally selected the calf they would eat, and when it was cooked he himself hasted to dress it, serving it, along with the luxuries of butter and milk, before his guests and then standing to attention as they ate in order to offer service. It was truly a joint family accomplishment in which everyone pulled together under Abraham's leadership and enthusiasm to a greater good and to the embracing of others outside the immediate family circle.

Mourning

The final cameo which will close this book is one of the few scriptural scenes of marital bereavement. All good things must come to an end in this life until the great day dawns when the Lord comes – and this includes the joy of marriage. It is all the more poignant to observe in Abraham and Sarah's case because we have travelled so far with them: through so many incidents in so many chapters. We have seen something of their love and respect for one another, the challenges they faced, and most importantly the commitment which bound them together through it all:

> "And Sarah died in Kirjath-arba; the same is Hebron in the land of Canaan: and Abraham came to mourn for Sarah, and to weep for her."   (Genesis 23:2)

The importance of the scene which follows is brought out by the fact that a whole twenty-verse chapter is devoted to the mourning of Sarah and the securing of a burying place for her – a long passage dedicated to a seemingly minor detail, even in the context of an overall narrative arc which is reasonably long.

But it is not in point of fact a minor detail at all; it is rich in significance. Abraham places great stock in the burial of his beloved wife and in the fact that her burial place should specifically and contractually be in the Promised Land in a permanent inheritance. The negotiation with the men of Heth is told in detail and with deliberation to make this point: twice Abraham stands up and twice he bows, insisting on paying for the land so that it is incontrovertibly his possession – the first fulfilment of God's vital promise that He would give him the land on which he stood. His first possession and inheritance in the Promised Land is for his wife.

It isn't until Sarah has died that securing an actual physical inheritance in the land as opposed to merely a promise of it becomes top of mind for Abraham, but this change in his focus makes a fitting tribute to his love for his wife. What he wants to do is to ensure that she is buried in the land that God has promised and that the place in which he chooses for this is incontrovertibly his. He is securing the burial of a princess, after all, and she in fact becomes the first person in the line of Abraham's relatives and descendants to be so buried in the inherited land and the first to receive this promise. This is a fine example of a husband seeking above all things the salvation of his wife, a beautiful symbolic acting out of the very thing Paul tells us that husbands should prioritise in Ephesians 5.

The patriarchs who follow like Jacob and Joseph will also place great store at the end of Genesis in ensuring that they are buried in the Promised Land. But the one who *first* ensured that this could be possible was Abraham when he sought out a burial place for his wife. Thus she becomes the first person to be buried in the Promised Land awaiting the return of Christ. A man can't do better for his wife than ensuring she is as closely associated as that with the promises of God.

Epilogue: the next chapter

"And I saw a new heaven and a new earth: for the first heaven and the first earth were passed away; and there was no more sea. And I John saw the holy city, new Jerusalem, coming down from God out of heaven, prepared as a bride adorned for her husband. And I heard a great voice out of heaven saying, Behold, the tabernacle of God is with men, and he will dwell with them, and they shall be his people, and God himself shall be with them, and be their God. And God shall wipe away all tears from their eyes; and there shall be no more death, neither sorrow, nor crying, neither shall there be any more pain: for the former things are passed away."

(Revelation 21:1-4)

Scripture index